The Ancient Egyptian Path to Enlightenment

MAUI

"TO THINK, TO PONDER, TO FIX ATTENTION"

"Contemplate thy powers, contemplate thy wants and thy connections; so shalt thou discover the duties of life, and be directed in all thy ways."

"When an idea exclusively occupies the mind, it is transformed into an actual physical state."

"Reason of Divinity may not be known except by a concentration of the senses like onto it."

"Get thyself ready and make the thought in you a stranger to the world-illusion."

Ancient Egyptian Proverbs

MEDITATION

On the Cover: **An Ancient Egyptian Yogi sitting in the Lotus Posture, from the Tomb of Ptahotep.**

Cruzian Mystic Books / Sema Institute of Yoga
P.O.Box 570459
Miami, Florida, 33257
(305) 378-6253 Fax: (305) 378-6253

First U.S. edition 1997

© 1997 By Reginald Muata Abhaya Ashby

© 2002 By Reginald Muata Abhaya Ashby

© 2003 By Reginald Muata Abhaya Ashby

All rights reserved. No part of this book may be used or reproduced in any manner whatsoever without written permission (address above) except in the case of brief quotations embodied in critical articles and reviews. All inquiries may be addressed to the address above.

Ashby, Muata
Meditation: The Path To Enlightenment
ISBN: 1-884564-26-7

Library of Congress Cataloging in Publication Data

1 Meditation 2 Spirituality 3 Yoga 5 Self Help.

Cruzian Mystic Books

The Ancient Egyptian Path to Enlightenment

Sema Institute of Yoga

Sema (☥) is an Ancient Egyptian word and symbol meaning *union*. The Sema Institute is dedicated to the propagation of the universal teachings of spiritual evolution which relate to the union of humanity and the union of all things within the universe. It is a non-denominational organization which recognizes the unifying principles in all spiritual and religious systems of evolution throughout the world. Our primary goals are to provide the wisdom of ancient spiritual teachings in books, courses and other forms of communication. Secondly, to provide expert instruction and training in the various yogic disciplines including Ancient Egyptian Philosophy, Christian Gnosticism, Indian Philosophy and modern science. Thirdly, to promote world peace and Universal Love.

A primary focus of our tradition is to identify and acknowledge the yogic principles within all religions and to relate them to each other in order to promote their deeper understanding as well as to show the essential unity of purpose and the unity of all living beings and nature within the whole of existence.

The Institute is open to all who believe in the principles of peace, non-violence and spiritual emancipation regardless of sex, race, or creed.

MEDITATION
About the author Dr. Muata Abhaya Ashby

About The Author

Reginald Muata Ashby holds a Doctor of Philosophy Degree in Religion, and a Doctor of Divinity Degree in Holistic Healing. He is also a Pastoral Counselor and Teacher of Yoga Philosophy and Discipline. Dr. Ashby is an adjunct faculty member of the American Institute of Holistic Theology and an ordained Minister. Dr. Ashby has studied advanced Jnana, Bhakti and Kundalini Yogas under the guidance of Swami Jyotirmayananda, a world renowned Yoga Master. He has studied the mystical teachings of Ancient Egypt for many years and is the creator of the Egyptian Yoga concept. He is also the founder of the Sema Institute, an organization dedicated to the propagation of the teachings of Yoga and mystical spirituality.

Karen Clarke-Ashby "Vijaya-Asha" is the wife and spiritual partner of Muata. She is an independent researcher, practitioner and teacher of Yoga, a Doctor in the Sciences and a Pastoral Counselor, the editor of Egyptian Proverbs and Egyptian Yoga by Muata. ♀

Sema Institute
P.O. Box 570459, Miami, Fla. 33257
(305) 378-6253, Fax (305) 378-6253
©2002

The Ancient Egyptian Path to Enlightenment
TABLE OF CONTENTS

- Sema Institute of Yoga 3
- **FOREWORD** 8
- **PREFACE** 8
- **INTRODUCTION TO THE HISTORY AND SPIRITUALITY OF ANCIENT EGYPT** .. 10
  - Early Beginnings: The First Religion 11
    - *A Long History* 11
    - *Where Was Shetaut Neter Practiced in Ancient Times?* 13
    - *The Land of Ancient Egypt-Nile Valley* 14
    - *The Term Kamit and the Origins of the Ancient Egyptians* 15
    - *The Term Kamit and the Origins of the Ancient Egyptians* 16
    - *Ancient Origins* 16
    - *The Hieroglyphic Text for the Name Qamit* 17
    - *When Was Neterian Religion Practiced?* 18
    - *OLD KINGDOM PERIOD* 19
    - *MIDDLE KINGDOM PERIOD* 19
    - *NEW KINGDOM PERIOD* 20
  - Who Were the Ancient Egyptians and What is Yoga Philosophy? 21
    - *Ancient Kemetic Terms and Ancient Greek Terms* 24
- **INTRODUCTION TO SHETAUT NETER ANCIENT EGYPTIAN AFRICAN RELIGION) AND SEMA TAWI (EGYPTIAN YOGA)** 25
  - Why is it Necessary to study Religion? 26
  - The Fundamental Principles of Ancient Egyptian Religion 27
    - *Summary of Ancient Egyptian Religion* 28
    - *"The practice of the Shedy disciplines leads to knowing oneself and the Divine. This is called being True of Speech"* 28
    - *Neterian Great Truths* 29
    - *Summary of The Great Truths and the Shedy Paths to their Realization* .. 31
    - *The Spiritual Culture and the Purpose of Life: Shetaut Neter* 32
  - Shetaut Neter 32
  - Who is Neter in Kamitan Religion? 33
    - *Sacred Scriptures of Shetaut Neter* 34
  - Neter and the Neteru 35
  - The Neteru 35
    - *The Neteru and Their Temples* 36
    - *The Neteru and Their Interrelationships* 37
    - *Listening to the Teachings* 39
    - *The Anunian Tradition* 40
    - *The Theban Tradition* 42
    - *The Goddess Tradition* 43
    - *The Aton Tradition* 45
    - *Akhnaton, Nefertiti and Daughters* 45
  - The General Principles of Shetaut Neter 46
    - *The Forces of Entropy* 47
    - *The Great Awakening of Neterian Religion* 48
  - What is Egyptian Yoga? What is Yoga? 49

MEDITATION

What is Egyptian Yoga? 51
- The Study of Yoga 55
- The Sema Tawi of Wisdom 57
- The Sema Tawi of Right Action 59
- The Sema Tawi of Divine Love 60
- The Yogic Postures in Ancient Egypt 62
- The Sema Tawi of Tantrism 67

INTRODUCTION TO THE SEMA TAWI OF MEDITATION 71
- Uaa Shedy 71

PART I MEDITATION: THE PATH TO SPIRITUAL ENLIGHTENMENT 76
INTRODUCTION 77
- What is Meditation? 77
WHAT IS THE PURPOSE OF MEDITATING? 79
SHETAUT NETER – SHEDI 79
PURPOSE OF MEDITATION – PURIFYING THE MIND 79
- 3 states of mind 80

LISTENING (MEH MESTCHERT.) → REFLECTION (MAUI) → MEDITATION (UAH) 80
- 3 steps in meditation 80
- Establishment in Higher Consciousness 81
- What is the Mind? 82
KARMA AND REINCARNATION 94
YOGA AND RELIGION 95
INTEGRAL YOGA 96
- The Search for True Happiness and Inner Peace 98
- The Process of YOGA 99
HOW DOES MEDITATION WORK? 100
- The Therapeutic Value of Meditation 103

PART II: THE ANCIENT HISTORY OF MEDITATION 105
THE ANCIENT HISTORY OF MEDITATION: 106
- The Destruction of Evil Men and Women 106
- The Story of Hetheru and Djehuti 109
GLOSS ON THE DESTRUCTION OF EVIL MEN AND WOMEN 109
- The Goddess Hat-Hor (Hetheru) 114
- The Three States of Consciousness 115
- The Mystical Experience: Pure Consciousness 116
- The Distracted State (Agitation) 116
- The State of Dullness 119
- The State of Lucidity (Harmony, Purity and Balance) 120

PART III: FORMAL MEDITATION PRACTICE AND ITS EFFECTS ON THE MIND 126
INTRODUCTION 127
- Concentration 128

Aids to Concentration 129
Extended Concentration (Meditation) 133
Cosmic Consciousness 133
Objects of Meditation 134
The Neteru and Their Interrelationships 137
The Mystical Circle 139
Abstract Meditation 139
Meditation In Life: How to Develop a Meditative Lifestyle 140
The Diet 145
Tips for Formal Meditation Practice 146
Rituals Associated With Meditation Practice 146
The Development of Devotional Feeling 148
Choosing a Word(s) of Power 149
The Daily Schedule for Yoga Practice 150
Basic Schedule of Spiritual Practice 151
Proper Breathing 152
Meditation Postures 154
WORDS OF POWER IN MEDITATION: 155
Chanting the Divine Name: 155
Meditation Technique #1: Simple Meditation Technique 162
Meditation Technique #2: The Integrated Meditation 163
Meditation Technique #3: The Basic Serpent Power Meditation based on Ancient Egyptian Wisdom Teachings 165
Meditation Technique #4: The Supreme Self Meditation: Based on the hieroglyphic text of the "Destruction of Humankind" 171
Meditation Technique #5: The Highest Form of Meditation: Identification With the Divine 172
MEDITATION AS MEDICINE: For Peace, Health and Spiritual Enlightenment 174
Weathering the Storm of Uncontrolled Thoughts: How to Handle the Restless Mind 176

INDEX **193**

AUDIO SEMINAR WORKSHOP SERIES 197

BECOME A CERTIFIED KEMETIC MEDITATION INSTRUCTOR .... ERROR! BOOKMARK NOT DEFINED.

Uaa Shedy .... *Error! Bookmark not defined.*
Uaa Shedy .... *Error! Bookmark not defined.*

OTHER BOOKS FROM C M BOOKS .... ERROR! BOOKMARK NOT DEFINED.

SELF-PUBLISH FOR PROFIT, SPIRITUAL FULFILLMENT AND SERVICE TO HUMANITY .... **ERROR! BOOKMARK NOT DEFINED.**

MUSIC BASED ON THE PRT M HRU AND OTHER KEMETIC TEXTS .... ERROR! BOOKMARK NOT DEFINED.

MEDITATION

Foreword

Meditation: the way to freedom from anxiety, depression, slothfulness, insanity, unrest and ignorance? How is it possible?

Meditation can indeed prevent mental illness, and promote the development of a highly integrated and advanced mind that can not only be free of mental complexes but even unravel the mysteries of the universe. Meditation is the same power that allowed the great achievements of the past such as the great pyramids, to be possible. This is the declaration of the sages and it is up to the individual to prove it in their own lives. Those who have implemented the teachings have discovered the value of meditation and you will too. Countless scientific studies have proven the efficacy of meditation. Start today and discover its benefits to transform your life.

-Sebai Muata Ashby

Preface

When one normally speaks of meditation, the picture of someone sitting in a cross-legged position in a quiet area, seeking to experience inner peace, comes to mind. While this form of discipline is important in the practice of yoga for spiritual enlightenment, success in meditation has deeper implications. It means experiencing a state of inner peace and bliss which remains with you not only when you are involved in the formal practice of meditation, but all throughout your day, in all conditions and situations. To most this attainment may seem to be an impossibility, however, through the practice of yoga it is possible to achieve such a state, forevermore.

A metaphor is given to illustrate how, through the practice of meditation, you can become eternally peaceful and blissful. In certain countries cloth is dyed by placing a white piece of cloth into the dye, and then placing it on a clothes line to dry in the light of the sun. As the rays of the sun dry the cloth, it also bleaches it out. The process of dipping the cloth in the dye and placing it to dry in the sun continues. Each time the cloth is left in the sun, the color is bleached out, however, never as much as the previous time. Each time it retains a little more of the dye. Finally, when the color of the cloth no longer fades when hung to dry in the hot sun, the process is completed. When you sit in formal meditation and experience inner peace, you are submerging yourself in the the bliss and peace of your innermost essence, your Higher Self. However, the moment your eyes open, you are once again bombarded by the world of objects clamoring for your attention, pulling you away from the state of inner peace. Your inner peace is constantly being bleached by the sun of the world process. However, with the continued practice of meditation you will find that you are able to abide in the experience of inner peace of the Self for longer and longer periods of time after your practice of formal meditation. Thus you become more and more able to withstand the deleterious effects of the blazing heat of the world process. You no longer become angry or frustrated at things which normally would have angered or frustrated you before because internally you are having a more profound experience. However, until this practice is perfected, you must make a conscious effort preserve your experience of inner peace by not allowing yourself to become upset and angry. In other words, you must put forth every effort to maintain a balanced and serene (calm) mind.

The Ancient Egyptian Path to Enlightenment

The importance of keeping the mind calm is emphasized in yoga. It is said that there are four gatekeepers to the palace of Enlightenment: Serenity, Contentment, Spiritual Inquiry, and Good Association (gathering in a group to listen to spiritual teachings being espoused by Enlightened Sages). The importance of serenity is illustrated by the following metaphor. Picture a lake on a calm day where there is no breeze. As you can imagine, the sun and surrounding trees will be perfectly reflected in the water. Likewise, when the mind is calm, when there are no thoughts creating ripples in the lake of consciousness, then the Higher Self can clearly reflect in the mind of the individual, providing a feeling of inner expansion and the experience of supreme peace and bliss.

So the experience of inner peace and supreme bliss can be yours at every moment, by stilling the mind. It becomes a choice you make on a daily basis. There is a parable about a jeweler who, while waiting on a customer, is told by an employee that a valuable diamond is missing. The jeweler smiles and nods his head in acknowledgment. A few minutes later the employee returns and informs him that they found the missing diamond. Again the jeweler smiles and nods his head, and continues his business with the customer. The customer, puzzled by the lack of concern on the part of the jeweler, asks the jeweler why did he not become upset when he was told about the lost jewel and elated when it was found. The jeweler replied that he had reflected within himself when he was told that the jewel was lost, and he realized that the diamond was merely a perishable object, and its loss meant nothing compared to treasure of inner peace he was experiencing. Likewise, when the diamond was found he did not become elated because he was experiencing a more profound treasure, the bliss of the Self. Like the jeweler, you too must choose to protect that which is truly valuable, your mental serenity, and not discard it for the seemingly valuable, but perishable, objects of the world. Mental serenity is the key to experiencing the eternal peace and bliss of the Supreme (Higher) Self.

May you discover the bliss and peace of the Soul in deep mystic meditation.

Dr. Karen "Vijaya-Asha" Ashby

Dr. Karen "Vijaya-Asha" Ashby is the author of *Yoga Mystic Metaphors,* the editor of numerous works by Dr. Muata Ashby and the spiritual partner of Dr. Muata Abhaya Ashby.

MEDITATION

Introduction to The History and Spirituality of Ancient Egypt

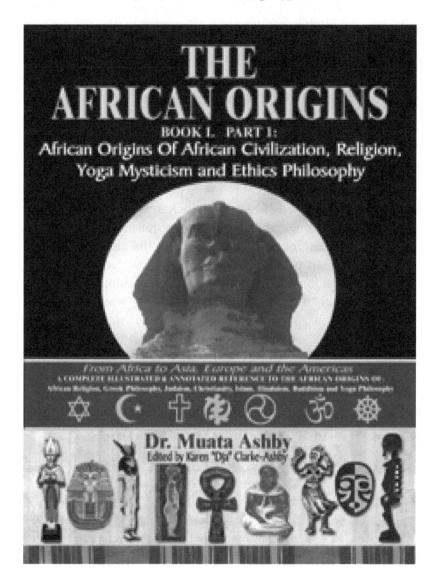

The Ancient Egyptian Path to Enlightenment

Early Beginnings: The First Religion

Shetaut Neter is the Ancient Egyptian Religion and Philosophy. Ancient Egypt was the first and most ancient civilization to create a religious system that was complete with all three stages of religion, as well as an advanced spiritual philosophy of righteousness, called Maat Philosophy, that also had secular dimensions. Several temple systems were developed in Kamit; they were all related. The pre-Judaic/Islamic religions that the later Jewish and Muslim religions drew from in order to create their religions developed out of these, ironically enough, only to later repudiate the source from whence they originated. In any case, the Great Sphinx remains the oldest known religious monument in history that denotes high culture and civilization as well. Ancient Egypt and Nubia produced the oldest religious systems and their contact with the rest of the world led to the proliferation of advanced religion and spiritual philosophy. People who were practicing simple animism, shamanism, nature based religions and witchcraft were elevated to the level of not only understanding the nature of the Supreme Being, but also attaining salvation from the miseries of life through the effective discovery of that Transcendental being, not as an untouchable aloof Spirit, but as the very essence of all that exists.

NETERIANISM 10.000 B.C.E. – 2001 A.C.E.

A Long History

For a period spanning over 10,000 years the Neterian religion served the society of ancient Kamit. It is hard to comprehend the vastness of time that is encompassed by Ancient Egyptian culture, religion and philosophy. Yet the evidence is there to be seen by all. It has been collected and presented in the book *African Origins of Civilization, Religion and Yoga Philosophy*. That volume will serve as the historical record for the Neterian religion and as record of its legacy to all humanity. It serves as the basis or foundation for the work contained in all the other books in this series that have been created to elucidate on the teachings and traditions as well as disciplines of the varied Neterian religious traditions.

MEDITATION

The book *African Origins of Civilization, Religion and Yoga Philosophy,* and the other volumes on the specific traditions detail the philosophies and disciplines that should be practiced by those who want to follow the path of Hm or Hmt, to be practitioners of the Shetaut Neter religion and builders of the Neterian faith worldwide.

The Ancient Egyptian Path to Enlightenment
Where Was Shetaut Neter Practiced in Ancient Times?

Below left: A map of North East Africa showing the location of the land of *Ta-Meri* or *Kamit*, also known as Ancient Egypt and South of it is located the land which in modern times is called Sudan.

Egypt IS In Africa and Ancient Egyptian Religion and Philosophy are African Religion and African Philosophy

MEDITATION
The Land of Ancient Egypt-Nile Valley

The cities wherein the major theologies of Neterianism developed were:

A. Sais (temple of Net),

B. Anu (Heliopolis- temple of Ra),

C. Men-nefer or Hetkaptah (Memphis, temple of Ptah),

D. Sakkara (Pyramid Texts),

E. Akhet-Aton (City of Akhenaton, temple of Aton),

F. Abdu (temple of Asar),

G. Denderah (temple of Hetheru),

H. Waset (Thebes, temple of Amun),

I. Edfu (temple of Heru),

J. Philae (temple of Aset). The cities wherein the theology of the Trinity of Asar-Aset-Heru was developed were Anu, Abydos, Philae, Edfu, Denderah and Edfu.

The Ancient Egyptian Path to Enlightenment

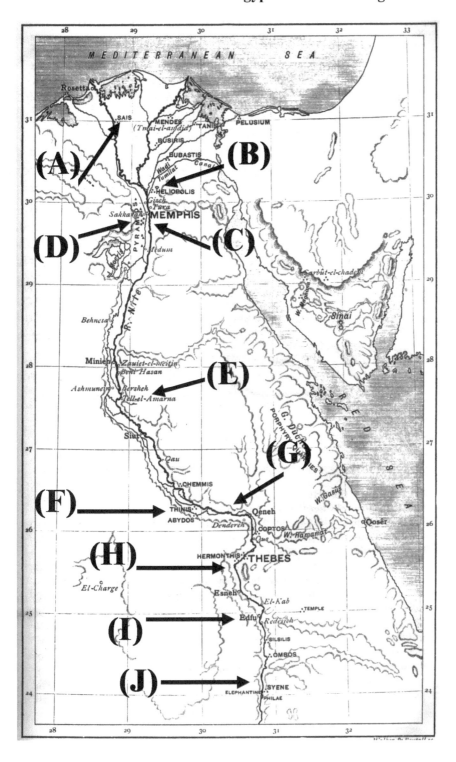

MEDITATION
The Term Kamit and the Origins of the Ancient Egyptians

Ancient Origins

The Ancient Egyptians recorded that they were originally a colony of Ethiopians from the south who came to the north east part of Africa. The term "Ethiopian," "Nubian," and "Kushite" all relate to the same peoples who lived south of Egypt. In modern times, the land which was once known as Nubia ("Land of Gold"), is currently known as the Sudan, and the land even further south and east towards the coast of east Africa is referred to as Ethiopia (see map above).

Recent research has shown that the modern Nubian word *kiji* means "fertile land, dark gray mud, silt, or black land." Since the sound of this word is close to the Ancient Egyptian name Kish or Kush, referring to the land south of Egypt, it is believed that the name Kush also meant "the land of dark silt" or "the black land." Kush was the Ancient Egyptian name for Nubia. Nubia, the black land, is the Sudan of today. Sudan is an Arabic translation of *sûd* which is the plural form of *aswad*, which means "black," and *ân* which means "of the." So, Sudan means "of the blacks." In the modern Nubian language, *nugud* means "black." Also, *nuger, nugur*, and *nubi* mean "black" as well. All of this indicates that the words Kush, Nubia, and Sudan all mean the same thing — the "black land" and/or the "land of the blacks."[1] As we will see, the differences between the term Kush and the term Kam (Qamit - name for Ancient Egypt in the Ancient Egyptian language) relate more to the same meaning but different geographical locations.

As we have seen, the terms "Ethiopia," "Nubia," "Kush" and "Sudan" all refer to "black land" and/or the "land of the blacks." In the same manner we find that the name of Egypt which was used by the Ancient Egyptians also means "black land" and/or the "land of the blacks." The hieroglyphs below reveal the Ancient Egyptian meaning of the words related to the name of their land. It is clear that the meaning of the word Qamit is equivalent to the word Kush as far as they relate to "black land" and that they also refer to a differentiation in geographical location, i.e. Kush is the "black land of the south" and Qamit is the "black land of the north." Both terms denote the primary quality that defines Africa, "black" or "Blackness" (referring to the land and its people). The quality of blackness and the consonantal sound of K or Q as well as the reference to the land are all aspects of commonality between the Ancient Kushitic and Kamitan terms.

---

[1] "Nubia," *Microsoft® Encarta® Africana.* © 1999 Microsoft Corporation. All rights reserved.

The Ancient Egyptian Path to Enlightenment
The Hieroglyphic Text for the Name Qamit

Qamit - Ancient Egypt

Qamit - blackness – black

Qamit - literature of Ancient Egypt – scriptures

Qamiu or variant -

Ancient Egyptians-people of the black land.

MEDITATION

When Was Neterian Religion Practiced?

c. 65,000 B.C.E. Paleolithic – Nekhen (Hierakonpolis)
c. 10,000 B.C.E. Neolithic – period

PREDYNASTIC PERIOD

c. 10,500 B.C.E.-7,000 B.C.E. Creation of the Great Sphinx Modern archeological accepted dates – Sphinx means Hor-m-akhet or Heru (Heru) in the horizon. This means that the King is one with the Spirit, Ra as an enlightened person possessing an animal aspect (lion) and illuminated intellect. Anunian Theology – Ra - Serpent Power Spirituality

c. 10,000 B.C.E.-5,500 B.C.E. The Sky GOD- Realm of Light-Day – NETER Androgynous – All-encompassing –Absolute, Nameless Being, later identified with Ra-Herakhti (Sphinx)

>7,000 B.C.E. Kemetic Myth and Theology present in architecture

The Ancient Egyptian Path to Enlightenment
OLD KINGDOM PERIOD

5500+ B.C.E. to 600 A.C.E. Amun -Ra - Ptah (Heru) – Amenit - Rai – Sekhmet (male and female Trinity-Complementary Opposites)

5500+ B.C.E. Memphite Theology – Ptah

5500+ B.C.E. Hermopolitan Theology- Djehuti

5500+ B.C.E. The Asarian Resurrection Theology - Asar

5500+B.C.E. The Goddess Principle- Theology, Aset-Hetheru-Net-Mut-Sekhmet-Buto

5500 B.C.E. (Dynasty 1) Beginning of the Dynastic Period (Unification of Upper and Lower Egypt)

5000 B.C.E. (5th Dynasty) Pyramid Texts - Egyptian Book of Coming Forth By Day - 42 Precepts of MAAT and codification of the Pre-Dynastic theologies (Pre-Dynastic period: 10,000 B.C.E.-5,500 B.C.E.) Coming Forth By Day (Book of the Dead)

4241 B.C.E. The Pharaonic (royal) calendar based on the Sothic system (star Sirius) was in use.

MIDDLE KINGDOM PERIOD

3000 B.C.E. WISDOM TEXTS-Precepts of Ptahotep, Instructions of Any, Instructions of Amenemope, Etc.

2040 B.C.E.-1786 B.C.E. *COFFIN TEXTS* Coming Forth By Day (Book of the Dead)

1800 B.C.E.-Theban Theology - Amun

MEDITATION
NEW KINGDOM PERIOD

1570 B.C.E.-Books of Coming Forth By Day (Book of the Dead)

1353 B.C.E. Atonism- Non-dualist Pre-Dynastic Philosophy was redefined by Akhenaton.

712-657 B.C.E. The Nubian Dynasty

657 B.C.E. - 450 A.C.E. This is the last period of Ancient Egyptian culture which saw several invasions by foreigners from Asia Minor (Assyrians, Persians) and Europe (Greeks and Romans) and finally the closing of the temples, murdering of priests and priestesses, the forced conversion to the foreign religions and destruction of Neterian holy sites by Christians and Muslims. The teaching went dormant at this time until the 20th century A.C.E.

The Ancient Egyptian Path to Enlightenment
Who Were the Ancient Egyptians and What is Yoga Philosophy?

The Ancient Egyptian religion (*Shetaut Neter*), language and symbols provide the first "historical" record of Yoga Philosophy and Religious literature. Egyptian Yoga is what has been commonly referred to by Egyptologists as Egyptian "Religion" or "Mythology", but to think of it as just another set of stories or allegories about a long lost civilization is to completely miss the greatest secret of human existence. Yoga, in all of its forms and disciplines of spiritual development, was practiced in Egypt earlier than anywhere else in history. This unique perspective from the highest philosophical system which developed in Africa over seven thousand years ago provides a new way to look at life, religion, the discipline of psychology and the way to spiritual development leading to spiritual Enlightenment. Egyptian mythology, when understood as a system of Yoga (union of the individual soul with the Universal Soul or Supreme Consciousness), gives every individual insight into their own divine nature and also a deeper insight into all religions and Yoga systems.

> **Diodorus Siculus (Greek Historian) writes in the time of Augustus (first century B.C.):**
>
> *"Now the Ethiopians, as historians relate, were the first of all men and the proofs of this statement, they say, are manifest. For that they did not come into their land as immigrants from abroad but were the natives of it and so justly bear the name of autochthones* (sprung from the soil itself), *is, they maintain, conceded by practically all men..."*
>
> *"They also say that the Egyptians are colonists sent out by the Ethiopians, Asar having been the leader of the colony. For, speaking generally, what is now Egypt, they maintain, was not land, but sea, when in the beginning the universe was being formed; afterwards, however, as the Nile during the times of its inundation carried down the mud from Ethiopia, land was gradually built up from the deposit...And the larger parts of the customs of the Egyptians are, they hold, Ethiopian, the colonists still preserving their ancient manners. For instance, the belief that their kings are Gods, the very special attention which they pay to their burials, and many other matters of a similar nature, are Ethiopian practices, while the shapes of their statues and the forms of their letters are Ethiopian; for of the two kinds of writing which the Egyptians have, that which is known as popular* (demotic) *is learned by everyone, while that which is called sacred* (hieratic), *is understood only by the priests of the Egyptians, who learnt it from their Fathers as one of the things which are not divulged, but among the Ethiopians, everyone uses these forms of letters. Furthermore, the orders of the priests, they maintain, have much the same position among both peoples; for all are clean who are engaged in the service of the gods, keeping themselves shaven, like the Ethiopian priests, and having the same dress and form of staff, which is shaped like a plough and is carried by their kings who wear high felt hats which end in a knob in the top and are circled by the serpents which they call asps; and this symbol appears to carry the thought that it will be the lot who shall dare to attack the king to encounter death-carrying stings. Many other things are told by them concerning their own antiquity and the colony which they sent out that became the Egyptians, but about this there is no special need of our writing anything."*

MEDITATION

The Ancient Egyptian texts state:
"Our people originated at the base of the mountain of the Moon, at the origin of the Nile river."

"KMT"
"Egypt", "Burnt", "Land of Blackness","Land of the Burnt People."

KMT (Ancient Egypt) is situated close to Lake Victoria in present day Africa. This is the same location where the earliest human remains have been found, in the land currently known as Ethiopia-Tanzania. Recent genetic technology as reported in the new encyclopedias and leading news publications has revealed that all peoples of the world originated in Africa and migrated to other parts of the world prior to the last Ice Age 40,000 years ago. Therefore, as of this time, genetic testing has revealed that all humans are alike. The earliest bone fossils which have been found in many parts of the world were those of the African Grimaldi type. During the Ice Age, it was not possible to communicate or to migrate. Those trapped in specific locations were subject to the regional forces of weather and climate. Less warmer climates required less body pigment, thereby producing lighter pigmented people who now differed from their dark-skinned ancestors. After the Ice Age when travel was possible, these light-skinned people who had lived in the northern, colder regions of harsh weather during the Ice Age period moved back to the warmer climates of their ancestors, and mixed with the people there who had remained dark-skinned, thereby producing the Semitic colored people. "Semite" means mixture of skin color shades.

Therefore, there is only one human race who, due to different climactic and regional exposure, changed to a point where there seemed to be different "types" of people. Differences were noted with respect to skin color, hair texture, customs, languages, and with respect to the essential nature (psychological and emotional makeup) due to the experiences each group had to face and overcome in order to survive.

From a philosophical standpoint, the question as to the origin of humanity is redundant when it is understood that <u>ALL</u> come from one origin which some choose to call the "Big Bang" and others "The Supreme Being."

> **"Thou makest the color of the skin of one race to be different from that of another, but however many may be the varieties of mankind, it is thou that makes them all to live."**
> —Ancient Egyptian Proverb from *The Hymns of Amun*

> **"Souls, Heru, son, are of the self-same nature, since they came from the same place where the Creator modeled them; nor male nor female are they. Sex is a thing of bodies not of Souls."**
> —Ancient Egyptian Proverb from *The teachings of Aset to Heru*

Historical evidence proves that Ethiopia-Nubia already had Kingdoms at least 300 years before the first Kingdom-Pharaoh of Egypt.

> *"Ancient Egypt was a colony of Nubia - Ethiopia. ...Asar having been the leader of the colony..."*

The Ancient Egyptian Path to Enlightenment

"And upon his return to Greece, they gathered around and asked, "tell us about this great land of the Blacks called Ethiopia." And Herodotus said, "There are two great Ethiopian nations, one in Sind (India) and the other in Egypt."

Recorded by Egyptian high priest *Manetho* (300 B.C.)
also Recorded by *Diodorus* (Greek historian 100 B.C.)

The pyramids themselves however, cannot be dated, but indications are that they existed far back in antiquity. The Pyramid Texts (hieroglyphics inscribed on pyramid walls) and Coffin Texts (hieroglyphics inscribed on coffins) speak authoritatively on the constitution of the human spirit, the vital Life Force along the human spinal cord (known in India as *"Kundalini"*), the immortality of the soul, reincarnation and the law of Cause and Effect (known in India as the Law of Karma).

Below., Egyptian man and woman-(tomb of Payry) 18th Dynasty displaying the naturalistic style (as people really appeared in ancient times).

MEDITATION
Ancient Kemetic Terms and Ancient Greek Terms

In keeping with the spirit of the culture of Kemetic Spirituality, in this volume we will use the Kemetic names for the divinities through which we will bring forth the Philosophy of the Prt M Hru. Therefore, the Greek name Osiris will be converted back to the Kemetic (Ancient Egyptian) Asar (Ausar), the Greek Isis to Aset (Auset), the Greek Nephthys to Nebthet, Anubis to Anpu or Apuat, Hathor to Hetheru, Thoth or Hermes to Djehuti, etc. (see the table below) Further, the term Ancient Egypt will be used interchangeably with "Kemit" ("Kamit"), or "Ta-Meri," as these are the terms used by the Ancient Egyptians to refer to their land and culture.

Kemetic (Ancient Egyptian) Names	Greek Names
Amun	Zeus
Ra	Helios
Ptah	Hephastos
Nut	Rhea
Geb	Kronos
Net	Athena
Khonsu	Heracles
Set	Ares or Typhon
Bast	Artemis
Uadjit	Leto
Asar (Ausar)	Osiris or Hades
Aset (Auset)	Isis or Demeter
Nebthet	Nephthys
Anpu or Apuat	Anubis
Hetheru	Hathor (Aphrodite)
Heru	Horus or Apollo
Djehuti	Thoth or Hermes
Maat	Astraea or Themis

Introduction to Shetaut Neter Ancient Egyptian African Religion) and Sema Tawi (Egyptian Yoga)

MEDITATION

Why is it Necessary to study Religion?

In order to fully understand the process of Kamitan meditation it is necessary to have a basic understanding of Kamitan religion, as the two aspects of Ancient Egyptian-African culture are related. Firstly, meditation is the ultimate goal of all religions and all disciplines that promote spiritual evolution. Meditation is the final outcome of a life lived righteously, intelligently, lovingly and with strength of will on the spiritual path. So the yogic disciplines have been designed to augment the practice of religion. Religion means to return or rejoin the spirit with the higher self.

The religion of Ancient Kamit incorporated several traditions, each of which enjoined a variation on the practice of divine worship and meditation based on the particular divinity of that tradition. However, it was always recognized that all the divinities are in reality aspects of the transcendental divinity which has neither shape nor form nor name. So just as in other African religions (see the book African Origins by Muata Ashby) the religion of Ancient Egypt (Shetaut Neter) is composed of an advanced system by which human beings can discover the transcendental divine.

Therefore, this first section of this book will present an overview of Shetaut Neter or Neterian religion (Neterianism) of ancient Egypt-Africa and also the Sema disciplines or what is in modern times refered to as "Yoga" that was practiced in ancient times and can be practiced today in order to advance on the path of Kamita Spirituality (spiritual traditions of Ancient Egypt-Africa).

The Ancient Egyptian Path to Enlightenment
The Fundamental Principles of Ancient Egyptian Religion

NETERIANISM
(The Oldest Known Religion in History)

The term "Neterianism" is derived from the name "Shetaut Neter." Shetaut Neter means the "Hidden Divinity." It is the ancient philosophy and mythic spiritual culture that gave rise to the Ancient Egyptian civilization. Those who follow the spiritual path of Shetaut Neter are therefore referred to as "Neterians." The fundamental principles common to all denominations of Ancient Egyptian Religion may be summed up in four "Great Truths" that are common to all the traditions of Ancient Egyptian Religion.

MEDITATION
Summary of Ancient Egyptian Religion

Maa Ur n Shetaut Neter
"Great Truths of The Shetaut Neter Religion"

I

Pa Neter ua ua Neberdjer m Neteru
"The Neter, the Supreme Being, is One and alone and as Neberdjer, manifesting everywhere and in all things in the form of Gods and Goddesses."

II

an-Maat swy Saui Set s-Khemn
"Lack of righteousness brings fetters to the personality and these fetters cause ignorance of the Divine."

III

s-Uashu s-Nafu n saiu Set
"Devotion to the Divine leads to freedom from the fetters of Set."

IIII

ari Shedy Rekh ab m Maakheru
"The practice of the Shedy disciplines leads to knowing oneself and the Divine. This is called being True of Speech"

The Ancient Egyptian Path to Enlightenment
Neterian Great Truths

1. ***"Pa Neter ua ua Neberdjer m Neteru"*** -"The Neter, the Supreme Being, is One and alone and as Neberdjer, manifesting everywhere and in all things in the form of Gods and Goddesses."

Neberdjer means "all-encompassing divinity," the all-inclusive, all-embracing Spirit which pervades all and who is the ultimate essence of all. This first truth unifies all the expressions of Kamitan religion.

2. **"an-Maat swy Saui Set s-Khemn"** - "Lack of righteousness brings fetters to the personality and these fetters lead to ignorance of the Divine."

When a human being acts in ways that contradict the natural order of nature, negative qualities of the mind will develop within that person's personality. These are the afflictions of Set. Set is the neteru of egoism and selfishness. The afflictions of Set include: anger, hatred, greed, lust, jealousy, envy, gluttony, dishonesty, hypocrisy, etc. So to be free from the fetters of set one must be free from the afflictions of Set.

3. **"s-Uashu s-Nafu n saiu Set"** -"Devotion to the Divine leads to freedom from the fetters of Set."

To be liberated (Nafu - freedom - to breath) from the afflictions of Set, one must be devoted to the Divine. Being devoted to the Divine means living by Maat. Maat is a way of life that is purifying to the heart and beneficial for society as it promotes virtue and order. Living by Maat means practicing Shedy (spiritual practices and disciplines).

Uashu means devotion and the classic pose of adoring the Divine is called "Dua," standing or sitting with upraised hands facing outwards towards the image of the divinity.

4. **"ari Shedy Rekh ab m Maakheru"** - "The practice of the Shedy disciplines leads to knowing oneself and the Divine. This is called being True of Speech."

Doing Shedy means to study profoundly, to penetrate the mysteries (Shetaut) and discover the nature of the Divine. There have been several practices designed by the sages of Ancient Kamit to facilitate the process of self-knowledge. These are the religious (Shetaut) traditions and the Sema (Smai) Tawi (yogic) disciplines related to them that augment the spiritual practices.

All the traditions relate the teachings of the sages by means of myths related to particular gods or goddesses. It is understood that all of these neteru are related, like brothers and sisters, having all emanated from the same source, the same Supremely Divine parent, who is neither male nor female, but encompasses the totality of the two.

MEDITATION
The Great Truths of Neterianism are realized by means of Four Spiritual Disciplines in Three Steps

The four disciples are: Rekh Shedy (Wisdom), Ari Shedy (Righteous Action and Selfless Service), Uashu (Ushet) Shedy (Devotion) and Uaa Shedy (Meditation)

The Three Steps are: Listening, Ritual, and Meditation

SEDJM REKH SHEDY

L I S T E N

- *Sedjm REKH Shedy* - **Listening** to the WISDOM of the Neterian Traditions
    - Shetaut Asar — Teachings of the Asarian Tradition
    - Shetaut Anu — Teachings of the Ra Tradition
    - Shetaut Menefer — Teachings of the Ptah Tradition
    - Shetaut Waset — Teachings of the Amun Tradition
    - Shetaut Netrit — Teachings of the Goddess Tradition
    - Shetaut Aton — Teachings of the Aton Tradition

ARI SHEDY

R I T U A L

- *Ari Maat Shedy* – **Righteous Actions** – Purifies the GROSS impurities of the Heart
    - Maat Shedy — True Study of the Ways of hidden nature of Neter
    - Maat Aakhu — True Deeds that lead to glory
    - Maat Aru — True Ritual

UASHU (USHET) SHEDY

- *Ushet Shedy* – **Devotion to the Divine** – Purifies the EMOTIONAL impurities of the Heart
    - Shmai — Divine Music
    - Sema Paut — Meditation in motion
    - Neter Arit — Divine Offerings – Selfless-Service – virtue -

UAA SHEDY

M E D I T A T E

1) *Uaa m Neter Shedy* - 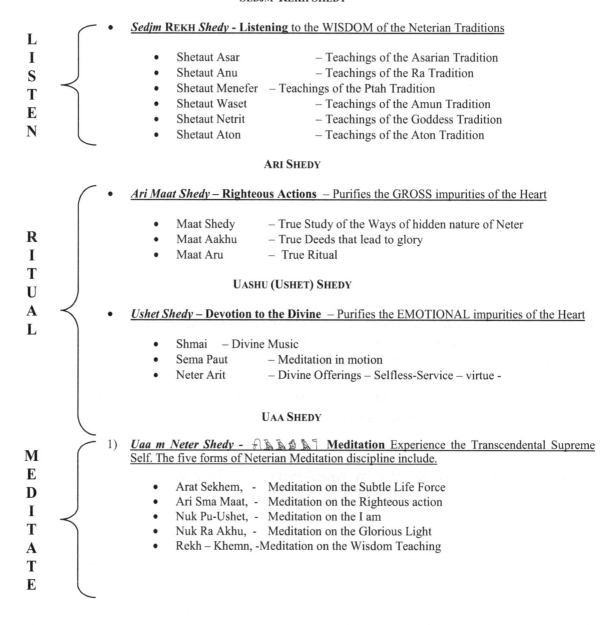 **Meditation** Experience the Transcendental Supreme Self. The five forms of Neterian Meditation discipline include.
    - Arat Sekhem, - Meditation on the Subtle Life Force
    - Ari Sma Maat, - Meditation on the Righteous action
    - Nuk Pu-Ushet, - Meditation on the I am
    - Nuk Ra Akhu, - Meditation on the Glorious Light
    - Rekh – Khemn, -Meditation on the Wisdom Teaching

The Ancient Egyptian Path to Enlightenment
Summary of The Great Truths and the Shedy Paths to their Realization

Great Truths

I
God is One and in all things manifesting through the Neteru

II
Unrighteousness brings fetters and these cause ignorance of truth (#1)

III
Devotion to God allows the personality to free itself from the fetters

IIII
The Shedy disciplines are the greatest form of worship of the Divine

Shedy Disciplines

I
Listen to the Wisdom Teachings (Become Wise)
Learn the mysteries as taught by an authentic teacher which allows this profound statement to be understood.

II
Acting (Living) by Truth
Apply the Philosophy of right action to become virtuous and purify the heart

III
Devotion to the Divine
Worship, ritual and divine love allows the personality purified by truth to eradicate the subtle ignorance that binds it to mortal existence.

IIII
Meditation
Allows the whole person to go beyond the world of time and space and the gross and subtle ignorance of mortal human existence to discover that which transcends time and space.

Great Awakening
Occurs when all of the Great Truths have been realized by perfection of the Shedy disciplines to realize their true nature and actually experience oneness with the transcendental Supreme Being.

MEDITATION

The Spiritual Culture and the Purpose of Life: Shetaut Neter

"Men and women are to become God-like through a life of virtue
and the cultivation of the spirit through scientific knowledge,
practice and bodily discipline."

-Ancient Egyptian Proverb

The highest forms of Joy, Peace and Contentment are obtained when the meaning of life is discovered. When the human being is in harmony with life, then it is possible to reflect and meditate upon the human condition and realize the limitations of worldly pursuits. When there is peace and harmony in life, a human being can practice any of the varied disciplines designated as Shetaut Neter to promote {his/her} evolution towards the ultimate goal of life, which Spiritual Enlightenment. Spiritual Enlightenment is the awakening of a human being to the awareness of the Transcendental essence which binds the universe and which is eternal and immutable. In this discovery is also the sobering and ecstatic realization that the human being is one with that Transcendental essence. With this realization comes great joy, peace and power to experience the fullness of life and to realize the purpose of life during the time on earth. The lotus is a symbol of Shetaut Neter, meaning the turning towards the light of truth, peace and transcendental harmony.

Shetaut Neter

We have established that the Ancient Egyptians were African peoples who lived in the north-eastern quadrant of the continent of Africa. They were descendants of the Nubians, who had themselves originated from farther south into the heart of Africa at the Great Lakes region, the sources of the Nile River. They created a vast civilization and culture earlier than any other society in known history and organized a nation that was based on the concepts of balance and order as well as spiritual enlightenment. These ancient African people called their land Kamit, and soon after developing a well-ordered society, they began to realize that the world is full of wonders, but also that life is fleeting, and that there must be something more to human existence. They developed spiritual systems that were designed to allow human beings to understand the nature of this secret being who is the essence of all Creation. They called this spiritual system "Shtaut Ntr (Shetaut Neter)."

Shetaut means secret.

Neter means Divinity.

The Ancient Egyptian Path to Enlightenment
Who is Neter in Kamitan Religion?

"Ntr"

The symbol of Neter was described by an Ancient Kamitan priest as:
"That which is placed in the coffin"

The term Ntr, or Ntjr, comes from the Ancient Egyptian hieroglyphic language which did not record its vowels. However, the term survives in the Coptic language as *"Nutar."* The same Coptic meaning (divine force or sustaining power) applies in the present as it did in ancient times. It is a symbol composed of a wooden staff that was wrapped with strips of fabric, like a mummy. The strips alternate in color with yellow, green and blue. The mummy in Kamitan spirituality is understood to be the dead but resurrected Divinity. So the Nutar (Ntr) is actually every human being who does not really die, but goes to live on in a different form. Further, the resurrected spirit of every human being is that same Divinity. Phonetically, the term Nutar is related to other terms having the same meaning, such as the latin "Natura," the Spanish Naturalesa, the English "Nature" and "Nutriment", etc. In a real sense, as we will see, Natur means power manifesting as Neteru and the Neteru are the objects of creation, i.e. "nature."

MEDITATION
Sacred Scriptures of Shetaut Neter

The following scriptures represent the foundational scriptures of Kamitan culture. They may be divided into three categories: **Mythic Scriptures**, **Mystical Philosophy** and **Ritual Scriptures**, and **Wisdom Scriptures** (Didactic Literature).

MYTHIC SCRIPTURES Literature	Mystical (Ritual) Philosophy Literature	Wisdom Texts Literature
SHETAUT ASAR-ASET-HERU The Myth of Asar, Aset and Heru (Asarian Resurrection Theology) - Predynastic **SHETAUT ATUM-RA** Anunian Theology Predynastic Shetaut Net/Aset/Hetheru Saitian Theology – Goddess Spirituality Predynastic **SHETAUT PTAH** Memphite Theology Predynastic Shetaut Amun Theban Theology Predynastic	Coffin Texts (C. 2040 B.C.E.-1786 B.C.E.) Papyrus Texts (C. 1580 B.C.E.- Roman Period)[2] Books of Coming Forth By Day Example of famous papyri: Papyrus of Any Papyrus of Hunefer Papyrus of Kenna Greenfield Papyrus, Etc.	Wisdom Texts (C. 3,000 B.C.E. – PTOLEMAIC PERIOD) Precepts of Ptahotep Instructions of Any Instructions of Amenemope Etc. **Maat Declarations** Literature (All Periods) Blind Harpers Songs

---

[2] After 1570 B.C.E they would evolve into a more unified text, the Egyptian Book of the Dead.

The Ancient Egyptian Path to Enlightenment
Neter and the Neteru

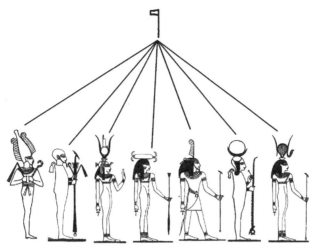

The Neteru (Gods and Goddesses) proceed from the Neter (Supreme Being)

As stated earlier, the concept of Neter and Neteru binds and ties all of the varied forms of Kamitan spirituality into one vision of the gods and goddesses all emerging from the same Supreme Being. Therefore, ultimately, Kamitan spirituality is not polytheistic, nor is it monotheistic, for it holds that the Supreme Being is more than a God or Goddess. The Supreme Being is an all-encompassing Absolute Divinity.

The Neteru

The term "Neteru" means "gods and goddesses." This means that from the ultimate and transcendental Supreme Being, "Neter," come the Neteru. There are countless Neteru. So from the one come the many. These Neteru are cosmic forces that pervade the universe. They are the means by which Neter sustains Creation and manifests through it. So Neterianism is a monotheistic polytheism. The one Supreme Being expresses as many gods and goddesses. At the end of time, after their work of sustaining Creation is finished, these gods and goddesses are again absorbed back into the Supreme Being.

All of the spiritual systems of Ancient Egypt (Kamit) have one essential aspect that is common to all; they all hold that there is a Supreme Being (Neter) who manifests in a multiplicity of ways through nature, the Neteru. Like sunrays, the Neteru emanate from the Divine; they are its manifestations. So by studying the Neteru we learn about and are led to discover their source, the Neter, and with this discovery we are enlightened. The Neteru may be depicted anthropomorphically or zoomorphically in accordance with the teaching about Neter that is being conveyed through them.

MEDITATION
The Neteru and Their Temples

Diagram: The Ancient Egyptian Temple Network

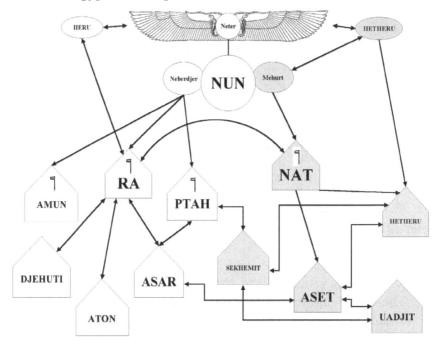

The sages of Kamit instituted a system by which the teachings of spirituality were espoused through a Temple organization. The major divinities were assigned to a particular city. That divinity or group of divinities became the "patron" divinity or divinities of that city. Also, the Priests and Priestesses of that Temple were in charge of seeing to the welfare of the people in that district as well as maintaining the traditions and disciplines of the traditions based on the particular divinity being worshipped. So the original concept of "Neter" became elaborated through the "theologies" of the various traditions. A dynamic expression of the teachings emerged, which though maintaining the integrity of the teachings, expressed nuances of variation in perspective on the teachings to suit the needs of varying kinds of personalities of the people of different locales.

In the diagram above, the primary or main divinities are denoted by the Neter symbol. The house structure represents the Temple for that particular divinity. The interconnections with the other Temples are based on original scriptural statements espoused by the Temples that linked the divinities of their Temple with the other divinities. So this means that the divinities should be viewed not as separate entities operating independently, but rather as family members who are in the same "business" together, i.e. the enlightenment of society, albeit through variations in form of worship, name, form (expression of the Divinity), etc. Ultimately, all the divinities are referred to as Neteru and they are all said to be emanations from the ultimate and Supreme Being. Thus, the teaching from any of the Temples leads to an understanding of the others, and these all lead back to the source, the highest Divinity. Thus, the teaching within any of the Temple systems would lead to the attainment of spiritual enlightenment, the Great Awakening.

The Ancient Egyptian Path to Enlightenment
The Neteru and Their Interrelationships

Diagram : The Primary Kamitan Neteru and their Interrelationships

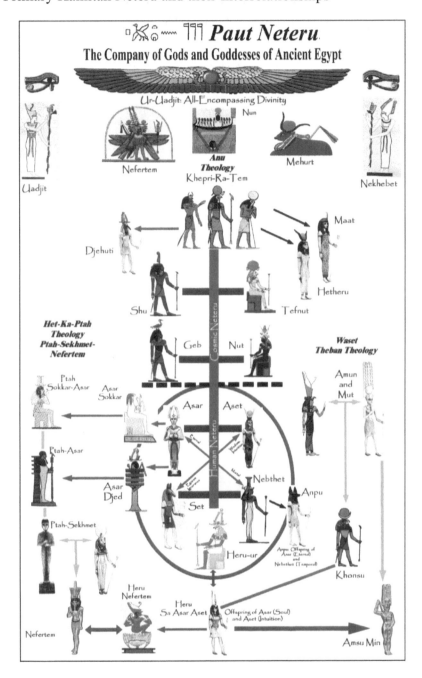

The same Supreme Being, Neter, is the winged all-encompassing transcendental Divinity, the Spirit who, in the early history, is called "Heru." The physical universe in which the Heru lives is called "Hetheru" or the "house of Heru." This divinity (Heru) is also the Nun or primeval substratum from which all matter is composed. The various divinities and the material universe are composed from this primeval substratum. Neter is actually androgynous and Heru, the Spirit, is related as a male aspect of that androgyny. However, Heru in the androgynous aspect, gives rise to the solar principle and this is seen in both the male and female divinities.

The image above provides an idea of the relationships between the divinities of the three main Neterian spiritual systems (traditions): Anunian Theology, Wasetian (Theban) Theology and Het-Ka-Ptah (Memphite) Theology. The traditions are composed of companies or groups of gods and goddesses. Their actions,

MEDITATION

teachings and interactions with each other and with human beings provide insight into their nature as well as that of human existence and Creation itself. The lines indicate direct scriptural relationships and the labels also indicate that some divinities from one system are the same in others, with only a name change. Again, this is attested to by the scriptures themselves in direct statements, like those found in the ***Prt m Hru*** text Chapter 4 (17).[3]

---

[3] See the book *The Egyptian Book of the Dead* by Muata Ashby

The Ancient Egyptian Path to Enlightenment
Listening to the Teachings

"Mestchert"

"Listening, to fill the ears, listen attentively-"

What should the ears be filled with?

The sages of Shetaut Neter enjoined that a Shemsu Neter (follower of Neter, an initiate or aspirant) should listen to the WISDOM of the Neterian Traditions. These are the myth related to the gods and goddesses containing the basic understanding of who they are, what they represent, how they relate human beings and to the Supreme Being. The myths allow us to be connected to the Divine.

An aspirant may choose any one of the 5 main Neterian Traditions.

- Shetaut Anu – Teachings of the Ra Tradition
- Shetaut Menefer – Teachings of the Ptah Tradition
- Shetaut Waset – Teachings of the Amun Tradition
- Shetaut Netrit – Teachings of the Goddess Tradition
- Shetaut Asar – Teachings of the Asarian Tradition
- Shetaut Aton – Teachings of the Aton Tradition

MEDITATION
The Anunian Tradition

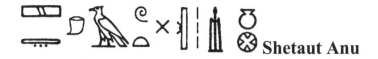 **Shetaut Anu**

The Mystery Teachings of the Anunian Tradition are related to the Divinity Ra and his company of Gods and Goddesses.[4] This Temple and its related Temples espouse the teachings of Creation, human origins and the path to spiritual enlightenment by means of the Supreme Being in the form of the god Ra. It tells of how Ra emerged from a primeval ocean and how human beings were created from his tears. The gods and goddesses, who are his children, go to form the elements of nature and the cosmic forces that maintain nature.

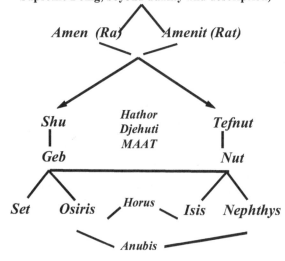

Below: The Heliopolitan Cosmogony.

The city of Anu (Amun-Ra)

Top: Ra. From left to right, starting at the bottom level- The Gods and Goddesses of Anunian Theology: Shu, Tefnut, Nut, Geb, Aset, Asar, Set, Nebthet and Heru-Ur

---

[4] See the Book Anunian Theology by Muata Ashby

The Ancient Egyptian Path to Enlightenment
The Memphite Tradition

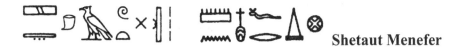 Shetaut Menefer

The Mystery Teachings of the Menefer (Memphite) Tradition are related to the Neterus known as Ptah, Sekhmit, Nefertem. The myths and philosophy of these divinities constitutes Memphite Theology.[5] This temple and its related temples espoused the teachings of Creation, human origins and the path to spiritual enlightenment by means of the Supreme Being in the form of the god Ptah and his family, who compose the Memphite Trinity. It tells of how Ptah emerged from a primeval ocean and how he created the universe by his will and the power of thought (mind). The gods and goddesses who are his thoughts, go to form the elements of nature and the cosmic forces that maintain nature. His spouse, Sekhmit has a powerful temple system of her own that is related to the Memphite teaching. The same is true for his son Nefertem.

Below: The Memphite Cosmogony.

The city of Hetkaptah (Ptah)

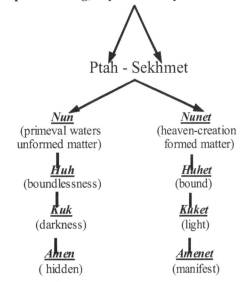

The Neters of Creation -
The Company of the Gods and Goddesses.
Neter Neteru
Nebertcher - Amun (unseen, hidden, ever present, Supreme Being, beyond duality and description)

Ptah - Sekhmet

Nun (primeval waters unformed matter) — *Nunet* (heaven-creation formed matter)

Huh (boundlessness) — *Huhet* (bound)

Kuk (darkness) — *Kuket* (light)

Amen (hidden) — *Amenet* (manifest)

Ptah, Sekhmit and Nefertem

---

[5] See the Book Memphite Theology by Muata Ashby

MEDITATION
The Theban Tradition

Shetaut Amun

The Mystery Teachings of the Wasetian Tradition are related to the Neterus known as Amun, Mut Khonsu. This temple and its related temples espoused the teachings of Creation, human origins and the path to spiritual enlightenment by means of the Supreme Being in the form of the god Amun or Amun-Ra. It tells of how Amun and his family, the Trinity of Amun, Mut and Khonsu, manage the Universe along with his Company of Gods and Goddesses. This Temple became very important in the early part of the New Kingdom Era.

Below: The Trinity of Amun and the Company of Gods and Goddesses of Amun

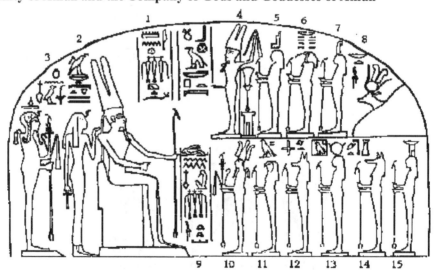

See the Book *Egyptian Yoga Vol. 2* for more on Amun, Mut and Khonsu by Muata Ashby

The Ancient Egyptian Path to Enlightenment
The Goddess Tradition

Shetaut Netrit

"Arat"

The hieroglyphic sign Arat means "Goddess." General, throughout ancient Kamit, the Mystery Teachings of the Goddess Tradition are related to the Divinity in the form of the Goddess. The Goddess was an integral part of all the Neterian traditions but special temples also developed around the worship of certain particular Goddesses who were also regarded as Supreme Beings in their own right. Thus as in other African religions, the goddess as well as the female gender were respected and elevated as the male divinities. The Goddess was also the author of Creation, giving birth to it as a great Cow. The following are the most important forms of the goddess.[6]

Aset, Net, Sekhmit, Mut, Hetheru

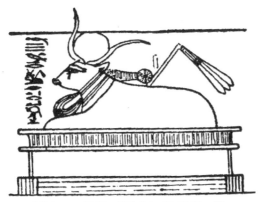

Mehurt ("The Mighty Full One")

---

[6] See the Books, *The Goddess Path, Mysteries of Isis, Glorious Light Meditation, Memphite Theology* and *Resurrecting Osiris* by Muata Ashby

MEDITATION
The Asarian Tradition

 Shetaut Asar

This temple and its related temples espoused the teachings of Creation, human origins and the path to spiritual enlightenment by means of the Supreme Being in the form of the god Asar. It tells of how Asar and his family, the Trinity of Asar, Aset and Heru, manage the Universe and lead human beings to spiritual enlightenment and the resurrection of the soul. This Temple and its teaching were very important from the Pre-Dynastic era down to the Christian period. The Mystery Teachings of the Asarian Tradition are related to the Neterus known as: Asar, Aset, Heru (Osiris, Isis and Horus)

The tradition of Asar, Aset and Heru was practiced generally throughout the land of ancient Kamit. The centers of this tradition were the city of Abdu containing the Great Temple of Asar, the city of Pilak containing the Great Temple of Aset[7] and Edfu containing the Ggreat Temple of Heru.

---

[7] See the Book Resurrecting Osiris by Muata Ashby

The Ancient Egyptian Path to Enlightenment
The Aton Tradition

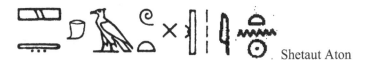 Shetaut Aton

This temple and its related temples espoused the teachings of Creation, human origins and the path to spiritual enlightenment by means of the Supreme Being in the form of the god Aton. It tells of how Aton with its dynamic life force created and sustains Creation. By recognizing Aton as the very substratum of all existence, human beings engage in devotional exercises and rituals and the study of the Hymns containing the wisdom teachings of Aton explaining that Aton manages the Universe and leads human beings to spiritual enlightenment and eternal life for the soul. This Temple and its teaching were very important in the middle New Kingdom Period. The Mystery Teachings of the Aton Tradition are related to the Neter Aton and its main exponent was the Sage King Akhnaton, who is depicted below with his family adoring the sundisk, symbol of the Aton.

Akhnaton, Nefertiti and Daughters

For more on Atonism and the Aton Theology see the Essence of Atonism Lecture Series by Sebai Muata Ashby ©2001

MEDITATION
The General Principles of Shetaut Neter
(Teachings Presented in the Kamitan scriptures)

1. The Purpose of Life is to Attain the Great Awakening-Enlightenment-Know thyself.

2. SHETAUT NETER enjoins the Shedy (spiritual investigation) as the highest endeavor of life.

3. SHETAUT NETER enjoins that it is the responsibility of every human being to promote order and truth.

4. SHETAUT NETER enjoins the performance of Selfless Service to family, community and humanity.

5. SHETAUT NETER enjoins the Protection of nature.

6. SHETAUT NETER enjoins the Protection of the weak and oppressed.

7. SHETAUT NETER enjoins the Caring for hungry.

8. SHETAUT NETER enjoins the Caring for homeless.

9. SHETAUT NETER enjoins the equality for all people.

10. SHETAUT NETER enjoins the equality between men and women.

11. SHETAUT NETER enjoins the justice for all.

12. SHETAUT NETER enjoins the sharing of resources.

13. SHETAUT NETER enjoins the protection and proper raising of children.

14. SHETAUT NETER enjoins the movement towards balance and peace.

The Ancient Egyptian Path to Enlightenment

The Forces of Entropy

In Neterian religion, there is no concept of "evil" as is conceptualized in Western Culture. Rather, it is understood that the forces of entropy are constantly working in nature to bring that which has been constructed by human hands to their original natural state. The serpent Apep (Apophis), who daily tries to stop Ra's boat of creation, is the symbol of entropy. This concept of entropy has been referred to as "chaos" by Western Egyptologists.

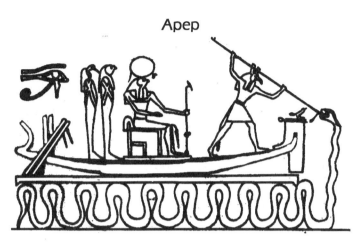

Above: Set protecting the boat of Ra from the forces of entropy (symbolized by the serpent Apep).

As expressed previously, in Neterian religion there is also no concept of a "devil" or "demon" as is conceived in the Judeo-Christian or Islamic traditions. Rather, it is understood that manifestations of detrimental situations and adversities arise as a result of unrighteous actions. These unrighteous actions are due to the "Setian" qualities in a human being. Set is the Neteru of egoism and the negative qualities which arise from egoism. Egoism is the idea of individuality based on identification with the body and mind only as being who one is. One has no deeper awareness of their deeper spiritual essence, and thus no understanding of their connectedness to all other objects (includes persons) in creation and the Divine Self. When the ego is under the control of the higher nature, it fights the forces of entropy (as above). However, when beset with ignorance, it leads to the degraded states of human existence. The vices (egoism, selfishness, extraverted ness, wonton sexuality (lust), jealousy, envy, greed, gluttony) are a result.

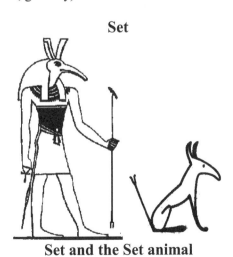

Set and the Set animal

MEDITATION
The Great Awakening of Neterian Religion

"Nehast"

Nehast means to "wake up," to Awaken to the higher existence. In the Prt m Hru Text it is said:

Nuk pa Neter aah Neter Uah asha ren[8]

"I am that same God, the Supreme One, who has myriad of mysterious names."

The goal of all the Neterian disciplines is to discover the meaning of "Who am I?," to unravel the mysteries of life and to fathom the depths of eternity and infinity. This is the task of all human beings and it is to be accomplished in this very lifetime.

This can be done by learning the ways of the Neteru, emulating them and finally becoming like them, Akhus, (enlightened beings), walking the earth as giants and accomplishing great deeds such as the creation of the universe!

Udjat
The Eye of Heru is a quintessential symbol of awakening to Divine Consciousness, representing the concept of Nehast.

---

[8] (Prt M Hru 9:4)

The Ancient Egyptian Path to Enlightenment
What is Egyptian Yoga? What is Yoga?

In order to have a full understanding of what meditation is you will first be introduced to the basic concept of yoga and its main disciplines. Then we will explore its practice in Ancient Egypt. Then we will focus on the specific forms of meditation practiced in the Ancient Egyptian spiritual traditions.

Most students of yoga are familiar with the yogic traditions of India consider that the Indian texts such as the Bhagavad Gita, Mahabharata, Patanjali Yoga Sutras, etc. are the primary and original source of Yogic philosophy and teaching. However, upon examination, the teachings currently espoused in all of the major forms of Indian Yoga can be found in Ancient Egyptian scriptures, inscribed in papyrus and on temple walls as well as steles, statues, obelisks and other sources.

Yoga is the practice of mental, physical and spiritual disciplines which lead to self-control and self-discovery by purifying the mind, body and spirit, so as to discover the deeper spiritual essence which lies within every human being and object in the universe. In essence, the goal of Yoga practice is to unite or *yoke* one's individual consciousness with Universal or Cosmic consciousness. Therefore, Ancient Egyptian religious practice, especially in terms of the rituals and other practices of the Ancient Egyptian Temple system known as *Shetaut Neter* (the way of the hidden Supreme Being), also known in Ancient times as *Smai Tawi* "Egyptian Yoga," should as well be considered as universal streams of self-knowledge philosophy which influenced and inspired the great religions and philosophers to this day. In this sense, religion, in its purest form, is also a Yoga system, as it seeks to reunite the soul with its true and original source, God. In broad terms, any spiritual movement or discipline that brings one closer to self-knowledge is a "Yogic" movement. The main recognized forms of Yoga disciplines are:

- *Yoga of Wisdom,*
- *Yoga of Devotional Love,*
- *Yoga of Meditation,*
    - *Physical Postures Yoga*
- *Yoga of Selfless Action,*
- *Tantric Yoga*
    - *Serpent Power Yoga*

The diagram below shows the relationship between the Yoga disciplines and the path of mystical religion (religion practiced in its three complete steps: 1st receiving the myth {knowledge}, 2nd practicing the rituals of the myth {following the teachings of the myth} and 3rd entering into a mystical experience {becoming one with the central figure of the myth}).

MEDITATION

```
                    Myth    Ritual   Mystical
    Path of ──────→   ↓       ↓        ↓
    Religion       Devotion  Action  Meditation
   ↗                   ↕       ↕    and Wisdom*
Spiritual    Three                      ↕
Aspiration   Stages → ASPIRATION → STRIVING → ESTABLISHED
   ↘                                            → Meditation ─┐
         Path of                                → Devotion    ├→ Spiritual
         Yoga    ─────────────────────────────→ Wisdom*       │  Enlightenment
         Mysticism                              → Action      │
                                                → Tantrism ───┘
```

The disciplines of Yoga fall under five major categories. These are: *Yoga of Wisdom, Yoga of Devotional Love, Yoga of Meditation, Tantric Yoga* and *Yoga of Selfless Action.* When these disciplines are practiced in a harmonized manner this practice is called "Integral Yoga." Within these categories there are subsidiary forms which are part of the main disciplines. The emphasis in the Kamitan Asarian (Osirian) Myth is on the Yoga of Wisdom, Yoga of Devotional Love and Yoga of Selfless Action. The important point to remember is that all aspects of Yoga can and should be used in an integral fashion to effect an efficient and harmonized spiritual movement in the practitioner. Therefore, while there may be an area of special emphasis, other elements are bound to become part of the Yoga program as needed. For example, while a Yogin (practitioner of Yoga, aspirant, initiate) may place emphasis on the Yoga of Wisdom, they may also practice Devotional Yoga and Meditation Yoga along with the wisdom studies. So the practice of any discipline that leads to oneness with Supreme Consciousness can be called Yoga. If you study, rationalize and reflect upon the teachings, you are practicing *Yoga of Wisdom*. If you meditate upon the teachings and your Higher Self, you are practicing *Yoga of Meditation*.

Thus, whether or not you refer to it as such, if you practice rituals which identify you with your spiritual nature, you are practicing *Yoga of Ritual Identification* (which is part of the Yoga of Wisdom {Kamitan-Rekh, Indian-Jnana} and the Yoga of Devotional Love {Kamitan-Ushet, Indian-Bhakti} of the Divine). If you develop your physical nature and psychic energy centers, you are practicing *Serpent Power* (Kamitan-*Uraeus* or Indian-*Kundalini*) *Yoga* (which is part of Tantric Yoga). If you practice living according to the teachings of ethical behavior and selflessness, you are practicing *Yoga of Action* (Kamitan-Maat, Indian-Karma) in daily life. If you practice turning your attention towards the Divine by developing love for the Divine, then it is called *Devotional Yoga* or *Yoga of Divine Love*. The practitioner of Yoga is called a Yogin (male practitioner) or Yogini (female practitioner), or the term "Yogi" may be used to refer to either a female or male practitioner in general terms. One who has attained the culmination of Yoga (union with the Divine) is also called a Yogi. In this manner, Yoga has been developed into many disciplines which may be used in an integral fashion to achieve the same goal: Enlightenment. Therefore, the aspirant is to learn about all of the paths of Yoga and choose those elements which best suit {his/her} personality or practice them all in an integral, balanced way.

Enlightenment is the term used to describe the highest level of spiritual awakening. It means attaining such a level of spiritual awareness that one discovers the underlying unity of the entire universe as well as the fact that the source of all creation is the same source from which the innermost Self within every human heart arises.

The Ancient Egyptian Path to Enlightenment
What is Egyptian Yoga?

The Term "Egyptian Yoga" and The Philosophy Behind It

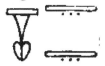

Smai Tawi (From Chapter 4 of the *Prt m Hru*)

As previously discussed, Yoga in all of its forms were practiced in Egypt apparently earlier than anywhere else in our history. This point of view is supported by the fact that there is documented scriptural and iconographical evidence of the disciplines of virtuous living, dietary purification, study of the wisdom teachings and their practice in daily life, psychophysical and psycho-spiritual exercises and meditation being practiced in Ancient Egypt, long before the evidence of its existence is detected in India (including the Indus Valley Civilization) or any other early civilization (Sumer, Greece, China, etc.).

The teachings of Yoga are at the heart of *Prt m Hru*. As explained earlier, the word "Yoga" is a Sanskrit term meaning to unite the individual with the Cosmic. The term has been used in certain parts of this book for ease of communication since the word "Yoga" has received wide popularity especially in western countries in recent years. The Ancient Egyptian equivalent term to the Sanskrit word yoga is: *"Smai." Smai* means union, and the following determinative terms give it a spiritual significance, at once equating it with the term "Yoga" as it is used in India. When used in conjunction with the Ancient Egyptian symbol which means land, *"Ta,"* the term "union of the two lands" arises.

In Chapter 4 and Chapter 17 of the *Prt m Hru*, a term "Smai Tawi" is used. It means "Union of the two lands of Egypt," ergo "Egyptian Yoga." The two lands refer to the two main districts of the country (North and South). In ancient times, Egypt was divided into two sections or land areas. These were known as Lower and Upper Egypt. In Ancient Egyptian mystical philosophy, the land of Upper Egypt relates to the divinity Heru (Heru), who represents the Higher Self, and the land of Lower Egypt relates to Set, the divinity of the lower self. So *Smai Taui* means "the union of the two lands" or the "Union of the lower self with the Higher Self. The lower self relates to that which is negative and uncontrolled in the human mind including worldliness, egoism, ignorance, etc. (Set), while the Higher Self relates to that which is above temptations and is good in the human heart as well as in touch with transcendental consciousness (Heru). Thus, we also have the Ancient Egyptian term *Smai Heru-Set,* or the union of Heru and Set. So Smai Taui or Smai Heru-Set are the Ancient Egyptian words which are to be translated as **"Egyptian Yoga."**

Above: the main symbol of Egyptian Yoga: *Sma*. The Ancient Egyptian language and symbols provide the first "historical" record of Yoga Philosophy and Religious literature. The hieroglyph Sma, "Sema," represented by the union of two lungs and the trachea, symbolizes

MEDITATION

that the union of the duality, that is, the Higher Self and lower self, leads to Non-duality, the One, singular consciousness.

The Ancient Egyptians called the disciplines of Yoga in Ancient Egypt by the term "*Smai Tawi.*" So what does Smai Tawi mean?

Smai Tawi
(From Chapter 4 of the *Prt m Hru*)

The Ancient Egyptian Symbols of Yoga

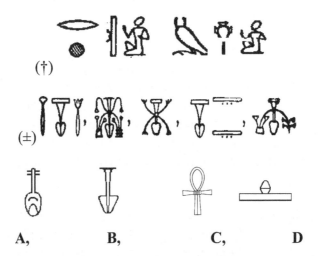

The theme of the arrangement of the symbols above is based on the idea that in mythological and philosophic forms, Egyptian mythology and philosophy merge with world mythology, philosophy and religion. The hieroglyphic symbols at the very top (†) mean: **"Know Thyself," "Self knowledge is the basis of all true knowledge"** and (±) abbreviated forms of **Smai taui,** signifies "Egyptian Yoga." The next four below represent the four words in Egyptian Philosophy, which mean **"YOGA."** They are: (A) **"Nefer"** (B) **"Sema"** (C) **"Ankh"** and (D) **"Hetep."**

The Ancient Egyptian Path to Enlightenment

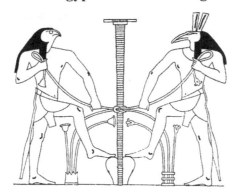

Above left: Smai Heru-Set, Heru and Set join forces to tie up the symbol of Union (Sema –see (B) above). The Sema symbol refers to the Union of Upper Egypt (Lotus) and Lower Egypt (Papyrus) under one ruler, but also at a more subtle level, it refers to the union of one's Higher Self and lower self (Heru and Set), as well as the control of one's breath (Life Force) through the union (control) of the lungs (breathing organs). The character of Heru and Set are an integral part of the Pert Em Heru.

The central and most popular character within Ancient Egyptian Religion of Asar is Heru, who is an incarnation of his father, Asar. Asar is killed by his brother Set who, out of greed and demoniac (Setian) tendency, craved to be the ruler of Egypt. With the help of Djehuti, the God of wisdom, Aset, the great mother and Hetheru, his consort, Heru prevailed in the battle against Set for the rulership of Kemit (Egypt). Heru's struggle symbolizes the struggle of every human being to regain rulership of the Higher Self and to subdue the lower self.

The most ancient writings in our historical period are from the Ancient Egyptians. These writings are referred to as hieroglyphics. The original name given to these writings by the Ancient Egyptians is *Metu Neter,* meaning "the writing of God" or *Neter Metu* or "Divine Speech." These writings were inscribed in temples, coffins and papyruses and contained the teachings in reference to the spiritual nature of the human being and the ways to promote spiritual emancipation, awakening or resurrection. The Ancient Egyptian proverbs presented in this text are translations from the original hieroglyphic scriptures. An example of hieroglyphic text was presented above in the form of the text of Smai Taui or "Egyptian Yoga."

Egyptian Philosophy may be summed up in the following proverbs, which clearly state that the soul is heavenly or divine and that the human being must awaken to the true reality, which is the Spirit, Self.

"Self knowledge is the basis of true knowledge."

"Soul to heaven, body to earth."

"Man is to become God-like through a life of virtue and the cultivation of the spirit through scientific knowledge, practice and bodily discipline."

"Salvation is accomplished through the efforts of the individual. There is no mediator between man and {his/her} salvation."

MEDITATION

"Salvation is the freeing of the soul from its bodily fetters, becoming a God through knowledge and wisdom, controlling the forces of the cosmos instead of being a slave to them, subduing the lower nature and through awakening the Higher Self, ending the cycle of rebirth and dwelling with the Neters who direct and control the Great Plan."

Egyptian Yoga is a revolutionary new way to understand and practice Ancient Egyptian Mysticism, the Ancient Egyptian mystical religion (*Shetaut Neter*). Egyptian Yoga is what has been commonly referred to by Egyptologists as Egyptian "Religion" or "Mythology," but to think of it as just another set of stories or allegories about a long lost civilization is to completely miss the greatest secret of human existence. What is Yoga? The literal meaning of the word YOGA is to *"YOKE"* or to *"LINK"* back. The implication is to link back individual consciousness to its original source, the original essence: Universal Consciousness. In a broad sense Yoga is any process which helps one to achieve liberation or freedom from the bondage to human pain and spiritual ignorance. So whenever you engage in any activity with the goal of promoting the discovery of your true Self, be it studying the wisdom teachings, exercise, fasting, meditation, breath control, rituals, chanting, prayer, etc., you are practicing yoga. If the goal is to help you to discover your essential nature as one with God or the Supreme Being or Consciousness, then it is Yoga. Yoga, in all of its forms as the disciplines of spiritual development, as practiced in Ancient Egypt earlier than anywhere else in history. The ancient scriptures describe how Asar, the first mythical king of Ancient Egypt, traveled throughout Asia and Europe establishing civilization and the practice of religion. This partially explains why the teachings of mystical spirituality known as Yoga and Vedanta in India are so similar to the teachings of Shetaut Neter (Ancient Egyptian religion - Egyptian Yoga. This unique perspective from the highest philosophical system which developed in Africa over seven thousand years ago provides a new way to look at life, religion, psychology and the way to spiritual development leading to spiritual Enlightenment. So Egyptian Yoga is not merely a philosophy but a discipline for promoting spiritual evolution in a human being, allowing him or her to discover the ultimate truth, supreme peace and utmost joy which lies within the human heart. These are the true worthwhile goals of life. Anything else is settling for less. It would be like a personality who owns vast riches thinking that he is poor and homeless. Every human being has the potential to discover the greatest treasure of all existence if they apply themselves to the study and practice of the teachings of Yoga with the proper guidance. Sema ( ) is the Ancient Egyptian word and symbol meaning *union or Yoga*. This is the vision of Egyptian Yoga.

The Ancient Egyptian Path to Enlightenment
The Study of Yoga

When we look out upon the world, we are often baffled by the multiplicity, which constitutes the human experience. What do we really know about this experience? Many scientific disciplines have developed over the last two hundred years for the purpose of discovering the mysteries of nature, but this search has only engendered new questions about the nature of existence. Yoga is a discipline or way of life designed to promote the physical, mental and spiritual development of the human being. It leads a person to discover the answers to the most important questions of life such as, Who am I? Why am I here? Where am I going?

As explained earlier, the literal meaning of the word *Yoga* is to *"Yoke"* or to *"Link"* back, the implication being to link the individual consciousness back to the original source, the original essence, that which transcends all mental and intellectual attempts at comprehension, but which is the essential nature of everything in Creation, termed "Universal Consciousness. While in the strict sense, Yoga may be seen as a separate discipline from religion, yoga and religion have been linked at many points throughout history and continue to be linked even today. In a manner of speaking, Yoga as a discipline may be seen as a non-sectarian transpersonal science or practice to promote spiritual development and harmony of mind and body thorough mental and physical disciplines including meditation, psycho-physical exercises, and performing action with the correct attitude.

The teachings which were practiced in the Ancient Egyptian temples were the same ones later intellectually defined into a literary form by the Indian Sages of Vedanta and Yoga. This was discussed in our book *Egyptian Yoga: The Philosophy of Enlightenment*. The Indian Mysteries of Yoga and Vedanta may therefore be understood as representing an unfolding exposition of the Egyptian Mysteries.

The question is how to accomplish these seemingly impossible tasks? How to transform yourself and realize the deepest mysteries of existence? How to discover "Who am I?" This is the mission of Yoga Philosophy and the purpose of yogic practices. Yoga does not seek to convert or impose religious beliefs on any one. Ancient Egypt was the source of civilization and the source of religion and Yoga. Therefore, all systems of mystical spirituality can coexist harmoniously within these teachings when they are correctly understood.

The goal of yoga is to promote integration of the mind-body-spirit complex in order to produce optimal health of the human being. This is accomplished through mental and physical exercises which promote the free flow of spiritual energy by reducing mental complexes caused by ignorance. There are two roads which human beings can follow, one of wisdom and the other of ignorance. The path of the masses is generally the path of ignorance which leads them into negative situations, thoughts and deeds. These in turn lead to ill health and sorrow in life. The other road is based on wisdom and it leads to health, true happiness and enlightenment.

The central and most popular character within ancient Egyptian Religion of Asar is Heru who is an incarnation of his father, Asar. Asar is killed by his brother Set who, out of greed and demoniac (Setian) tendency, craves to be the ruler of Egypt. With the help of Djehuti, the God of wisdom, Aset, the great mother and Hetheru, his consort, Heru prevails in the battle against Set for the rulership of Egypt. Heru' struggle symbolizes the struggle of every human being to regain rulership of the Higher Self and to subdue the lower self. With this understanding, the land of Egypt is equivalent to the Kingdom/Queendom concept of Christianity.

MEDITATION

The most ancient writings in our historical period are from the ancient Egyptians. These writings are referred to as hieroglyphics. Also, the most ancient civilization known was the ancient Egyptian civilization. The proof of this lies in the ancient Sphinx which is over 12,000 years old. The original name given to these writings by the ancient Egyptians is *Metu Neter*, meaning "the writing of God" or *Neter Metu* or "Divine Speech." These writings were inscribed in temples, coffins and papyruses and contained the teachings in reference to the spiritual nature of the human being and the ways to promote spiritual emancipation, awakening or resurrection. The —Ancient Egyptian Proverbs presented in this text are translations from the original hieroglyphic scriptures. An example of hieroglyphic text is presented on the front cover.

Egyptian Philosophy may be summed up in the following proverbs which clearly state that the soul is heavenly or divine and that the human being must awaken to the true reality which is the spirit Self.

"Self knowledge is the basis of true knowledge."

"Soul to heaven, body to earth."

"Man is to become God-like through a life of virtue and the cultivation of the spirit through scientific knowledge, practice and bodily discipline."

"Salvation is accomplished through the efforts of the individual. There is no mediator between man and his / her salvation."

"Salvation is the freeing of the soul from its bodily fetters, becoming a God through knowledge and wisdom, controlling the forces of the cosmos instead of being a slave to them, subduing the lower nature and through awakening the Higher Self, ending the cycle of rebirth and dwelling with the Neters who direct and control the Great Plan."

The Sema Tawi of Wisdom

In the Temple of Aset (Aset) in Ancient Egypt the Discipline of the Yoga of Wisdom is imparted in three stages:

THE THREE-FOLD PROCESS OF WISDOM YOGA IN EGYPT:

According to the teachings of *the Ancient Temple of Aset* the Yoga of Wisdom, entails the process of three steps:

Discipline of Wisdom Yoga in Ancient Egypt
1-<u>Listening</u> to the wisdom teachings on the nature of reality (creation) and the nature of the Self.
2-<u>Reflecting</u> on those teachings and incorporating them into daily life.
3-<u>Meditating</u> on the meaning of the teachings.

1-<u>Listening</u> to the wisdom teachings on the nature of reality (creation) and the nature of the Self.
2-<u>Reflecting</u> on those teachings and incorporating them into daily life.
3-<u>Meditating</u> on the meaning of the teachings.

Aset (Aset) was and is recognized as the goddess of wisdom and her temple strongly emphasized and espoused the philosophy of wisdom teaching in order to achieve higher spiritual consciousness. It is important to note here that the teaching which was practiced in the Ancient Egyptian Temple of Aset[9] of **Listening** to, **Reflecting** upon, and **Meditating** upon the teachings is the same process used in Vedanta-Jnana Yoga of India of today. **The Yoga of Wisdom** is a form of Yoga based on insight into the nature of worldly existence and the transcendental Self, thereby transforming one's consciousness through development of the wisdom faculty. Thus, we have here a correlation between Ancient Egypt that matches exactly in its basic factor respects.

---

[9] See the book *The Wisdom of Aset* by Dr. Muata Ashby

MEDITATION

Figure: The image of goddess Aset (Aset) suckling the young king is the quintecential symbol of initiation in Ancient Egypt.

Temple of Aset
GENERAL DISCIPLINE

Fill the ears, listen attentively- Meh mestchert.

Listening

1- Listening to Wisdom teachings. Having achieved the qualifications of an aspirant, there is a desire to listen to the teachings from a Spiritual Preceptor. There is increasing intellectual understanding of the scriptures and the meaning of truth versus untruth, real versus unreal, temporal versus eternal. The glories of God are expounded and the mystical philosophy behind the myth is given at this stage.

MAUI

"to think, to ponder, to fix attention, concentration"

Reflection

2- Reflection on those teachings that have been listened to and living according to the disciplines enjoined by the teachings is to be practiced until the wisdom teaching is fully understood. Reflection implies discovering, intellectually at first, the oneness behind the multiplicity of the world by engaging in intense inquiry into the nature of one's true Self. Chanting the hekau and divine singing *Hesi,* are also used here.

"Devote yourself to adore God's name."

—Ancient Egyptian Proverb

Meditation

3- Meditation in Wisdom Yoga is the process of reflection that leads to a state in which the mind is continuously introspective. It means expansion of consciousness culminating in revelation of and identification with the Absolute Self.

Note: It is important to note here that the same teaching which was practiced in ancient Egypt of **Listening** to, **Reflecting** upon, and **Meditating** upon the teachings is the same process used in Vedanta-Jnana Yoga (from India) of today.

The Ancient Egyptian Path to Enlightenment

The Sema Tawi of Right Action

GENERAL DISCIPLINE
In all Temples especially
The Temple of Heru and Edfu

Scripture: Prt M Hru and special scriptures including the Berlin Papyrus and other papyri.

1- Learn Ethics and Law of Cause and Effect-Practice right action
(42 Precepts of Maat)
to purify gross impurities of the personality
Control Body, Speech, Thoughts

2- Practice cultivation of the higher virtues
(selfless-service)
to purify mind and intellect from subtle impurities

3- Devotion to the Divine
See maatian actions as offerings to the Divine

4- Meditation
See oneself as one with Maat, i.e. United with the cosmic order which is the Transcendental Supreme Self.

Plate 1: The Offering of Maat-Symbolizing the Ultimate act of Righteousness (Temple of Seti I)

MEDITATION

The Sema Tawi of Divine Love

GENERAL DISCIPLINE
In all Temples

Scripture: Prt M Hru and Temple Inscriptions.

<u>Discipline of Devotion</u>

1– Listening to the myth
    Get to know the Divinity
    Empathize
    Romantisize

2- Ritual about the myth
    Offerings to Divinity – propitiation
    act like divinity
    Chant the name of the Divinity
    Sing praises of the Divinity
    COMMUNE with the Divinity

3– Mysticism
    Melting of the heart
    Dissolve into Divinity

    IDENTIFY-with the Divinity

In the Kamitan teaching of Devotional love:

God is termed *Merri,* "Beloved One"

Love and Be Loved
"That person is beloved by the Lord." PMH, Ch 4

Offering Oneself to God-Surrender to God- Become One with God

The Ancient Egyptian Path to Enlightenment
Figure 1: The Dua Pose- Upraised arms with palms facing out towards the Divine Image

MEDITATION
Sema Tawi of Postures

The Yogic Postures in Ancient Egypt

Since their introduction to the West, the exercise system of India known as "Hatha Yoga" has gained much popularity. The disciplines related to the yogic postures and movements were developed in India around the 10th century A.C.E. by a sage named Goraksha.[10] Up to this time, the main practice was simply to adopt the cross-legged meditation posture known as the lotus for the purpose of practicing meditation. The most popular manual on Hatha Yoga is the *Hatha Yoga-Pradipika ("Light on the Forceful Yoga).* It was authored by Svatmarama Yogin in mid. 14th century A.C.E.[11]

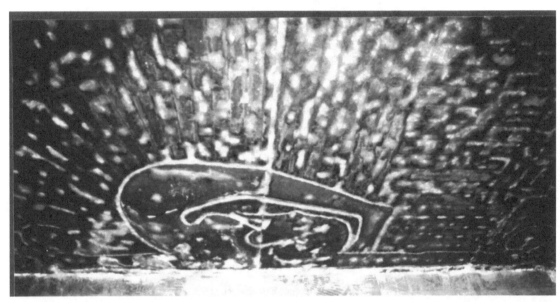

Above- The god Geb in the plough posture engraved on the ceiling of the antechamber to the Asarian Resurrection room of the Temple of Hetheru in Egypt. (photo taken by Ashby). Below: Illustration of the posture engraved on the ceiling.

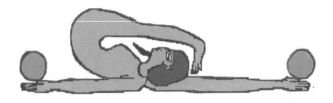

---

[10] Yoga Journal, {The New Yoga} January/February 2000
[11] **Hatha-Yoga-Pradipika,** <u>The Shambhala Encyclopedia of Yoga</u> by Georg Feuerstein, Ph. D.

The Ancient Egyptian Path to Enlightenment

Prior to the emergence of the discipline of the physical movements in India just before 1000 A.C.E.,[12] a series of virtually identical postures to those which were practiced in India can be found in various Ancient Egyptian papyruses and inscribed on the walls and ceilings of the temples. The Ancient Egyptian practice can be dated from 10,000 B.C.E to 300 B.C.E and earlier. Examples: Temple of Hetheru (800-300 B.C.E.), Temple of Heru (800-300 B.C.E.), Tomb of Queen Nefertari (reigned 1,279-1,212 B.C.E.), and various other temples and papyruses from the New Kingdom Era (c. 1,580 B.C.E). In Ancient Egypt the practice of the postures, called *Tjef Sema Paut Neteru* which means "Movements to promote union with the gods and goddesses" or simply *Sema Paut* (Union with the gods and goddesses), were part of the ritual aspect of the spiritual myth, which when practiced, served to harmonize the energies and promote the physical health of the body and direct the mind in a meditative capacity to discover and cultivate divine consciousness. These disciplines are part of a larger process called Sema or *Smai Tawi* (Egyptian Yoga). By acting and moving like the gods and goddesses one can essentially discover their character, energy and divine agency within one's consciousness, and thereby also become one of their retinue, that is, one with the Divine Self. In modern times, most practitioners of Indian Hatha Yoga see it primarily as a means to attain physical health only. However, even the practice in India had an origin in myth and a mythic component which is today largely ignored by modern practitioners.

(A) (B)

(C)

Above left: The Kamitan goddess Nut and god Geb and the higher planes of existence.
Above center and right: The goddess Nut performs the forward bend posture.

---

[12] *The Shambhala Encyclopedia of Yoga* by Georg Feuerstein, Ph. D.

MEDITATION

The figure above (left) depicts another conceptualization of the Netherworld, which is at the same time the body of Nut in a forward bend yoga exercise posture. The innermost goddess symbolizes the lower heaven where the moon traverses, the physical realm. The middle one symbolizes the course of the sun in its Astral journey. This shows a differentiation between the physical heavens and the Astral plane, as well as time and physical space and Astral time and space, i.e., the concept of different dimensions and levels of consciousness. The outermost symbolizes the causal plane.

Below- The Egyptian Gods and Goddesses act out the Creation through their movements: Forward bend -Nut, Spinal twist -Geb, Journey of Ra – Ra in his boat, and the squatting and standing motions of Nun and Shu.

The Ancient Egyptian Path to Enlightenment

Figure 2: The varied postures found in the Kamitan papyruses and temple inscriptions.

Figure 3: The practice of the postures is shown in the sequence below.

MEDITATION

20th Century A.C.E.
1. **Ananda Yoga** (Swami Kriyananda)
2. **Anusara Yoga** (John Friend)
3. **Ashtanga Yoga** (K. Pattabhi)
4. **Ashtanga Yoga** (Pattabhi Jois)
5. **Bikram Yoga** (Bikram Choudhury)
6. **Integral Yoga** (Swami Satchidananda b.
7. **Iyengar Yoga** (B.K.S. Iyengar)
8. **Kripalu Yoga** (Amrit Desai)
9. **Kundalini Yoga** (Yogi Bhajan)
10. **Sivananda Yoga** (Swami Vishnu-devananda)
11. **Svaroopa Yoga** (Rama Berch)

Women first admitted to Hatha Yoga practice

1893 A.C.E. — World Parliament of Religions – Vedanta Introduced to the West

1750 A.C.E. — Shiva Samhita – Hatha Yoga text – melds Vedanta with Hatha

1539 A.C.E. — Birth of Sikhism

1350 A.C.E. — Hatha Yoga Pradipika text - India

1000 A.C.E. — Goraksha – Siddha Yogis First Indian Hatha Yoga Practice

600 A.C.E. — Birth of Islam

Year 0 — Birth of Jesus – Christianity

300 B.C.E. — Arat, Geb, Nut Egyptian Yoga Postures – Late Period

1,680 B.C.E. — Geb, Nut, Ra, Asar, Aset, Sobek Egyptian Yoga Postures – New Kingdom

2,000 B.C.E. — Indus Valley – Kundalini – Serpent Power-Lotus Pose

3,600 B.C.E. — Nefertem Egyptian Yoga Posture – Old-Middle Kingdom Period

10,000 B.C.E. — Serpent Power-Horemakhet Egyptian Yoga Posture – Ancient Egyptian

The Ancient Egyptian Path to Enlightenment

The Sema Tawi of Tantrism

> Tantric influence, however, is not limited to India alone, and there is evidence that the precepts of tantrism traveled to various parts of the world, especially Nepal, Tibet, China, Japan and parts of South-East Asia; its influence has also been evident in Mediterranean cultures such as those of Egypt and Crete.[13]
> -Ajit Mookerjee (Indian Scholar-Author –from the book *The Tantric Way*)

Tantra Yoga is purported to be the oldest system of Yoga. Tantra Yoga is a system of Yoga which seeks to promote the re-union between the individual and the Absolute Reality, through the worship of nature and ultimately the Cosmos as an expression of the Absolute. Since nature is an expression of GOD, it gives clues as to the underlying reality that sustains it and the way to achieve wisdom, i.e. transcendence of it. The most obvious and important teaching that nature holds is the idea that creation is made up of pairs of opposites: Up-down, here-there, you-me, us-them, hot-cold, male-female, Ying-Yang, etc. The interaction, of these two complementary opposites, we call life and movement.

Insight (wisdom) into the true nature of reality gives us a clue as to the way to realize the oneness of creation within ourselves. By re-uniting the male and female principles in our own bodies and minds, we may reach the oneness that underlies our apparent manifestation as a man or woman. Thus, the term Tantra means to create a bridge between the opposites and in so doing the opposites dissolve, leaving unitary and transcendental consciousness. The union of the male and female principles may be effected by two individuals who worship GOD through GOD's manifestation in each other or by an individual who seeks union with GOD through uniting with his or her male or female spiritual partner. All men and women have both female and male principles within themselves.

In the Egyptian philosophical system, all Neteru or God principles emanate from the one GOD. When these principles are created, they are depicted as having a ***male and female*** principle. All objects and life forms appear in creation as either male or female, but underlying this apparent duality, there is a unity which is rooted in the pure consciousness of oneness, the consciousness of GOD, which underlies and supports all things. To realize this oneness consciously deep inside is the supreme goal.

In Tantrism, sexual symbolism is used frequently because these are the most powerful images denoting the opposites of Creation and the urge to unify and become whole, for sexuality is the urge for unity and self-discovery albeit limited to physical intercourse by most people. If this

---

[13] *The Tantric Way* by Ajit Mookerjee and Madhu Khanna

MEDITATION

force is understood, harnessed and sublimated it will lead to unity of the highest order that is unity with the Divine Self.

Above- the Kamitan God Geb and the Kamitan Goddess Nut separate after the sexual union that gave birth to the gods and goddesses and Creation. Below: three depictions of the god Asar in tantric union with Aset.

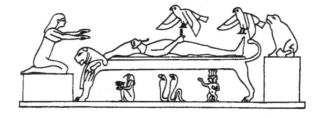

Above-The virgin birth of Heru (The resurrection of Asar - higher, Heru consciousness). Aset in the winged form hovers over the reconstructed penis of dead Asar. Note: Asar uses right hand.

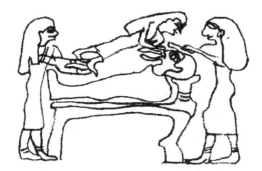

Drawing found in an Ancient Egyptian Building of The Conception of Heru[14]

Aset (representing the physical body-creation) and the dead body of Asar (representing the spirit, that essence which vivifies matter) are shown in symbolic immaculate union (compare

---

[14] *Sexual Life in Ancient Egypt* by Lise Manniche

The Ancient Egyptian Path to Enlightenment

to the "Kali Position" on the following page) begetting Heru, symbolizing to the immaculate conception which takes place at the birth of the spiritual life in every human: the birth of the soul (Ba) in a human is the birth of Heru.

-From a Stele at the British Museum 1372. 13th Dyn.

Above- the god Shiva and his consort Shakti

The "Kali position" (above) features **Shiva and Shakti (Kundalini-Prakriti)** in divine union (India). As with Asar and Aset of Egypt, Shiva is the passive, male aspect who "gives" the life essence (spirit) and creative impetus and Shakti is energy, creation, the active aspect of GOD. Thus Creation is akin to the idea of GOD making love with him/herself. Shiva and Shakti are the true essence of the human being, composed of spirit and matter (body). In the active aspect, the female is in the "active" position while the male is in the "passive" position. In Kamitan philosophy, the god Geb is the earth and the goddess Nut is the sky. Just as the earth is sedentary and the sky is dynamic so too are the divinities depicted in this way in Southern (African) and Eastern (India) iconography.

Above- Buddha and his consort.

Above: Tibetan Buddhist representation of The Dharmakaya, the cosmic father-mother. expressing the idea of the Supreme Being as a union of both male and female principals.

Notice that the female divinities are always on the top position. This is classic in Eastern and Kamitan mysticism. It is a recognition that the spirit (male aspect) is sedentary while matter, the female aspect, is in perpetual motion and the two complement and complete each other.

MEDITATION

Below left- The Triune ithyphallic form of Asar[15]
Below right- the Trilinga (Triune ithyphallic form) of Shiva.[16]

---

[15] For more details see the book *Egyptian Yoga Volume 1*
[16] For more details see the book *Egyptian Yoga Volume 1*

The Ancient Egyptian Path to Enlightenment

Introduction to The Sema Tawi of Meditation

It is well known and commonly accepted that meditation has been practiced in India from ancient times. Therefore, there is no need to site specific references to support that contention. Here we will concentrate on the evidence supporting the existence of the philosophy of meditation in Ancient Egypt.

The Paths of Meditation Practiced in Ancient Egypt

Uaa Shedy

M E D I T A T E

2) *Uaa m Neter Shedy* - **Meditation** Experience the Transcendental Supreme Self.

The forms of Neterian Meditation discipline include.

- Arat Sekhem, Meditation on the Subtle Life Force
- Ari Sma Maat, Meditation on the Righteous action
- Nuk Pu-Ushet, Meditation on the I am
- Nuk Ra Akhu, Meditation on the Glorious Light
- Rekh – Khemn, Meditation on the Wisdom Teaching
- Khet Ankh   Meditation on the Tree of Life

The paths of Kamitan meditation practice are varied so as to allow for the capacities and inclinations of a particular individual. This book will provide an overview of the practices. For detailed and specific aspects of a particular discipline please consult the additional resources listed below.

Glorious Light Meditation System of Ancient Egypt	Meditation on the Glorious Light
Mysteries of Isis	Meditation on the Wisdom Teaching
The Egyptian Book of the Dead	Meditation on the I am
The Path of Divine Love	Meditation on the Supreme Beloved
The Serpent Power	Meditation on the Subtle Life Force
Wisdom of Maati	Meditation on the Righteous action

MEDITATION

System of Meditation: **Glorious Light System** Specific location where it was practiced in ancient times: **Temple of Seti I, City of Waset (Thebes)** [17]

3) System of Meditation:

   a. **Wisdom System** Specific location where it was practiced in ancient times: **Temple of Aset – Philae Island, Aswan**
   b. **"I Am" System** Specific location where it was practiced in ancient times: **Prt M Hru (Book of the Dead)**

4) System of Meditation: **Serpent Power System** Specific location(s) where it was practiced in ancient times: **Temple of Hetheru, Temple of Djehuti, Temple of Aset, Temple of Uadjit (Serpent Goddess), Temple of Asar- City of Abdu**

5) System of Meditation: **Righteous Action Meditation** Specific location where it was practiced in ancient times: **IN ALL TEMPLES- GENERAL DISCIPLINE**

6) System of Meditation: **Devotional Meditation** Specific location where it was practiced in ancient times: **IN ALL TEMPLES- GENERAL DISCIPLINE**

---

[17] For More details see the book *The Glorious Light Meditation System of Ancient Egypt* by Dr. Muata Ashby.

The Ancient Egyptian Path to Enlightenment
Basic Instructions for the Glorious Light Meditation System- Given in the Tomb of Seti I. (1350 B.C.E.)

Formal meditation in Yoga consists of four basic elements: Posture, Sound (chant-words of power), Visualization, Rhythmic Breathing (calm, steady breath). The instructions, translated from the original hieroglyphic text contain the basic elements for formal meditation.

(1)-**Posture and Focus of Attention**

         iuf iri-f ahau maq b-phr nty hau iu
body do   make stand, within the Sundisk (circle of Ra)

This means that the aspirant should remain established as if in the center of a circle with a dot in the middle.

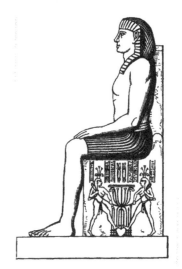

(2)- **Words of power-chant**[18]

Nuk Hekau (I am the word* itself)
Nuk Ra Akhu (I am Ra's Glorious Shinning** Spirit)
Nuk Ba Ra (I am the soul of Ra)
Nuk Hekau (I am the God who creates*** through sound)

(3)- **Visualization**

         Iuf mi Ra heru mestu-f n-shry chet
"My body is like Ra's on the day of his birth

This teaching is what in Indian Vedanta Philosophy is referred to as Ahamgraha Upashama – or visualizing and meditating upon oneself as being one with God. This teaching is the main focus of the Prt m Hru (Book of Enlightenment) text of Ancient Egypt. It is considered as the highest form of meditation practice amongst Indian mystics.[19]

---

[18] The term "Words of Power" relates to chants and or recitations given for meditation practice. They were used in a similar way to the Hindu "Mantras."
[19] Statement made by Swami Jyotirmayananda in class with his disciples.

MEDITATION

Basic Instructions for the Glorious Light Meditation System- Given in the Tomb of Seti I. (c. 1350 B.C.E.)

As we have seen, the practice of meditation in Ancient Egypt and its instruction to the masses and not just to the priests and priestesses, can be traced to at least 800 years earlier.

How should the paths of yoga work in concert? The following diagram shows the integral process that is engendered by the practice of all of the yogic disciplines. They lead to the integration of the main aspects of the personality and the discovery of the same underlying mystery of the inner Self.

Integral (Wholistic) Yoga

The process of personality Integration.

Love Contentment · Understanding · Peace · Fulfillment

The Paths of Smai Tawi

Love Contentment	Understanding	Peace	Fulfillment
↑	↑	↑	↑
Emotion	**Reason**	**Action**	**Will**
↑	↑	↑	↑
Sema of Devotional Love	Sema of Wisdom	Sema of Righteousness Virtue	Sema of Meditation
Control of feeling. Directed towards the Divine	Understanding the Divine	Self-control Selfless service. Purity of Heart.	Study of Mind and development of inner powers.

MEDITATION

PART I MEDITATION: THE PATH TO SPIRITUAL ENLIGHTENMENT

"TO THINK, TO PONDER, TO FIX ATTENTION, MEDITATION"

The Ancient Egyptian Path to Enlightenment
INTRODUCTION

What is Meditation?

Meditation may be thought of or defined as the practice of mental exercises and disciplines to enable the aspirant to achieve control over the mind, specifically, to stop the vibrations of the mind due to unwanted thoughts, imaginations, etc. But why is this necessary? Why should one need to control the thoughts and vibrations of the mind? Ordinarily, people profess to believe in something greater than their physical existence but what is this something? If a person on the street is asked, "Who are You?", most likely he or she will point to their body and say "this is me." But is this all there is to life? Many people profess to believe in a soul but do they really understand what it is? If they did why would they mourn at funerals or fear their own death? A human being is not just a physical body with a mind and five senses. In reality there is a deeper existence, a vast ocean of reality of which most people are not aware. This is the realm of the Higher Self which all the teachings of yoga and the various practices of meditation are directed toward discovering. This "hidden" aspect of ourselves which is beyond the thoughts is known as *Neter Neteru, Amun, Asar* or *Amenta* in the Ancient Egyptian mystical philosophy system of spirituality, as *Brahman*, in Indian Vedanta philosophy, as *God* in Christianity and as *The Self*. Due to mental distraction and erroneous thoughts and lifestyles, people are unable to discover their true higher nature, and thus they experience a limited existence as ordinary human beings until the time of their death. The Higher Self in a human being is like air. Air is free; moving in an unobstructed manner it circles the earth. However, if a certain volume of air were caught in an airtight bottle, the air would seem to be caught, trapped in the bottle existence. In the same manner, the human soul is part of the cosmos and it is all pervasive. However, as it associates with an individual existence and becomes involved with the desires, thoughts, fears and ignorance of human existence, it loses sight of its all-pervasive and transcendental nature. Thus, the body, mind, senses, thoughts, emotions and ignorance which together constitute the personality of a human being, are in reality like a bottle which closes off the vision of the truth. The soul, which is innately free and boundless, is as if caught by the reality of the individual personality, and the pressure of desires, longings and imaginations from this limited reality as if mesmerizes the Higher Self. This limited existence is known as the ego-consciousness. So from being Universal, the soul begins to believe itself to be individual. However, in reality the soul never stopped being Universal. The personality of a human being is like a transient veil like a magical illusion. At night the stars appear to be minuscule but if you were to get closer you would see that they are massive heavenly bodies. In the same way if you were to get closer to your real Self you would see that it is expansive and limitless. In most people their ego-personality is so prominent that they cannot see beyond its reality. Through the process of Yoga Philosophy and Meditation, a human being has the possibility of breaking through the confinement of individuality in order to discover universality and limitless expansion. So in reality every human being is not limited and finite. There is a greater reality which can and must be discovered.

Ancient Egyptian mysticism expresses the true nature of every human being (individual soul) as composed of a Causal Body, an Astral or Subtle Body and a Physical Body. The Universal Soul or the Self is singular and pure. Therefore, it is likened to a dot. The Soul develops a mental process and through this process, a form of ignorance or forgetfulness of its true nature develops. This is the development of the individual soul. The soul becomes submerged, as it were, in the sea of thoughts and impulses from the mind and senses. It remains as a latent witness in the deep unconscious level of the mind. It is caught in the powerlessness produced by the web of

MEDITATION

ignorance it has spun for itself. Through the mind and senses it experiences the universe, life, death, happiness, sadness, etc. However, in reality, the Universal Soul is never touched or affected by the occurrences of life, but the individual soul nevertheless experiences them as being real and compelling. In addition, the individual soul is really one with the Universal Soul. The belief in mortal existence as being real prevents the individual soul from discovering its deeper, transcendental reality, therefore, the soul travels on a journey which involves many experiences of birth death into a physical existence, death as well as the myriad experiences which occur in dreams and in the after death state (Heaven or Hell).

The Ancient Egyptian Path to Enlightenment
What is the purpose of meditating?

Ignorant- *Khemn*

ALL human beings desire to experience peace, fulfillment, and abiding happiness as well as self-knowledge and to know the secrets of the universe, including Why am I here?, Who am I? Where do I come from? And Who or what is God? There is one obstacle that prevents them from attaining this knowledge, ignorance. The practice of religion and spiritual studied is to resolve the ignorance and allow a human being to discover the truth about themselves and about what there is beyond death.

HOW IS THE HIGHER VISION ATTAINED?

Shetaut Neter – Shedi

The disciplines of Shetaut Neter (Ancient Egyptian-African religion) and Shety (study of the spiritual mysteries through the practice of the Sema Tawi (yogic disciplines).

PURPOSE OF MEDITATION – PURIFYING THE MIND

2 stages – informal (virtue)   and   formal (disciplinary)
↑   ↑
gross imp.   and   subtle imp.

The ultimate goal of life is to attain the great state of NEHAST or spiritual awakening. Many mystics around the world call it by different names (resurrection, liberation, enlightenment, etc.). This great goal of life is attained when the mind is purified through the two stages of meditation practice. The first mode of meditative practice is informal. Informal means all of the time when the formal mode is not being engaged. The formal mode is when a person makes a special time to sit and concentrate on meditating. A person cannot be meditating constantly all day long. They have to go to work, to pay bills, take care of family matters, etc. those times are the informal times. During those times an aspirant learns to live life in a "meditative" manner so that the peace is not disturbed and so that the mind remains pure and in this manner be ready for the formal practice. Therefore, both aspects are important.

MEDITATION
3 states of mind

According to the Ancient Egyptian Myth of Hetheru and Djehuti we learn that there are three states of mind. In order to achieve success in meditation and to reach the great goal of Nehast, these states must be understood and the complexes of the mind that allow it to be affected and afflicted by the lower states (agitated, dull) must be overcome. These states will be discussed in detail later in the text.

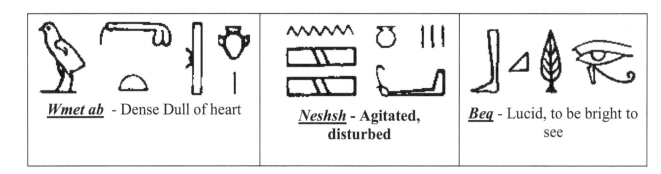

Listening (Meh mestchert.) ➔ Reflection (Maui) ➔ Meditation (Uah)

3 steps in meditation

Concentration - Meditation – superconsciousness
Mau – Uah – Syh .

There are three steps in the practice of meditation. Each step is to be understood and practiced so as to gradually lead the mind to expanding experiences of higher consciousness *Syh*. Experiences of Ecstasy allow the ordinary consciousness to be elevated because the mind is presented with a state of consciousness otherwise unbeknown to it. When sufficient experiences of superconsciousness occur the mind becomes established in that higher consciousness and then a person is said to be "Awakened." *Hefd*, the next level of experience, is a form of immersion in divine consciousness wherein the mind dissolves completely and subsides so there is no time and space or awareness of individuality but rather all-encompassing experience. But the experience is recognized by the mind after it is over. During the experience itself the personality ceases to exist as an ego conscious being that is aware of objects separate from itself –therefore, there is oneness, homogeneity, between individual and the Divine –the experience of transcendental consciousness is described as blissful-meaning unencumbered abiding happiness and the personality eventually recognizes that state to be more comfortable and normal than the usual conscious state and awareness as a mortal individual with a body and with finite sense experience and separated from all else.

The Ancient Egyptian Path to Enlightenment
Establishment in Higher Consciousness

Men ab mans firm of heart establish, firm I higher consciousness. This is achieved through *Ar maat,* or living in harmony righteousness (informal and forma meditation), which leads to *nehast* or spiritual awakening.

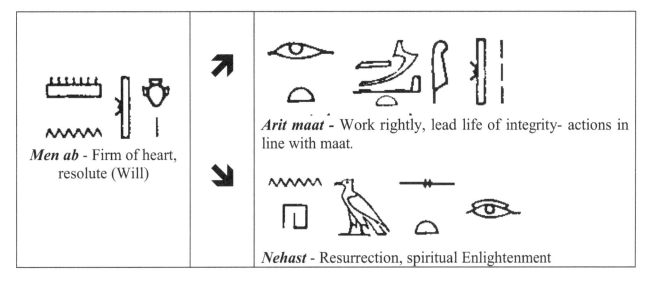

Men ab - Firm of heart, resolute (Will)

Arit maat - Work rightly, lead life of integrity- actions in line with maat.

Nehast - Resurrection, spiritual Enlightenment

MEDITATION
What is the Mind?

In order to begin to understand what meditation is all about it will first be necessary to gain a simple understanding of what the mind is and how it relates to a human being. Many people have been educated with the notion that the mind is an emanation or secretion of the physical brain and the body, and that the feelings, desires and emotions which all together form the complex which is referred to as a human being are all products of the physical self. Further, the popular notion in the scientific disciplines of modern society is that the mind in an individual human being is like a unique cell which contains only the information which is put into it through the senses.

If this notion is true how can science explain why modern parapsychologists have documented cases where people have exhibited knowledge of occurrences across the world. How can they explain the fact that many small children have recalled exact, detailed memories of a past life and that these memories have been confirmed by the families which the child lived in during a previous life time? How is it possible to explain when a mother somehow knows that her child is in imminent danger, even if the child is on the other side of the world?

The answer is that they cannot explain it through scientific means so these occurrences are brushed off as flukes or coincidences. Indeed many scientists have refused to acknowledge the evidence which points to the fact that the mind, or what every human being calls the essence of who they are and what makes them unique, is not confined to a locality. It is aware of activities from far away. Further, the memories which together combine to form the content of a person's history are not just the summation of a person's experiences in the present lifetime, but of previous ones as well.

The mind is in reality an expression of an ocean of consciousness in much the same way as a wave is an expression of the vast ocean. The individual mind of a human being is an emanation of the universal mind and the universal mind is all-pervasive, and therefore all-knowing. Therefore, if the limitations of the individual mind are overcome it can discover its universal and all-encompassing nature which is the higher reality.

The mind may be likened to a prism. In science a prism may be used to refract normal daylight. When this is done it is possible to see that daylight is composed of a spectrum of pure colors. The prism separates the daylight into seven colors. Each of these colors has a different wavelength allowing them to be placed in seven bands: red, orange, yellow, green, blue, indigo, and violet. These colors can be mixed to produce other colors. Interestingly, any color can be obtained by mixing the three primary colors, red, green and black, in the right proportions. So the existence of different wavelengths is what allows the human eye to perceive the different colors but in reality they are all emanations from the single light.

In the same way, the physical body and brain (nervous system) in a human being act like a prism. The light of consciousness which pervades the entire universe is seemingly refracted and thereby all the different forms, textures and colors of nature become discernible. This is what makes it possible for an individual human being to discern the different forms and colors of nature. This is also the source of notions about individuality, separation, time and space. This is the basis of human experience. All human experiences are related to the senses and their perception of colors, time and space.

The Ancient Egyptian Path to Enlightenment

Many people consider that their physical self is the only reality about them, yet in their dream they experience a different reality. Further, in the dreamless sleep state there is still another personality. So which is the true personality? The essence is that all of these personalities are relative, and therefore illusory (unreal). That is to say, they are only relative expressions of a higher reality which is the absolute and abiding truth. The soul or individual cell of human consciousness is the source which sustains the mind and the physical self. Thus the spirit essence of a human being is responsible for the existence of the mind and body, and not the other way around.

The mind in a human being is always concentrating on either the past, present or future. From the time you wake up in the morning until the time you go to sleep, you are constantly bombarded with the ideas of what you have done, what is going on now or what the future will bring. But what happened when you went to sleep? What happened to your thoughts which were so important and pressing? The past, present and future faded away into the mist of sleep as if they never existed. Most people do not give much importance to sleep even though the average person spends one third of human existence in the sleep state. What would happen if you were able to transcend yesterday, today and tomorrow as well as the waking time and the dream time? What would happen if this light of consciousness which seems to fragment into waking, dream and dreamless sleep and the various thoughts of the mind were not refracted? What would happen if all of the wavelengths were re-converged into one again?

The practice of meditation acts as a focusing device. It is a process by which the separated rays of consciousness within a human being are once again made whole. In much the same way as a magnifying glass focuses the rays of the sun into a powerful force which can ignite a fire, meditation focuses the rays of the mind and develops a one-pointed vision with the power to burn away all illusions, ignorance and negativity. When this occurs a new vision emerges; a new understanding about the universe and the very nature of who one really is emerges like the sun on a cloudy day. So meditation is like a process through which the scattered ideas, thoughts, feelings, emotions and psychic energies which make up the consciousness of a human being are converged in order to discover what lies beyond the multiplicity and apparent differentiation of nature as well as the human heart.

MEDITATION

Soul
⬇
Unconscious Mind - Causal Body
⬇
Subconscious Mind - Astral Body
⬇
Conscious Mind (waking state) - Physical Body

The Universal Soul is eternal, bodiless and all-pervasive.   The Soul - Spirit (GOD)

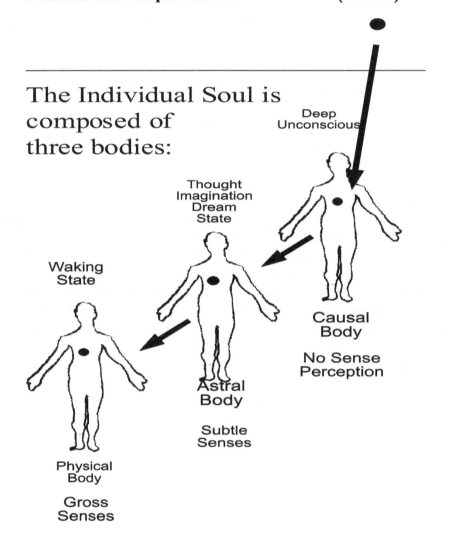

The Ancient Egyptian Path to Enlightenment

The mind and nervous system are instruments of the Self which it uses to have experiences in the realm of time and space, which it has created in much the same way as a person falls asleep and develops an entire dream world out of his/her own consciousness. It is at the unconscious and subconscious levels where the most intensive work of yoga takes place because it is here that the conscious identification of a person creates impressions in the mind and where desires based on those impressions develop. It is these desires that keep the aspirant involved in the realm of time and space or frees the aspirant from the world of time and space if they are sublimated into the spiritual desire for enlightenment. The desire to attain enlightenment is not viewed in the same manner as ego based desires; it is viewed as being aspiration which is a positive movement. Enlightenment is the term used to describe the highest level of spiritual awakening. It means attaining such a level of spiritual awareness that one discovers the underlying unity of the entire universe as well as the fact that the source of all creation is the same source from which the innermost Self within every human heart arises.

Externalized consciousness - distracted by egoism and worldly objects. ◄◄◄

The light of the Self (consciousness) shines through the mind and this is what sustains life. The flow of consciousness in most people is from within moving outward. This causes them to be externalized and distracted and they lose energy. Where the mind goes, energy flows. Have you ever noticed that you can "feel" someone looking at you? This is because there is a subtle energy being transmitted through their vision (which is an extension of the mind). Those who live in this externalized state of mind are not aware of the source of consciousness. Meditation as well as the other disciplines of yoga serve to reverse the flow of consciousness on itself so that the mind acts as a mirror which reveals the true Self.

Internalized consciousness of a yoga practitioner. ►►►

Most people are unaware that there are deeper levels to their being just as they are unaware of the fact that physical reality is not "physical". Quantum physics experiments have proven that the physical world is not composed of matter but of energy. This supports the findings of the ancient sages who have taught for thousands of years that the reality which is experienced by the human senses is not an "absolute" reality but a conditional one. Therefore, you must strive to rise beyond your conditioned mind and senses in order to perceive reality as it truly is.

Just as the sun is revealed when the clouds disperse, so the light of the Self is revealed when the mind is free of thoughts, imaginations, ideas, delusions, gross emotions, sentimental attachments, etc. In fact these thoughts, imaginations, ideas, delusions, gross emotions, sentimental attachments, etc., are refractions of the light of the Self, the light of your innermost consciousness. The Self, your true identity, is visible to the conscious mind. How is this possible? This is the teaching and goal of all meditation practices.

MEDITATION
Universal Ba (Soul)

Individual Soul
↙ ↓ ↘
Mind and Senses
(Astral Body and Astral World - the Tuat or Underworld)

↙ ↓ ↘
Physical Body and Physical World

When you are active and not practicing or experiencing the wisdom of yoga, you are distracted from the real you. This distraction which comes from the desires, cravings and endless motion of thoughts in the mind is the *veil* which blocks your perception of your deeper essence, The Self. These distractions keep you involved with the mind, senses, and body that you have come to believe is the real you. When your body is motionless and you are thinking and feeling, you are mostly associated with your mind. At times when you are not thinking, such as in the dreamless sleep state, then you are associated with your Higher Self. However, this connection in the dreamless sleep state is veiled by ignorance because you are asleep and not aware of the experience. During this time you do however, experience profound peace and rest. This is possible because you are turning away from your ego-personality, your individual self and you are going into the realm of the inner Self. In essence you are moving closer to that which is universal and turning away from that which is limited. In order to discover this realm you must consciously turn away from the phenomenal world, the world of your ego and its problems, concerns, worries and anxieties, which is distracting you from this inner reality. The practice of yoga accomplishes this task. Meditation, when backed up by the practice of yoga philosophy, is the most powerful agent of self-discovery. The practice of meditation allows you to develop a higher awareness which will affect all aspects of your life, but most importantly, it gives you, the aspirant, experiential knowledge of your true Self.

The Ancient Egyptian Path to Enlightenment

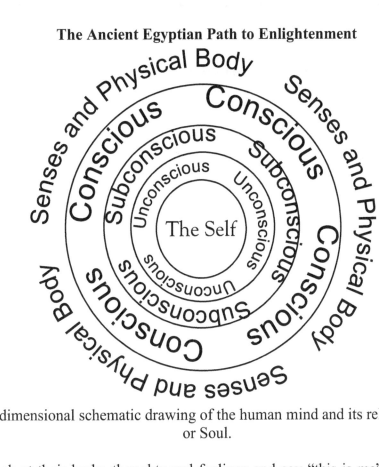

Above: A two dimensional schematic drawing of the human mind and its relationship to the Self or Soul.

Most people look at their body, thoughts and feelings and say "this is me". In reality a human being is in reality a complex organism composed of Conscious Mind, Subconscious Mind and Unconscious Mind. These form your personality or the person you have come to know as "you," with your particular tastes, family associations, religious and social affiliations, etc. Underlying all of this is the universal consciousness which is like an ocean. On the surface of this ocean is the personality and supporting it is the ocean of consciousness, The Self. The project of spiritual life and meditation practice is to go deep into this ocean by controlling the mind with its thoughts, desires, etc. (surface), through the various practices of Yoga.

MEDITATION

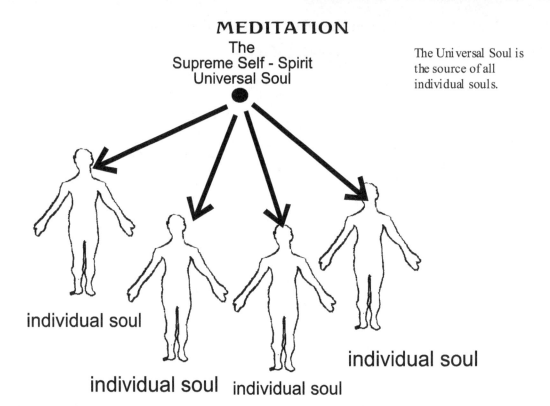

The Universal Soul is the source of all individual souls.

The distraction of the soul in the world of human experience leads to mental impressions which are based on the external reality (physical reality) and on ignorance of the truth (the Higher Soul reality). These impressions lead the mind to experience desires, thoughts and aspirations which lead a human being to experience more desires and more distractions. Desires born of ignorance cannot be satisfied through the mind and senses because these are limited and the experiences are fleeting. No matter how long they last during a person's life they are only transient experiences and never wholly fulfilling. Since the desires of the mind and senses based on ignorance can never be fulfilled, the soul is led to experience repeated situations of frustration and mental unrest and further away from the inner peace of the Self within. The individual soul of every human being is in reality seeking to discover the wholeness and peace of its true nature, the Universal Soul, within. However, the ignorant search to fulfill the desires of the mind leads it to countless situations in the realm of human experiences which in turn lead to more experiences in an endless cycle which continues even after death and causes the soul to return to human form again and again, in a futile effort to satisfy the desires based on ignorance. These teachings of the cycles of birth and death which the individual soul experiences are known as the doctrines of Karma and Reincarnation.

The Ancient Egyptian Path to Enlightenment

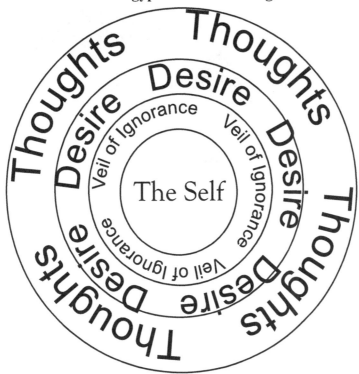

Above: A two dimensional schematic drawing of the human existence. The Self assumes the role of every individual soul and through the veil of ignorance experiences desires, thoughts and life as an individual being.

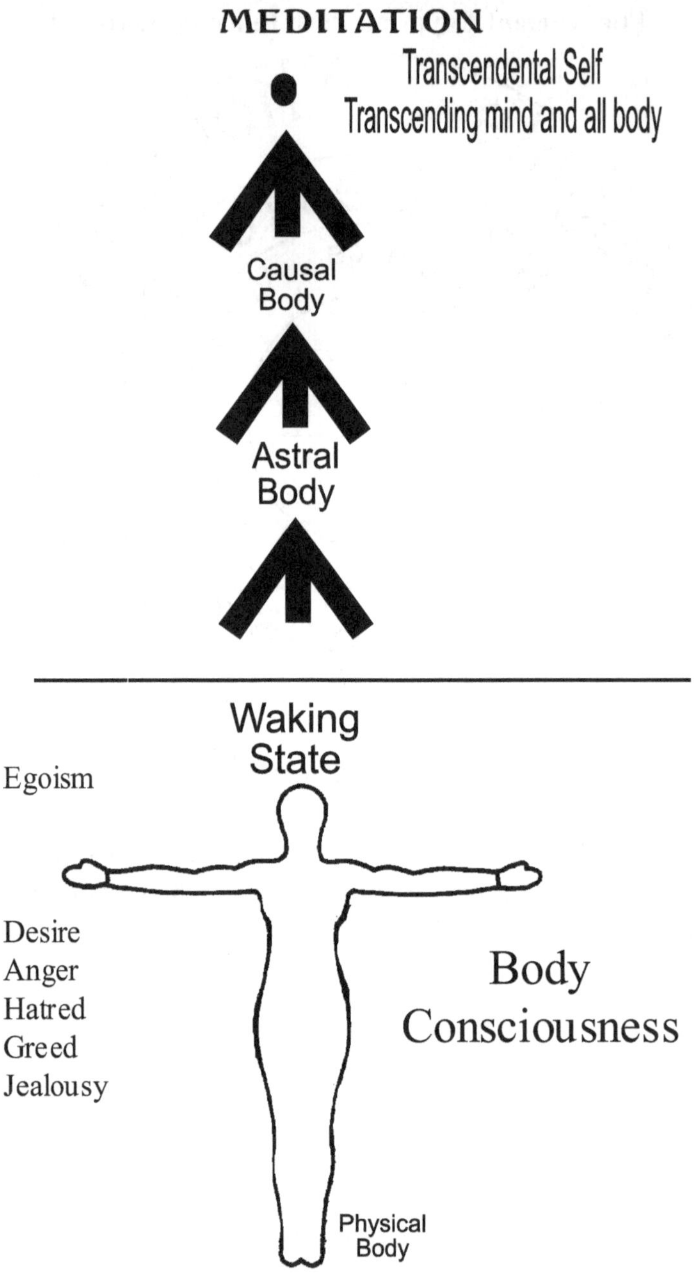

MEDITATION

Transcendental Self
Transcending mind and all body

Causal Body

Astral Body

Waking State

Egoism

Desire
Anger
Hatred
Greed
Jealousy

Body Consciousness

Physical Body

"The soul is a prisoner of its own ignorance. In this condition it is fettered with the chains of ignorance to an existence where it has no control over its fate in life. The purpose of each virtue is to remove one fetter."

Ancient Egyptian Proverb

The Ancient Egyptian Path to Enlightenment

The Supreme Self - Spirit

FETTERED MIND
Ignorance and Delusion caused by
Egoism ● Desire ● Anger   Hatred
Greed ● Jealousy

The Fetters cloud the mind and the higher vision is not visible. The intellect is dull so reason fails, and delusion, mental weakness and emotionality control the mind and prevent a person from seeing beyond their meager individual, mortal existence. This mind is a fog of thoughts and feelings which blocks the vision of the Higher Self.

MEDITATION
The Supreme Self - Spirit

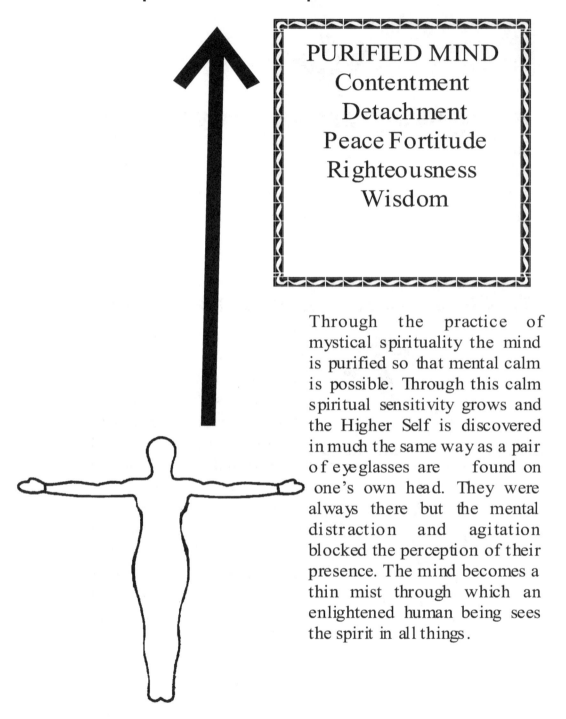

PURIFIED MIND
Contentment
Detachment
Peace Fortitude
Righteousness
Wisdom

Through the practice of mystical spirituality the mind is purified so that mental calm is possible. Through this calm spiritual sensitivity grows and the Higher Self is discovered in much the same way as a pair of eyeglasses are found on one's own head. They were always there but the mental distraction and agitation blocked the perception of their presence. The mind becomes a thin mist through which an enlightened human being sees the spirit in all things.

The
Supreme Self - Spirit
Cosmic Mind

The objective of all yoga disciplines is to purify the mind so that it can achieve a transcendental vision through meditation.

The objective of meditation is to unite the individual mind with the cosmic mind, the mortal with the eternal, the individual with the universal.

Individual
Ego Mind

MEDITATION
Karma and Reincarnation

The concept that has come to be known as "Karma" was known in Ancient Egypt before the advent of yoga in India. In ancient Africa it was called "Ari" or "actions, deeds." Ari should be thought of as the total effect of a person's actions and conduct during the successive phases of his/her existence. But how does this effect operate? How do the past actions affect the present and the future? If you consider your present lifetime you will notice that your actions of the past have led you to where you are today in much the same way as a fruit tree planted today will bear fruit in a few years. Your experiences from the present life or from previous lifetimes cause unconscious impressions which stay with the individual soul at the level of the causal body in the deep unconscious level of mind even after death. These unconscious impressions are what constitute the emerging thoughts, desires, and aspirations of every individual and they "cause" future incarnations because they impel the soul to continue on the journey of seeking fulfillment of the desires. These impressions are not exactly like memories, however, they work like memories. For example, if you had a fear in a previous lifetime or the childhood of your present lifetime you may not remember the event that caused the fear, but you will remember the "strange feeling" you have when you come into contact with certain objects or certain people. These feelings are caused by the unconscious impressions which are coming up to the surface of the conscious mind. It is this conglomerate of unconscious impressions which are "judged" in the Hall of MAAT and determine where the soul will go to next in the spiritual journey toward evolution or devolution also known as the cycle of birth and death or reincarnation as well as the experiences of heaven or hell. The following segment from the Ancient Egyptian "Instruction to Mer-ka-Ré" explains this point.

> *"You know that they are not merciful the day when they judge the miserable one..... Do not count on the passage of the years; they consider a lifetime as but an hour. After death man remains in existence and His acts accumulate beside him. Life in the other world is eternal, but he who arrives without sin before the Judge of the Dead, he will be there as a Neter and he will walk freely as do the masters of eternity."*

The reference above to "His acts accumulate beside him" alludes to the unconscious impressions which are formed as a result of one's actions while still alive. These impressions can be either positive or negative. Positive impressions are developed through positive actions by living a life of righteousness (MAAT) and virtue. This implies living according to the precepts of mystical wisdom or being a follower of Heru (*Shemsu Hor*) and Aset. These actions draw one closer to harmony and peace, thus paving the way to discover the Self within. The negative impressions are developed through sinful actions. They are related to mental agitation, disharmony and restlessness. This implies acts based on anger, fear, desire, greed, depression, gloom, etc. These actions draw one into the outer world of human desires. They distract the mind and do not allow the intellect (Saa) to function. Thus, existence at this level is closer to an animal, being based on animal instincts and desires of the body (selfishness), rather than to a spiritually mature human being, being based on reason, selflessness, compassion, etc.

(Purification of the heart)

The Ancient Egyptian Path to Enlightenment

How then is it possible to eradicate negative karmic impressions and to develop positive ones? The answer lies in your practice of the spiritual disciplines collectively known as yoga. When you study the teachings and live according to them, your mind undergoes a transformation at all levels. This transformation is the "purification of heart" so often spoken about throughout the *Egyptian Book of Coming Forth By Day*. It signifies an eradication of negative impressions, which renders the mind pure and subtle. When the mind is rendered subtle, then spiritual realization is possible. This discipline of purifying the heart by living according to the teachings is known as the Yoga of Action or MAAT.

Yoga and Religion

Yoga is the practice of mental, physical and spiritual disciplines which lead to self-control and self-discovery by purifying the mind, body and spirit, so as to discover the deeper spiritual essence which lies within every human being and object in the universe. In essence, the goal of yoga practice is to unite or *yoke* one's individual consciousness with universal or cosmic consciousness. Therefore, Ancient Egyptian religious practice, especially in terms of the rituals and other practices of the Ancient Egyptian temple system known as *Shetaut Neter* (the way of the hidden Supreme Being), may be termed as a yoga system: *Egyptian Yoga*. In this sense, religion, in its purest form, is a yoga system, as it seeks to reunite people with their true and original source.

In its complete form, religion is composed of three aspects, *mythology, ritual* and *metaphysical* or the *mystical experience* (mysticism - mystical philosophy). While many religions contain rituals, traditions, metaphors and myths, there are few professionals trained in the understanding of their deeper aspects and psychological implications (metaphysics and mystical). Thus, there is disappointment, frustration and disillusionment among many followers as well as leaders within many religions, particularly in the Western Hemisphere, because it is difficult to evolve spiritually without the proper spiritual guidance. Through introspection and spiritual research, it is possible to discover mythological vistas within religion which can rekindle the light of spirituality, and at the same time increase the possibility of gaining a fuller experience of life. The exoteric (outer, ritualistic) forms of religion with which most people are familiar is only the tip of an iceberg so to speak; it is only a beginning, an invitation or prompting to seek a deeper (esoteric) discovery of the transcendental truths of existence.

The disciplines of Yoga fall under five major categories, these are *Yoga of Wisdom, Yoga of Devotional Love, Yoga of Meditation, Tantric Yoga* and *Yoga of Selfless Action.* Within these categories there are subsidiary forms which are part of the main disciplines. The important point to remember is that all aspects of yoga can and should be used in an integral fashion to effect an efficient and harmonized spiritual movement in the practitioner. Therefore, while there may be an area of special emphasis, other elements are bound to become part of the yoga program as needed. For example, while a yogin may place emphasis on the yoga of wisdom, they may also practice devotional yoga and meditation yoga along with the wisdom studies.

So the practice of any discipline that leads to oneness with Supreme Consciousness is called yoga. If you study, rationalize and reflect upon the teachings, you are practicing *Yoga of Wisdom*. If you meditate upon the teachings and your Higher Self, you are practicing *Yoga of Meditation*. If you practice rituals which identify you with your spiritual nature, you are practicing *Yoga of Ritual Identification* (which is part of the yoga of wisdom and the yoga of devotional love of the Divine). If

MEDITATION

you develop your physical nature and psychic energy centers, you are practicing *Serpent Power* (Arat Shekhem) *Yoga* (which is part of Tantric Yoga). If you practice living according to the teachings of ethical behavior and selflessness, you are practicing *Yoga of Action* (Maat) in daily life. If you practice turning your attention towards the Divine by developing love for the Divine, then it is called *Devotional Yoga* or *Yoga of Divine Love*. The practitioner of yoga is called a yogin (male practitioner) or yogini (female practitioner), and one who has attained the culmination of yoga (union with the Divine) is called a yogi. In this manner, yoga has been developed into many disciplines which may be used in an integral fashion to achieve the same goal: Enlightenment. In this booklet we will concentrate on the practice of Yoga of Meditation.

Yoga is a tradition which has established a long proven record of success in teaching those who desire to discover the Self. The traditional approach to yoga instruction has been broken up into three stages. These are: **1-Listening, 2- Reflection and 3- Meditation**. In a broad sense, you will be instructed in this same manner throughout this book series. First you will receive the teaching, then you will be assisted in reflecting on that teaching and incorporating it into your life. You will then be instructed on how to intensify your reflective movement and gradually reach a meditative state of concentration on the Divine. A practitioner of Yoga must be able to integrate the main practices of Yoga into daily life. This means that you need to begin adding small amounts of time for Prayer, Repetition of the Divine Name (Hekau), Exercise (includes proper breathing exercise), Study of the Teachings, Silence, Selfless Service, Meditation, and Daily Reflection. This also means that you will gradually reduce the practices which go against yogic movement as you gain more time for Sheti (spiritual practice).

Integral Yoga

The personality of every human being is somewhat different from every other. However the Sages of Yoga have identified four basic factors which are common to all human personalities. These factors are: Emotion, Reason, Action and Will. This means that in order for a human being to evolve, all aspects of the personality must progress in an integral fashion. Therefore, four major forms of Yoga disciplines have evolved and each is specifically designed to promote a positive movement in one of the areas of personality. The Yoga of Devotional Love enhances and harnesses the emotional aspect in a human personality and directs it towards the Higher Self. The Yoga of Wisdom enhances and harnesses the reasoning aspect in a human personality and directs it towards the Higher Self. The Yoga of Action enhances and harnesses the Movement and Behavior aspect in a human personality and directs it towards the Higher Self. The Yoga of Meditation enhances and harnesses the Willing aspect in a human personality and directs it towards the Higher Self.

The Ancient Egyptian Path to Enlightenment

Emotion   Reason   Action   Will .
↑   ↑   ↑   ↑
Devotion Wisdom Service Meditation

Thus, Yoga is a discipline of spiritual living which transforms every aspect of personality in an integral fashion, leaving no aspect of a human being behind. This is important because an unbalanced movement will lead to frustration, more ignorance, more distraction and more illusions leading away from the Higher Self. For example, if a person develops the reasoning aspect of personality he or she may come to believe that they have discovered the Higher Self, however when it comes to dealing with some problem of life, such as the death of a loved one, they cannot control their emotions, or if they are tempted to do something unrighteous, such as smoking, they cannot control their actions and have no will power to resist. The vision of Integral Yoga is a lofty goal which every human being can achieve with the proper guidance, self-effort and repeated practice. There is a very simple philosophy behind Integral Yoga. During the course of the day you may find yourself doing various activities. Sometimes you will be quiet, at other times you will be busy at work, at other times you might be interacting with people, etc. Integral yoga gives you the opportunity to practice yoga at all times. When you have quiet time you can practice meditation, when at work you can practice righteous action and selfless service, when you have leisure time you can study and reflect on the teachings and when you feel the sentiment of love for a person or object you like you can practice remembering the Divine Self who made it possible for you to experience the company of those personalities or the opportunity to acquire those objects. From a higher perspective you can practice reflecting on how the people and objects in creation are expressions of the Divine and this movement will lead you to a spontaneous and perpetual state of ecstasy, peace and bliss which are the hallmarks of spiritual enlightenment. The purpose of Integral yoga is therefore to promote integration of the whole personality of a human being which will lead to complete spiritual enlightenment. Thus Integral Yoga should be understood as the most effective method to practice mystical spirituality.

MEDITATION
The Search for True Happiness and Inner Peace

Popular culture holds that happiness comes from hoarding objects and wealth as well as from promoting situations which provide pleasure and outer prosperity. Upon close reflection it will be quickly noticed that this is an illusion. Have you ever met anyone who was really happy all the time? Even those who seem to have everything they want in life are never satisfied. They are ever restless and unfulfilled. Look at your own life and reflect upon this. Objects, money and people do not and cannot bring true happiness or peace. In the end they are fleeting. True happiness and inner peace come when there is detachment from objects and sentimental worldly relationships, be they considered pleasurable or as sources of pain. Consider your sleep time. When you turn away from the world and your ego-personality do you not experience peace and tranquillity such as nothing you can experience in the world of human experiences? Yet people continue to search for a true source of peace and pleasure through ego based experiences. This is because of a lack of reflection and the distraction of the mind. True peace and fulfillment can only occur when there is "steadfastness" in the inner Self and no leaning upon illusions, externalities, desires, egoistic feelings or sentiments, etc. When these qualities have been developed, peace and joy can be experienced at all times, such as in a Sage. True happiness and peace is experienced when the mind is not affected by the waves of desire, pleasure or pain.

True happiness and prosperity are inner treasures which are to be discovered within the heart and not in the outside world. The goal of leading a meditative lifestyle is to discover the true treasure of inner peace. This treasure is more important than any form of outer prosperity no matter how secure it may seem to be. Anything outside of yourself can be lost but can you lose anything which you hold in your heart? Therefore that which is inside, the innermost reality within you, is more real and abiding than any outer development. So why do people search incessantly for worldly possessions and activities which they believe will bring happiness? This has been the central point in the study of yoga and mystical spirituality. All of the practices of spirituality are directed to answering this question as well as to showing the path which enables one to discover the true fountain of peace and joy.

The Ancient Egyptian Path to Enlightenment
The Process of YOGA

According to the instructions of the Temple of Aset in Ancient Egypt, a spiritual aspirant needs to engage in the following process of spiritual practice:

1- **Listening** to the teachings.

2- Constant study and **Reflection** on the teachings along with practicing them in everyday life situations.

3- **Meditation** on the meaning of the teachings.

According to the teachings of *Jnana Yoga* or the Yoga of Wisdom from India, the process of Yoga consists of three steps:

1- *Shravana:* **Listening** to Wisdom teachings. Having achieved the qualifications of an aspirant, there is a desire to listen to the teachings from a Spiritual Preceptor. There is increasing intellectual understanding of the scriptures and the meaning of truth versus untruth, real versus unreal, temporal versus eternal.

2- *Manana:* **Reflection** on those teachings and living according to the disciplines enjoined by the teachings until the wisdom is fully understood. Reflection implies discovering the oneness behind the multiplicity of the world by engaging in intense inquiry into the nature of one's true Self.

3- *Niddidhyasana:* The process of reflection leads to a state in which the mind is continuously introspective. This is termed **Meditation**. It means expansion of consciousness culminating in revelation of and identification with the Absolute Self: Brahman.

MEDITATION
How Does Meditation Work?

Meditation may be thought of or defined as the practice of mental exercises and disciplines to enable the meditator to achieve control over the mind, specifically, to stop the vibrations of the mind due to unwanted thoughts, imaginations, etc. Consciousness refers to the awareness of being alive and of having an identity. It is this characteristic which separates humans from the animal kingdom. Animals cannot become aware of their own existence and ponder the questions such as *Who am I?, Where am I going in life?, Where do I come from?,* etc. They cannot write books on history and create elaborate systems of social history based on ancestry, etc. Consciousness expresses itself in three modes. These are: Waking, Dream-Sleep and Dreamless-Deep-Sleep.

However, ordinary human life is only partially conscious. When you are driving or walking, you sometimes lose track of the present moment. All of a sudden you arrive at your destination without having conscious awareness of the road which you have just traveled. Your mind went into an "automatic" mode of consciousness. This automatic mode of consciousness represents a temporary withdrawal from the waking world. This state is similar to a day dream (a dreamlike musing or fantasy). This form of existence is what most people consider as "normal" everyday waking consciousness. It is what people consider to be the extent of the human capacity to experience or be conscious.

The "normal" state of human consciousness cannot be considered as "whole" or complete because if it was there would be no experience of lapses or gaps in consciousness. In other words, every instant of consciousness would be accounted for. There would be no trance-like states wherein one loses track of time or awareness of one's own activities, even as they are being performed. In the times of trance or lapse, full awareness or consciousness is not present, otherwise it would be impossible to not be aware of the passage of time while engaged in various activities. Trance here should be differentiated from the religious or mystical form of trance like state induced through meditation. As used above, it refers to the condition of being so lost in solitary thought as to be unaware of one's surroundings. It may further be characterized as a stunned or bewildered condition, a fog, stupor, befuddlement, daze, muddled state of mind. Most everyone has experienced this condition at some point or another. What most people consider to be the "awake" state of mind in which life is lived is in reality only a fraction of the total potential consciousness which a human being can experience.

The Ancient Egyptian Path to Enlightenment

Understanding the process of meditation.

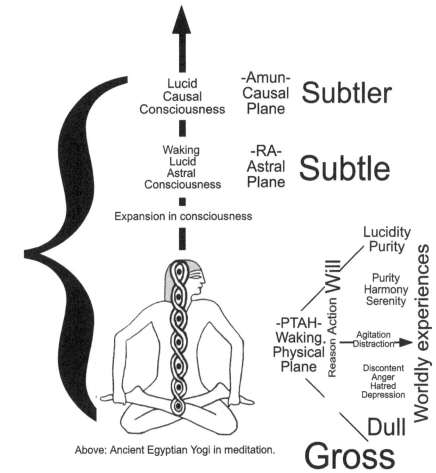

Above: The relative states of consciousness and the path of meditation. A figure from Ancient Egypt is sitting in the yoga lotus posture. Superimposed on him are the seven rings symbolizing the seven centers of psycho-spiritual energy consciousness known as Arat in Ancient Egypt Yoga mystical philosophy. Through the process of meditation a meditator lifts him/her self up beyond ordinary consciousness and discovers the transcendental realms and finally the Absolute Self.

The state of automatic consciousness is characterized by mental distraction, restlessness and extroversion. The automatic state of mind exists due to emotions such as desire, anger and hatred which engender desires in the mind, which in turn cause more movement, distractions, delusions and lapses or "gaps" in human consciousness. In this condition, it does not matter how many desires are fulfilled. The mind will always be distracted and agitated and will never discover peace and contentment. If the mind were under control, meaning, if you were to remain fully aware and conscious of every feeling, thought and emotion in your mind at any given time, it would be impossible for you to be swayed or deluded by your thoughts into a state of relative unconsciousness or un-awareness. Therefore, it is said that those who do not have their minds

MEDITATION

under control are not fully awake and not conscious human beings.

Meditation and Yoga Philosophy are disciplines which are directed toward increasing awareness. Awareness or consciousness can only be increased when the mind is in a state of peace and harmony. Thus, the disciplines of Meditation (which are part of the Yoga) are the primary means of controlling the mind and allowing the individual to mature psychologically and spiritually.

Psychological growth is promoted because when the mind is brought under control, the intellect becomes clear and psychological complexes such as anxiety and other delusions which have an effect even in ordinary people can be cleared up. Control of the mind and the promotion of internal harmony allows the meditator to integrate their personality and to resolve the hidden issues of the present, of childhood and of past lives.

When the mind has been brought under control, the expansion in consciousness leads to the discovery that one's own individual consciousness is not the total experience of consciousness. Through the correct practice of meditation, the individual's consciousness and awareness expands to the point wherein there is a discovery that one is more than just an individual. The state of "automatic consciousness" becomes reduced in favor of the experiences of increasing levels of continuous awareness. In other words, there is a decrease in daydreaming as well as the episodes of carrying out activities and forgetting oneself in them until they are finished (driving for example). Also, there is a reduced level of loss of awareness of self during the dreaming-sleep and dreamless-sleep states. Normally, most people at a lower level of consciousness-awareness become caught in a swoon or feinting effect which occurs at the time when one "falls" asleep or when there is no awareness of dreams while in the deep sleep state (dreamless-sleep). This swooning effect causes an ordinary person to lose consciousness of their own "waking state" identity and to assume the identity of their "dream subject" and thus, to feel that the dream subject as well as the dream world are realities in themselves.

This shift in identification from the waking personality to the dream personality to the absence of either personality in the dreamless-sleep state led ancient philosophers to discover that these states are not absolute realities. Philosophically, anything that is not continuous and abiding cannot be considered as real. Only what exists and does not change in all periods of time can be considered as "real". Nothing in the world of human experience qualifies as real according to this test. Nature, the human body, everything has a beginning and an end. Therefore, they are not absolutely real. They appear to be real because of the limited mind and senses along with the belief in the mind that they are real. In other words, people believe that matter and physical objects are real even though modern physics has proven that all matter is not "physical" or "stable". It changes constantly and its constituent parts are in reality composed of "empty spaces". Think about it. When you fall asleep, you "believe" that the dream world is "real" but upon waking up you believe it was not real. At the same time, when you fall asleep, you forget the waking world, your relatives and life history, and assume an entirely new history, relatives, situations and world systems. Therefore, philosophically, the ordinary states of consciousness which a human being experiences are limited and illusory. The waking, dream and dreamless-sleep states are only transient expressions of the deeper underlying consciousness. This underlying consciousness which witnesses the other three states is what Carl Jung referred to as the "Collective Unconscious". In Indian Philosophy this "fourth" state of consciousness-awareness is known as *Turia*. It is also referred to as "God Consciousness" or "Cosmic Consciousness".

The Ancient Egyptian Path to Enlightenment

The theory of meditation is that when the mind and senses are controlled and transcended, the awareness of the transcendental state of consciousness becomes evident. From here, consciousness-awareness expands, allowing the meditator to discover the latent abilities of the unconscious mind. When this occurs, an immense feeling of joy emerges from within, the desire for happiness and fulfillment through external objects and situations dwindles and a peaceful, transcendental state of mind develops. Also, the inner resources are discovered which will allow the practitioner to meet the challenges of life (disappointments, disease, death, etc.) while maintaining a poised state of mind.

When the heights of meditative experience are reached, there is a more continuous form of awareness which develops. It is not *lost* at the time of falling asleep. At this stage there is a discovery that just as the dream state is discovered to be "unreal" upon "waking up" in the morning, the waking state is also discovered to be a kind of dream which is transcended at the time of "falling asleep". There is a form of "continuous awareness" which develops in the mind which spans all three states of consciousness and becomes a "witness" to them instead of a subject bound by them.

Further, there is a discovery that there is a boundless source from which one has originated and to which one is inexorably linked. This discovery brings immense peace and joy wherein the worldly desires vanish in the mind and there is absolute contentment in the heart. This level of experience is what the Buddhists call *Mindfulness*. However, the history of mindfulness meditation goes back to the time of Ancient Egypt as we will see in the following section. In India, the higher level of consciousness wherein automatic consciousness is eradicated and there is continuous awareness is called *Sakshin Buddhi*. From Vedanta and Yoga Philosophy, the teaching of the "witnessing consciousness" found even greater expression and practice in Buddhist philosophy and Buddhist meditation. Buddhi or higher intellect is the source of the word *Buddha*, meaning one who has attained wakefulness at the level of their higher intellect.

The Therapeutic Value of Meditation

The main source of unhappiness, restlessness, and agitation in the human heart is due to the fact that human existence is un-fulfilling. No matter how much money one has, no matter how much power one has, no matter how many parties one attends, no matter how many sensual pleasures are indulged or how much fame one has, it is never enough to allow one to feel lasting *contentment*. This is because the innermost desire of the heart, the desire to experience the boundless bliss and peace of the Higher Self, has been misunderstood. The mind and senses can never be quenched in the world of ordinary human experience. In reality you are seeking the inner peace and supreme love which transcends all human bounds, and due to ignorance you try to fulfill this need by acquiring possessions and having relationships with other human beings. In essence you have forgotten your true Self and have accepted the body and personality as your true essence. This predicament is the source of all mental aberrations and negative thoughts which lead to negative feelings such as anger, jealousy, vanity, envy, hatred, greed, conceit, covetousness, lust, selfishness, etc. Since the true state of the Soul is peace, contentment and bliss, any of the negative thoughts and feeling which are experienced are in reality a separation from the truth. These negative thoughts rob a human being from the possibility of discovering true peace and contentment. They lead to experiences of degraded human existence and are the cause of animosity, violence, vices and anguish in human relations. In their intensified form these negative thoughts and feelings cause mental illness, addictions, and various forms of

MEDITATION

psychosis and after the death of the physical body lead a soul to experience hellish experiences in the astral plane.

Meditation allows you to go beyond the ignorance of ordinary human existence and to gain strength of will to practice virtuous living. It calms the mind so that it can reach the level of intuitional awareness wherein the higher reality of existence is to be discovered. Meditation is like a churning process which cleanses the mind just as a washing machine cleanses clothes. Therefore, meditation is the provenance of peace, contentment, goodwill and love. If the mind has not experienced the joy of true meditation experience it has not truly experienced its higher existence and therefore, it remains in the degraded state of being susceptible to the frailties and weaknesses of human desire. This state makes it possible to experience the frustrations, sorrows and disappointments of human existence. Therefore, the meditative process alleviates human pain and suffering by leading the practitioner to the true source of contentment and happiness. One who has experienced the truth which is discovered through meditation will not be susceptible to the adversities of life. Rather, he or she will be in a better position to deal with negative emotions and to solve problems rationally, without attachment or regret. One who has experienced the truth which is discovered through meditation will not have a covetous personality because he or she has begun to discover the true source of contentment in the heart. So the meditative experience which allows one to discover the inner reaches of the heart is the source of sanity, intellectual expansion, compassion, goodwill, supreme peace and boundless bliss.

PART II: The Ancient History of Meditation

MEDITATION
The Ancient History of Meditation:

The practice of meditation has received much publicity due to the resurgence of interest in Eastern religions; so much so that most people in modern times consider the practice of meditation as having originated in India or China. However, a deeper research into Ancient Egyptian mythology and philosophy reveals that the practices which are today known as "Yoga" were practiced thousands of years ago in Ancient Egypt. These practices included Meditation and Vegetarianism as well as the other major forms of yoga which survive to this day. Perhaps the earliest recorded meditation practice and instruction comes from the teaching of the "Destruction of Mankind" which is inscribed in hieroglyphic text on the walls of a chamber in the tomb of king Seti I of Ancient Egypt who lived between 2000 and 1250 BCE or earlier. It describes the words of power, visualization and posture elements of meditation and the procedure for practicing the meditation. A compendium of the myth is included below because it contains important mystical teachings in reference to mystical psychology and the nature of human consciousness. Following the compendium there will be a *Gloss* or brief commentary to elucidate the mystical implications of the myth. A meditation based on the teaching of the myth will be presented in the final section of this manual.

The Creation
(From the hieroglyphic text entitled: The History of Creation.)

Ra and the Company of Gods and Goddesses in the Barque of Millions of Years

Here is the story of Ra, the God who was self-begotten and self-created. He created men and women from his own being. He assumed the sovereignty over men and women, and gods, and all things, the ONE God. Upon rising for the first time out of Nu, the Primeval Ocean, Ra emitted from himself Shu (air and space or ether) and Tefnut (moisture). These two gave rise to Geb (earth, physical matter) and Nut (sky, heaven). Maat is a daughter of Ra. It is said that Maat is the foundation of creation and that Maat is what everything is based on since Ra stands in his boat of creation on the pedestal of Maat.

The Destruction of Evil Men and Women
(From the hieroglyphic text entitled: The Destruction of Evil Men and Women.)

Now men and women were speaking words of complaint, saying: "Behold, his Majesty (Life, Strength, and Health to him! has grown old, and his bones have become like silver, and his members have turned into gold and his hair is like unto real lapis-lazuli." His Majesty heard the words of complaint which men and women were uttering, and his Majesty (Life, Strength, and Health to him!) said unto those who were in his train: "Cry out, and bring to me my Eye, and Shu, and Tefnut, and Seb (Geb), and Nut, and the father-gods, and the mother-gods who were with me, even when I was in Nu side by side with my

The Ancient Egyptian Path to Enlightenment

god Nu. Let there be brought along with my Eye, its ministers, and let them be led to me here secretly, so that men and women may not perceive them coming, and may not therefore take to flight with their hearts. Come thou with them to the Great House, and let them declare their plans fully, for I will go from Nu into the place wherein I brought about my own existence, and let those gods be brought unto me there. Now the gods were drawn up on each side of Ra, and they bowed down before his Majesty until their heads touched the ground, and the maker of men and women, the King of those who have knowledge, spake his words in the presence of the Father of the first-born gods.

And the gods spoke in the presence of his Majesty, saying: "Speak unto us, for we are listening to your words." Then Ra spoke unto Nu, saying: "0 you first born god from whom I came into being, 0 ye gods of ancient time, my ancestors, take ye heed to what men and women are doing; for behold, those who were created by my Eye are uttering words of complaint against me. Tell me what ye would do in the matter, and consider this thing for me, and seek out a plan for me, for I will not slay them until I have heard what ye shall say to me concerning it." Then the Majesty of Nu, to son Ra, spoke, saying: "You are the god who are greater than he who made thee. You are the sovereign of those who were created with thee. Thy throne is set, and the fear of thee is great; let thine Eye go against those who have uttered blasphemies against thee." And the Majesty of Ra said: "Behold, they have betaken themselves to flight into the mountain lands, for their hearts are afraid because of the words which they have uttered." The gods spoke in the presence of his Majesty, saying: "Let thine Eye go forth and let it destroy for thee those who revile thee with words of evil, for there is no eye whatsoever that can go before it and resist thee and it when it journeyeth in the form of Hetheru."

Thereupon this goddess went forth and slew the men and the women who were on the mountains and desert lands. And the Majesty of this god said, "Come, come in peace, O Hetheru, for the work is accomplished." Then this goddess said, "You have made me to live, for when I gained the mastery over men and women it was sweet to my heart. I should like to continue feeding upon men and women." Then the Majesty of Ra said, "I myself will be master over them as their King, and I will destroy them." And it came to pass that *She of the offerings*, Hetheru, waded about in the night season in their blood, beginning at Suten-henen. Then the Majesty of Ra spake saying:, "Cry out, and let there come to me swift and speedy messengers who shall be able to run like the wind . . . ." and straightway, these messengers were brought unto him. And the Majesty of this god spake saying: "Let these messengers go to Abu, and bring unto me mandrakes in great numbers"; and when these mandrakes were brought unto him the Majesty of this god gave them to Sekhet, the goddess who dwelleth in Annu (Heliopolis) to crush. And behold, when the maidservants were bruising the grain for making beer, these mandrakes were placed in the vessels which were to hold the beer, and some of the blood of the men and women who had been slain. Now they made seven thousand vessels of beer. Now when the Majesty of Ra, the King of the South and North, had come with the gods to look at the vessels of beer, and behold, the daylight had appeared after the slaughter of men and women by the goddess in their season as she sailed up the river, the Majesty of Ra, said: "It is good, it is good that she has displayed the power of righteousness and punished the evil ones, nevertheless I must protect men and women against her." And Ra, said, "Let them take up the vases and carry them to the place where the men and women were slaughtered by her."

MEDITATION

Then the Majesty of the King of the South and North, in the three-fold beauty of the night, caused to be poured out these vases of beer which make men to lie down (sleep), and the meadows of the Four Heavens (the South, North, West, and East of the sky) were filled with beer (divine nectar) by reason of the Souls of the Majesty of this God. And it came to pass that when this goddess arrived at the dawn of day, she found these Heavens flooded with the nectar, and she was pleased thereat; and she drank of the beer and blood, and her heart rejoiced, and she became drunk, and she gave no further attention to men and women. Then said the Majesty of Ra, to this goddess, "Come in peace, come in peace, O Amit (most beautiful one)" and thereupon beautiful women came into being in the city of Amit (or, Amem). And the Majesty of Ra spake in homage to this goddess, saying: "Let there be made for her vessels of the beer which produceth sleep at every holy time and season of the year, and they shall be in number according to the number of my hand-maidens." And from that early time until now men have been wont to make on the occasions of the festival of Hetheru vessels of the beer which make them to sleep in number according to the number of the hand-maidens of Ra.

And the Majesty of Ra spake unto this goddess, saying: "I am smitten with the pain of the fire of sickness; whence cometh to me this pain?" And the Majesty of Ra said, "I live, but my heart has become exceedingly weary with existence with these men and women who have forgotten me and become boastful, prideful and full of themselves. I have slain some of them, but there is a remnant of worthless ones, for the destruction which I wrought among them was not as great as my power." Then the gods who were in his following said unto him, "Be not overcome by thy inactivity, for thy might is in proportion to thy will." And the Majesty of this God (Ra) said unto the Majesty of Nu, "My members are weak and have suffered pain since primeval time, and I shall not recover until another period comes".

And the Majesty of the god Nu said, "Son Shu, be thou the Eye for thy father . . . . . and assist him, and you goddess Nut, place him on your back." And the goddess Nut said, "How can this be then, "0 my father Nu ?" " Hail," said Nut . . . . . to the god Nu, and the goddess straightway became a cow, and she set the Majesty of Ra upon (her) back . . . . . And when these things had been done, men and women saw the god Ra upon the back of the cow. Then these men and women said, "Remain with us, and we will overthrow thine enemies who speak words of blasphemy against thee, and destroy them."

Then his Majesty, Ra, set out for the Great House, and the gods who were in the train of Ra remained with the men and women; during that time the earth was in darkness. And when the earth became light again, and the morning had dawned, the men came forth with their bows and their other weapons, and they set their arms in motion to shoot the enemies of Ra.

Then said the Majesty of this god, "Your transgressions of violence are placed behind you, for the slaughtering of the enemies is above the slaughter of sacrifice." Thus came into being the slaughter of enemies. And the Majesty of this god said unto Nut, "I have placed myself upon my back in order to stretch myself out."

The Ancient Egyptian Path to Enlightenment

And the Majesty of this God said, "Call to me the god Djehuti," and one brought the god to him forthwith. And the Majesty of this god said unto Djehuti, "Let us depart to a distance from heaven, from my place, because I would make light and the god of light in the Ṭuat and the Land of Gaves. You shall write down the things which are in it, and you shall punish those who are sinful, that is to say, the workers who have worked iniquity (rebellion-unrighteousness). Through thee I will keep away from the servants whom this heart of mine loathes. You shall be in my place ASTI (ast-throne or support), and you shall therefore be called, O Djehuti, the "ASTI of Ra." Moreover, I give thee power to send forth light. . . . . ; thereupon shall come into being the Ibis (jcabi) bird of Djehuti. I moreover give thee "power" to lift up thine hand before the two Companies of the gods who are better than you, and what you do shall be fairer than (the work of the god KHEN; therefore shall the divine bird of Djehuti come into being. Moreover, I give thee power to embrace the two heavens with thy beauties and with thy rays of light; therefore shall come into being the Moon-god of Djehuti. Moreover, I give thee power to drive back the Ha-nebu (unrighteous northerners); therefore shall come into being the dog-headed Ape (anan) of Djehuti, and he shall act as governor for me. Moreover, you are now in my place in the sight of all those who see thee and who present offerings to thee, and every being shall ascribe praise unto thee, O you who are God."

The Story of Hetheru and Djehuti

Some say that Hetheru, the goddess of beauty, the eye of Ra, transformed herself into the form of a lioness or lynx and killed the evil people who plotted against the Lord of All. Having killed all those who were evil, she forgot her true identity and became addicted to the taste of human blood. She continued to kill everyone she could find as she roamed the earth. Then, seeing that humankind would soon come to an end, Ra sent the messenger of wisdom, Djehuti, to bring his daughter back. Straightway Djehuti transformed himself into a baboon and found Hetheru. At first she threatened to devour him but he cleverly enticed her into listening to the divine stories of gods and goddesses. He told her about Ra, her father and reminded her of her beautiful human form. He spoke of her glory as the Eye of Ra, and the honor which the people of Egypt bestowed upon her. Gradually her desire for blood and killing dwindled and she began to desire to regain her former place as the mighty goddess of beauty and passion. Thus, Djehuti led her back to Egypt and back to her rightful place among the pantheon of gods and goddesses.

Gloss on The Destruction of Evil Men and Women

The *Destruction of Evil Men and Women* (Myth of Hetheru and Djehuti) is extremely important teaching in reference to the nature of human consciousness, the source of the human soul and the way and process of spiritual enlightenment.

There are several variations in the Ancient Egyptian myths relating to the *"Eye"*. One tells that the Eye left Ra and went into Creation and was lost. Ra (Divine Self) sent Djehuti (wisdom) to find the Eye (individual soul) and bring it back. It was through the *Magic* (wisdom teachings) of the god Djehuti that the Eye realized who it was and agreed to return to Ra. Upon its return, however, it found that Ra had replaced it with another. In order to pacify it, Ra placed it on his *brow* in the form of a *Uraeus serpent, where it could rule the world.* One variation to the story holds that the Eye left Ra and went to Nubia in the form of a Lioness or a Lynx (Hetheru, in her

MEDITATION

aspect as destroyer of evil and unrighteousness). When Ra heard this, he sent the Nubian god, *Ari-Hems-Nefer* (a form of Shu), and Djehuti to bring the Eye back. They took the form of baboons (symbol of wisdom) and soon found the Eye near the Mountain of the Sunrise, where Asar was born. The Eye refused to leave because it learned to enjoy its new existence. It was destroying those who had committed sins (plotted against Ra) while on earth. Djehuti worked his magic on the Eye and brought it back to Ra. Another variation of the story holds that Ra sent *Shu* and *Tefnut* in search of the Eye. The Eye resisted, and in the struggle, shed tears, and from the tears grew men. This is a clever play on words because the word for "tears", **Remtu**, ⬯ 𓅓 𓂋 𓏏 𓁿 𓏥, (that fell from the eyes of Ra) and the word for "men", **Reth** or **Rethu**, ⬯ 𓂋 𓏏 𓀀 𓏥, have similar sounds in Ancient Egyptian language.

The Ancient Egyptian Path to Enlightenment

Below: Sample of the actual text from the Ancient Egyptian Scripture of the Myth of Hetheru and Djehuti and the Glorious Light Meditation instruction.

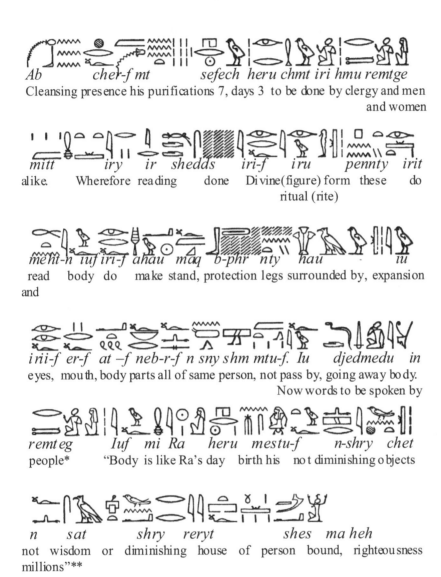

Rai-an-ir ab n Djehuti r shed si her Ra
Whoever in heart of Djehuti reads words these for Ra

Ab   cher-f mt   sefech heru chmt iri hmu remtge
Cleansing presence his purifications 7, days 3 to be done by clergy and men and women

mitt   iry   ir shedds   iri-f   iru   pennty   irit
alike.   Wherefore reading   done   Divine(figure) form these   do ritual (rite)

meni-n iuf iri-f ahau maq b-phr nty hau   iu
read   body   do   make stand, protection legs surrounded by, expansion and

iri-f er-f at –f neb-r-f n sny shm mtu-f. Iu   djedmedu   in
eyes, mouth, body parts all of same person, not pass by, going away body. Now words to be spoken by

remt eg   Iuf mi Ra   heru mestu-f   n-shry chet
people*   "Body is like Ra's day   birth his   not diminishing objects

n   sat   shry   reryt   shes ma heh
not wisdom or diminishing house of person bound, righteousness millions"**

The relationship of "tears" to "men" symbolizes the idea that humankind is the expression of the desire of the Divine Self to have experiences in the realm of time and space. Further, "tears" are a symbol of human experience. It implies that human experience is a sorrowful condition because consciousness has degraded itself to the level of gross, limited human experience in the form of an individual ego as opposed to the expansive, limitless Self. This contraction in consciousness is what allows the ego to emerge as an individual and distinct personality out of "nowhere", just as a dream personality emerges out of "nowhere". Instead of knowing itself as the immutable Soul, the soul sees the ego and the world of time and space as the reality. This development would be like the ocean forgetting that it is the ocean and believing itself to be one

MEDITATION

of the waves. Therefore, instead of seeing itself as encompassing all the waves, it is concerned with its transient experience, as an individual wave, and with comparing itself to other waves.

Life is "sorrowful" from the standpoint of wisdom because even conditions that appear to be pleasurable are in reality setting the individual up for disappointment and frustration later on, because no positive situation can last indefinitely. Also, the pursuit of worldly pleasure and pain sets up mental impressions that will survive the death of the body and lead the soul to further incarnations in search of fulfillment. Therefore, the Sages say that *all life is painful to the wise.* This is why Yoga philosophy emphasizes going beyond both pleasure *and* pain in order to transcend the bondage to time and space. This can be accomplished by turning away from the world which is illusory and seeking to discover the Self.

The masses of people who do not have spiritual sensitivity put up with the world and its ups and downs due to lack of reflectiveness. Having been taught from their youth by family and society to look for happiness in the world, they do not know any better. Through the development of wisdom and reflection, the aspirant can develop an intuition which transcends pleasure and pain and move beyond the world of ordinary human experience as a source of happiness. The following Ancient Egyptian teachings highlight the idea of the sorrowfulness of ordinary human experience and urge the aspirant to live according to the teachings of virtue and wisdom in order to avoid the sufferings of life.

Through the story of the Eye, very important mystical teachings are being conveyed. The Eye, *Udjat,* is a symbol of intuitional vision. Also, it represents the desire of the Divine to go into itself (Creation) and the subsequent forgetfulness that ensues. The resistance of the Eye to return to the divine abode is a symbol of the predicament of ordinary people who, through ignorance and intense desire, detest the idea of even considering the spiritual values of life because their hearts (minds) are consumed with passion. They are consumed with the desire to experience the pleasures of material existence. Having created the universe in itself, the Supreme Being sent its Eye (consciousness) into Creation. Consciousness then became "lost" in Creation and became the souls of human beings and all life forms, forgetting its true Self. The Eye, lost in Creation, is the human soul which is caught up in the cycle of birth-death-birth (reincarnation) due to forgetfulness and distraction (ignorance of its true nature). The Supreme Being (Ra) sent out its messenger of wisdom (Djehuti) in the forms of *Metu Neter* (ancient scriptures of wisdom) and *Sbai* (spiritual preceptor-Guru) to instruct the Eye in reference to its true nature. Having "remembered" who it was in reality, the Eye then returned to its rightful place.

The same teaching of the Eye is to be found in the Ancient Egyptian story of Heru and Set. Heru was the son of Asar and Aset. Set was the brother of Asar. Due to jealousy, anger, hatred and greed, Set murdered Asar. When Heru grew up he challenged Set over the throne of Ancient Egypt. Heru represents the forces of good and Set represents the forces of egoism, sinfulness and negativity. Heru also represents the human spirit which is being obstructed by Set who represents distraction and dullness in the human mind. During the conflict Set tore out Heru' Eye. Some

versions* of the story tell that Set threw filth into the eyes of Heru and this led Heru to despair, frustration, anger and dejection. It is Djehuti who restored the vision of Heru through the power of magical words of power (wisdom teaching). In this context, the whole teaching of wisdom which Djehuti applies (*Hekau* -Magic) to the Eye causes it to remember its essential nature and its glory as the Eye of Heru. Upon its return, the Eye provided Heru with the strength of will he needed to overthrow Set. This story mythologizes the journey of the human soul and its eventual redemption wherein it achieves the sublimation of the ego and attains to *Self-realization*.
*Ancient Egyptian Book of Coming Forth By Day.

In this aspect, the plight of the Eye and its subsequent restoration through the teachings of Djehuti, the transmitter of wisdom, embodies the principle of the teacher-disciple relationship though which spiritual knowledge is transmitted. We saw this same principle in the Initiation of Heru by Aset and it may be found in the Gnostic Christianity with the teachings of Jesus to his disciples and the story of Thecla as well as in the Indian Vedantic principle of the Guru-Disciple relationship such as Krishna and Arjuna and Vasistha and Rama. Djehuti is the master teacher who initiates the aspirant on the spiritual path of wisdom. In teaching others, the priest or priestess assumes the role of Djehuti. Djehuti is the *Guru* of the Eye. In Hinduism, this process is immortalized in the epics, the *Bhagavad Gita* and the *Yoga Vasistha Ramayana* scriptures. In these two scriptures, two aspirants are reminded of their divine essential nature by the Gurus who are themselves, one with the Divine Self. Gradually, they are led to realization of the Self through a process which involves the classical teachings of Yoga (wisdom, reflection and meditation). These texts are highly recommended for any serious student of Yoga scriptures.

When Heru' eye (the moon) was torn out and thrown away by Set, the god Djehuti, who presides as the moon (see verse 8) found it and using the formula below, turned it into the Moon. When the parts of the Eye of Heru are added up, gives the answer 63/64 which approximate the whole number 1. One is the number which symbolizes oneness, wholeness, All sight, All knowing, the Supreme Being, The Absolute. As long as the soul is involved in creation (matter), there will remain some small separation between the individual BA and the Universal BA, the ONE. In order to become completely unified, merged into infinity, the individual soul of the enlightened person dissolves into the Universal soul at the time of death; this is complete ONENESS with the divine. The missing part of the Eye of Heru, 1/64, is added by Djehuti through magic.

Thus through the magic of Djehuti (wisdom), the parts (representing our consciousness) may be reconstituted to wholeness. Djehuti is an aspect of Ptah, the Cosmic Mind. In this aspect Djehuti symbolizes the higher consciousness (mind) of those humans who are attuned to the Universal (Cosmic) Mind.
Thus Djehuti speaks:

> *"I came seeking the Eye of Heru, that I might bring it back and count it. I found it (now it is) complete, counted and sound, so that it can flame up to the sky and blow above and below..."*

Therefore, through the Eye (vision, consciousness) of Djehuti (wisdom), the Eye of Heru (inner vision) may be brought back to its original place, that it may attain the heights of heaven and achieve control over the spiritual domain (above) and the realm of matter (below). Djehuti is

MEDITATION

the God who brings MAAT (truth, righteousness, justice). Thus, through wisdom and righteousness our original condition may be restored. The name for the Eye of Heru may be pronounced as *"Wedjat", "Udjat" or "Utchat"* meaning: *"the whole or restored one"* and also *"that which protects."*

In the Pyramid of Unas, the Eye of Djehuti is called *"The Black Eye of Heru."* In the same text is said to Unas:

"Thou hast seized the two Eyes of Heru, the White Eye and the Black Eye and thou hast carried them off and set them in front of thee and they give light to thy face."

In the saga of the struggle of Heru and Set, the most central issue is the return of the Eye to its rightful place in the "brow" of Heru. This event is synonymous with the resurrection (redemption) of the soul of Asar (soul-initiate-aspirant), when he was killed by Set (ignorance-pride-ego). While the scriptures speak about two eyes (right and left) they are both indeed referring to the same inner spiritual vision which allows a human being to transcend the egoistic vision of life. Thus, through the restoration of spiritual vision (discovering the Eye of intuitional understanding) a human being (Asar) is *resurrected*.

The ego in a human being is what leads him or her into positive or negative situations and also makes a person susceptible to either pain or pleasure, adversity or prosperity in life. The Eye of intuitional vision protects one from any and all adversity and injury because once one attains intuitional vision, the light of understanding vanquishes all negative thoughts, fears, and desires in the human heart which could lead a person to situations of pain and sorrow; It also nullifies all negativity from outside (from people or nature) which might seek to cause harm to a person either in thought, word or deed. Therefore, an enlightened human being (Sage, Saint) is beyond the pain and sorrow of life because he or she has transcended the ego itself.

The Goddess Hat-Hor (Hetheru)

In a text from the Temple at Dier al-Medina, Hetheru is referred to as having the same divine attributes as Heru. She is described as *"The Golden One"* and *"The Queen of the Gods"*. Her shrines being even more numerous than those of Heru, Hetheru or *Het-Heru*, meaning *"The House of Heru"* and *"The House Above (sky),"* became identified, like Heru, with the salvation of the initiate. In the *Egyptian Book of Coming Forth By Day*, she is the one who urges the initiate to do battle with the monster Apep so as not to lose his / her heart as she cries out: *"Take your armor"*. In a separate papyrus, the initiate is told that she (Hetheru) is the one who:

"will make your face perfect among the Gods; she will open your eye so that you may see every day... she will make your legs able to walk with ease in the Underworld, Her name is Hetheru, Lady of Amenta."

The Ancient Egyptian Path to Enlightenment

Hetheru represents the power of the Ra (Supreme Spirit), therefore, associating with her implies coming into contact with the boundless source of energy which sustains the universe. Making contact with Hetheru implies the development of inner will-power which engenders clarity of vision that will lead to the discovery of what is righteous and what is unrighteous. A mind which is constantly distracted and beset with fetters (anger, hatred, greed, conceit, covetousness, lust, selfishness, etc.) cannot discern the optimal course in life. It becomes weak willed because the negative emotions and feelings drain the mental energy, thus unrighteous actions and sinful thoughts arise and the weak mind cannot resist them. Unrighteous actions lead to adverse situations and adverse situations lead to pain and sorrow in life. (see *The Asarian Resurrection* and *Egyptian Tantra Yoga* for more on Hetheru and the teachings of Egyptian Tantra Yoga)

In mystical philosophy the eyes are understood to be the seat of waking consciousness. When you wake someone you look at their eyes to see if they are awake. The right Eye in particular is seen as the dynamic aspect of consciousness, and Hetheru, as the right Eye of Ra, symbolizes exactly that concept. God (Ra) has projected consciousness (the Eye) into creation, and in so doing, the eye (waking consciousness) becomes involved in various activities within the world of time and space. Similarly, the human soul has projected its image into time and space (the ocean of creation), and in so doing, the psycho-physical self has emerged and human experience is possible. From this process arises the possibility of karmic involvement as well as ignorance and egoism.

The Three States of Consciousness

The Eye as a Metaphor

The Eye coming into physical form as the lynx or lioness is a symbol of human existence. It represents the human soul. In the same way that the Eye is a "ray" or "projection" of Ra, the Supreme Being, the human soul is a ray or projection of the Supreme Being. Thus, the plight of the Eye is a parable which the Sages of Ancient Egypt composed in order to explain human existence and to impart the knowledge of spiritual enlightenment for spiritual aspirants. In this context it is similar in most respects to other initiatic scriptures, especially those from India (The Upanishads, Bhagavad Gita, Yoga Vasistha).

The teachings are given through three main characters in the story. These are *Ra, Hat-Hor* and *Djehuti*. Hat-Hor displays three distinct states of consciousness throughout the myth. In so doing the myth outlines the three important states of religion and religious practice in a highly artistic and entertaining manner. True religious practice is made up of three stages of spiritual practice as previously discussed. Therefore, it requires three stages of teaching or initiatic education. The first stage is composed of the events of the myth. This includes the events of the story, the characters and/or deities within the story, the plot and basic themes within the story. The second stage is the Ritual. Ritual includes the observances, ceremonies, customs, etc., related to the myth. The third level of religion is the Mystical Experience. This third level is the true objective of all religious practices. Without this stage, religion becomes dry and ineffective. When people only practice the first and second levels of religion the practice often becomes personal and egoistic as well as dogmatic and subjective. This is the breeding ground for conflict between religions as well as misunderstanding about what true religious practice is all about.

MEDITATION
The Mystical Experience: Pure Consciousness

In the beginning Hat-hor is one with Ra. She experiences awareness of her essential nature as being united with the Supreme. This is the mystical experience. The mystical experience is the true state of being. It represents a full awareness of the spiritual Self as well as an awareness of the unity of everything in creation. This is the true state of human consciousness. This state of consciousness is characterized by all-pervasiveness, infinite expansion, infinite freedom, infinite awareness and infinite peace. In Indian mysticism the states of consciousness are called *"Gunas"* or modes of expression in which consciousness (God) expresses.

The Distracted State (Agitation)

When she (Hat-Hor) is sent (projected) into time and space (the phenomenal world) to perform a task in the service of the Divine she falls prey to human sentiment. In particular she becomes filled with anger and develops a need to satisfy her desire for flesh and blood. This a state in which she becomes forgetful of her original state. It is a condition wherein the soul is overpowered with delusion due to the overwhelming pressure of desires, thoughts and strong emotions. These act as clouds which block the human personality from having a clear vision of the Self. They are called fetters and anyone who is fettered is known as one who is in the state of bondage. This state of mind is characterized by restlessness, distraction, dissatisfaction, lack of fulfillment, constant movement, etc. In relation to the Gunas of Indian mysticism, this state of consciousness is known as *Rajas*.

The human soul uses the mind and senses in order to have human experiences in much the same way as a person uses glasses to see the world. When the glasses are colored, anything that is seen through them is colored. In the same way when the soul uses the mind and senses to "know," everything that is known in this manner is "colored" by the thoughts, feelings, sentiments, egoism, etc. Therefore, the mind that is beset with ignorance, anger, hatred, anxiety, delusion, etc. will act as a veil which blocks the vision of the innermost Self. This state is represented by Hetheru as she runs through the land seeking to satisfy her endless desire to slay and consume human beings. The desires in a mind that is constantly assaulted by the fetters are endless. No sooner does one desire become fulfilled before another arises. This is because ignorance is feeding on ignorance, and ignorance can never satiate ignorance. Hetheru in the state of delusion believes that she must continue to search out, kill and eat flesh and blood in order to satisfy her innermost urge. Since the desire is of the flesh (her body, mind and ego), it is never possible to satisfy it. As long as she continues to believe that this is her true desire and purpose she will continue in an endless search for fulfillment in this manner. This state of consciousness is characterized by a constriction in consciousness. No longer is there all-pervasiveness or peace but a squeezing pressure of desires.

"The Body belongs to the Earth,
Soul belongs to Heaven"

-Ancient Egyptian Proverb

This is the miserable predicament of human embodiment. When the human soul becomes embodied (associated with a human form-the body, mind and senses) the pressure of these (body, mind and senses) cause the soul to forget its true nature. It begins to believe that it is the body and that the feelings, sentiments, desires of the mind, senses and body are its own. This form of delusion leads people on an endless search through life trying to satisfy their need for companionship, comfort, happiness, etc., through worldly objects and other human personalities. However, the real need and innermost desire is to discover the Self, to know "Who am I".

In this state most people are concerned with getting rich or acquiring objects which they perceive as sources of pleasure. There is little thought given to why there is only a brief period of apparent fulfillment once an object or situation that was desired is finally acquired or achieved. There is only the thought: Somewhere in this world there is a situation or some thing which will make me supremely happy and which will fulfill my desires. However this "something" is never to be found in the world of time and space.

"Searching for one's self in the world is the pursuit of an illusion."

-Ancient Egyptian Proverb

People in the *Distracted State* are considered as "normal" by mainstream society. People in this state will often act out of selfishness and will not consider the consequences of their actions. They experience a *Thermometer Existence*. This means that they experience mood swings and a constant flow of emotions and desires. They may be reasonably honest under ordinary conditions but when under the pressure of temptation they may lie, cheat or steal.

Another characteristic of the *Distracted State* is that people meet in conversations and talk about any and all subjects without coherence, or rationality. For example, two people may meet at lunch time and discuss several subjects from the taste of their sandwich to the breakfast they had that day, to the new movie playing, to the weather forecast, to the latest intrigue of their favorite soap opera star, to the ugly tie of their boss and then go back to their job. The conversation flows from one subject to another without any rhyme or reason and it is all mindless and inane talk. A thoughtful person would not engage in such a confused dialogue. She or he would remain quiet. This would make them seem abnormal to the general population.

You must understand that what the masses consider to be good and normal is in reality abnormal. It is an aberration from the higher reality wherein it is possible to experience inner fulfillment and peace. The distracted manner in which most people carry on is an expression of their feeling of emptiness which must continuously be filled with excitement and action. A person who has experienced inner fulfillment does not require interaction with others for the sake of interaction and does not require action in order to feel as if something fulfilling is "going on" and "I am alive", etc. Such a person who displays calmness, self-sufficiency, mental poise, equanimity, peacefulness and who is not susceptible to stress under stressful conditions is seen as abnormal by a distracted personality. People who do not feel the need to seek excitement through parties, sports, entertainments of various types, overindulging in food, sex or drink, etc. are seen as social bores by the masses, and yet this advanced state of being is the real evidence of psycho-spiritual advancement in life.

There are many intellectuals in all fields, including spirituality, who engage in debates and intellectual discussions for the sake of argument. Logic is not studied for a higher purpose but for the sake of logic itself. Under these conditions the mind can construct any form of reasoning which will support its viewpoint.

The power of reasoning and speech is of paramount importance because what you understand is what determines your experiences in the outer world as well as in the inner. Your speech is an

MEDITATION

expression of your innermost beliefs and ideals, your consciousness. Therefore, you should not allow your intellectual capacity to become retarded, melancholic, gloomy, dejected or spiritless. Intellectualism with no higher, sublime purpose eventually leads to dullness. The proof of this is the long history of intellectuals who have committed crimes and created the most anti-humane forms of philosophy throughout the world. Two examples of this are the African Slave Trade and the racism of Nazi Germany, both of which were supported by many intellectuals of the time. Even today there are those who create elaborate treatises which seek to prove the superiority of one group over another based on sex, economics, genetics, etc. All of these criteria are relative and illusory. Therefore, anyone who engages in such intellectual activity is to be considered as being equally caught in the ignorance of egoism as a backward person who never went to school even for a day and who has not learnt to interact with people of other groups. Thus, intellectual persons, even those who may seem cultured and sophisticated, cannot automatically be considered more advanced than an illiterate person.

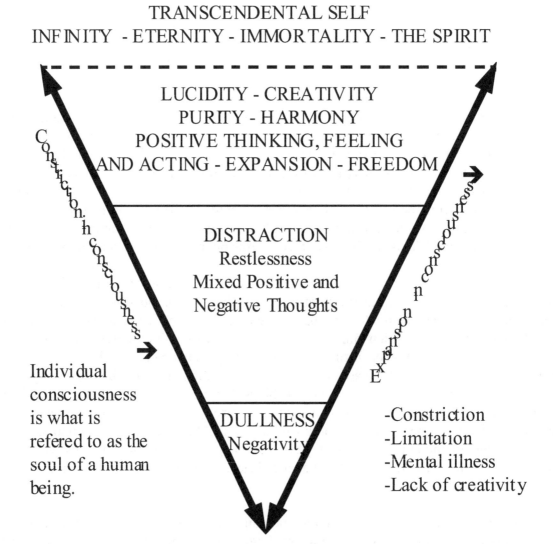

The personality of a human being may be understood as an inverted triangle. At the bottom there is constriction and at the top there is expansion.

In the state of Dullness there is awareness of negativity and all of the base feelings, anger, hatred, greed, lust, etc.

The Ancient Egyptian Path to Enlightenment

In the state of Distraction there is a mixture of positive and negative. If there is practice of Yoga a person in this state can have a glimpse of harmony, clarity and peace of mind.

In the state of purity there is joy, peace and harmony pervading in the mind. From here it is possible to glimpse the higher reality which transcends all states of mind. This higher reality is the true Self which is the objective of all spiritual disciplines. Thus, spiritual practice is the process of promoting positive feelings, understanding, harmony, love and righteousness and to going beyond the mind itself to discover the Absolute Self which is not affected by the modes of expression in which consciousness expresses.

The State of Dullness

When Hetheru is given the drugged beer she was immersed in a state of consciousness characterized by a deep stupor. This is a state of mind wherein there is such degradation that the personality expresses ignorance, negativity, animosity, grief, hatred, etc. which had previously been in a dormant state. Ra decreed that she should be given the potion because she was so deluded that she would not respond to any form of persuasion based on reason or relation of kinship. Have you ever tried to reason with a person who is in the throes of passion or anger? Have you tried to control yourself when in this state? In the *Distracted State*, the mind is clouded and the intellect or reasoning ability is weakened. People often fall in with bad company and are influenced by peer pressure. In the *Dullness State* the delusion has deepened so far that there is a lashing out, a desire for destruction of the environment as well as self-destruction. Hetheru has reached a state in which she will destroy anything which lies in her path. Thus, this state implies intensified anger and hatred as well as laziness, sleepiness, inertness, idleness, indolence, shiftlessness, slothfulness and sluggishness.

When consciousness sinks into deep dullness people may commit murder and/or enter into conflicts which could be life-threatening because they are compelled by their emotions and desires. They will consume substances which are poisonous such as cigarettes, drugs, or meat, even though they may find out that these substances are destroying their body and mind. They will indulge in sensual pleasures (anything that gives physical pleasure) and will become extremely angry if anything comes in the way of their satisfying their perceived desires. They will become violent with the slightest provocation. Sometimes the movement toward destruction is directed inward. This leads to self-inflicted injuries, insipidity, lassitude and deep depression.

When the degradation becomes severe people can commit the most heinous acts of violence and crimes of the most extreme, shocking and reprehensible nature. Others may become incapacitated due to inner negativity to such a degree that they can no longer sustain the practical realities of life. This leads to insanity, homelessness, suicide, etc. In Indian mysticism this state of consciousness is called *"Tamas"*.

MEDITATION

The State of Lucidity (Harmony, Purity and Balance)

(26) "I HAVE NOT STOPPED MY EARS AGAINST THE WORDS OF RIGHT AND WRONG."

From The Ancient Egyptian
Book of Coming Forth By Day

When Hetheru met with Djehuti a new form of awareness began to develop in her heart. At first she desired to kill and eat him, however, his beguiling charm and eloquence caught her interest. She spared his life and began to listen to him. In so doing she was opening the door to expansion in consciousness.

Most human beings are caught between the first two stages of consciousness at one time or another. There is a mixture of distraction, movement and dullness. In this state a human being does not want to sit still in order to listen to spiritual discourses about the nature of the soul and about the method to attain spiritual enlightenment, and if forced to do so, the mind falls into a state of dullness and she/he feels asleep (a state of extreme dullness).

It is only the stress of egoistic desires which is suppressing that which is positive, true and good within the human heart. In some brief and rare occasions there is an experience of peace, balance, contentment and tranquility. Many times these feelings are experienced for a brief period of time after an object of desire is acquired or a situation which one desired comes true. These experiences are only glimpses of the totality of happiness and peace which is in the heart. However, in order to discover this, the body, mind and senses must reach a state of balance, harmony and peace. This is possible though the practices of Yoga (Listening, Reflecting upon, Living in accordance* with and Meditating upon the teachings). *(practicing the teachings of MAAT)

When Yoga is practiced a purifying movement wherein the ignorance, delusion, restlessness, anger, anxiety, hatred, greed, lust, egoism, selfishness, and vices such as pride, covetousness, lust, anger, envy, gluttony, and sloth within the heart are cleansed. Therefore, Djehuti represents the light of reasoning and intuitional understanding about the innermost reality within the heart. Djehuti is the Sage who is sent by God to find the wayward child (the soul) to impart wisdom which leads to illumination of the heart and inner discovery of the truth. This principle is so pervasive in human culture that it has found expression in the Initiatic Way of Education as practiced first in ancient times in the Ancient Egyptian Temples, and later in the Indian Upanishads and epic myths of Krishna and Rama, and much later in the Christian baptism of Jesus by John the Baptist. These stories have one factor in common. It is the relationship of the Sage with the disciple wherein spiritual knowledge is imparted.

The myth of Hetheru and Djehuti is similar to the other important Initiatic myth of Ancient Egyptian, *The Asarian Resurrection* in which the young child Heru is taught about the mysteries of the soul and the universe by his mother and Spiritual Preceptor (teacher) Aset. In modern times this tradition of the *Spiritual Preceptor-Aspirant relationship* has been continued through the Gurus of Indian Yoga and the Sufi Gurus of the Near East and in Egypt. In popular culture this teaching has found expression through popular films such as *The Star Wars Trilogy* and *The*

The Ancient Egyptian Path to Enlightenment

Lion King.[20]

However, before spiritual knowledge can be imparted the spiritual aspirant must have aspiration. This implies a desire to go beyond the pettiness and sorrow of ordinary human existence as well as the maturity to accept responsibility for one's condition. This means that there can be no blaming of others for one's troubles. It is one's own Ari which has led one to one's present conditions, good or bad. Conversely, it is one's present self-effort in the area of *Shedi* (spiritual practice) which can lead one out of adversity and into spiritual as well as material prosperity.

Lucidity implies reason, clarity, wit, sanity, soundness, saneness. Also it implies righteousness, truthfulness, universal love, harmony, peace and selflessness. Therefore, in order to develop lucidity, a spiritual aspirant needs to practice these virtues in everyday life while at the same time studying the teachings at the feet of authentic Spiritual Preceptors (Sages and Saints). When a positive spiritual movement is engendered there is greater and greater awareness of the deeper spiritual reality culminating is Self-Discovery. This is symbolized by Hetheru's discovery of her true essential nature as one with Ra, the Supreme Being, and thus assuming her rightful place. Most human beings think their rightful place is as a member of some social, ethnic or political group, etc. In reality this is only an evanescent and minuscule expression of the totality of who they really are. It is like the sun expressing as a reflection in a pool of water falling into a delusion and thinking "I am this little reflection" and forgetting its true identity. So too every human being has forgotten his/her true identity. However, through the compassion and love of the Self (God), the message of truth which leads to spiritual enlightenment, a return home as it were, is brought by the genuine spiritual personalities who have emerged as great teachers throughout history. Their spiritual enlightenment (contact with the Self) allows them to transmit the teachings of the Self for all who wish to find true peace and happiness. Thus, their discourses and writings on the Self (spiritual scripture) are to be considered as authoritative sources for spiritual enlightenment and should be sought after and studied.

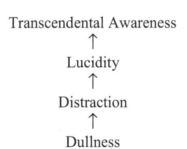

Transcendental Awareness
↑
Lucidity
↑
Distraction
↑
Dullness

(16) Do not prefer the well-born to the commoner,
Choose a man on account of his skills,
Then all crafts are done . . .
Guard your borders, secure your forts,
Troops are useful to their lord.

-From: **The Ancient Egyptian Instructions To Merikara**

This hekau (Ancient Egyptian utterance, verse or spiritual scripture) contains a profound teaching of mystical spirituality. It comes from a text in which an Ancient Egyptian Sage (Merikare) is teaching about the agitated state of mind by discussing the motivations and causes

---

[20] see the Book *Initiation Into Egyptian Yoga: The Secrets of Sheti* by Muata Ashby

MEDITATION

for the negativity of the "Asiatics" who were constantly attacking Egypt during that time and for several thousands of years before. It teaches the need to maintain equal vision or equanimity of mind. Since material wealth is transient and illusory as we discussed in the last passage, a person cannot be judged by his or her material condition. Rather, a person should be judged for their actions and abilities. Since every human being is innately a divine, immortal Soul, their potential is limitless. What holds people back is their ignorant understanding of life and egoistic feelings which lead to sinful behaviors (behaviors based on vices). If you judge others based on their level of material wealth you are engaging in sin because you are seeing them through your egoistic vision of what is true and real based on ignorance. Virtue is the only true wealth and it expresses in the form of compassion, non-violence, truth, universal love, harmony, sharing, etc. Virtue is an expression of one's understanding of the interconnectedness of life and one's own transcendental existence which is connected to the Supreme Spirit. To the extent that one is aware of one's own Divine nature, virtue manifests through the human personality. To the extent that one is in ignorance about one's own Divine nature, sinful (vice) behavior based on greed, jealousy, egoistic desires, etc., will manifest.

There is one more important point to realize about the various states of consciousness. Many people believe that when something which they feel is positive, occurs, then this means happiness, peace and harmony have been achieved. For example, people in general feel that when they experience some situation or acquire some object which brings them joy that this signifies happiness and is the goal of life. Upon reflection, in the light of Yogic Mystical Philosophy, it must be understood that both elation and depression, happiness and anger, etc., are both in reality only two forms of agitation. Elation causes one form of distraction and unrest while anger and negativity also cause a form of distraction and unrest. Dullness is also a form of distraction and unrest. As you study and reflect on the teachings of ancient mystical philosophy it should become increasingly clear to you that what most people consider to be true happiness and peace are in reality sources of agitation, stress and distraction from the real source of peace. This is why in Ancient Egyptian mystical philosophy as well as in the mystical philosophy from India there is an emphasis on the practice of balance (MAAT) as the following Hekau* explain.
*(Ancient Egyptian Spiritual Scripture)

Creativity is a factor of harmony and inner peace. When there is a raging storm of emotions, anxiety and tension in the mind the flow of inspiration from the transcendental Self is obstructed. Therefore, to promote creativity it is necessary to harmonize one's life in every aspect. All activities should be performed in such a way that promotes peace instead of tension. This way of life allows the Inner Self to guide your inner and outer life. This can be achieved if there is constant surrender of egoistic desire to the Divine Will by permitting yourself to be directed by the teachings of Yoga.

> (24) But this should be said to the Bowman:
> Lo, the miserable Asiatic,
> He is wretched because of the place he's in:
> Short of water, bare of wood,
> Its paths are many and painful because of mountains.
> He does not dwell in one place,
> Food propels his legs,
> He fights since the time of Heru,
> Not conquering nor being conquered,
> He does not announce the day of combat,

The Ancient Egyptian Path to Enlightenment

Like a thief who darts about a group.
But as I live and shall be what I am,
When the Bowmen were a sealed wall,
I breached [their strongholds],
I made Lower Egypt attack them,
I captured their inhabitants,
I seized their cattle,
Until the Asiatics abhorred Egypt.
Do not concern yourself with him,
The Asiatic is a crocodile on its shore,
It snatches from a lonely road,
It cannot seize from a populous town.

From:
The Instructions To Merikare

The preceding teaching speaks volumes about the nature of agitation. The general message is beware of your environment and beware of your surroundings. Harshness in surroundings and general environment can cause negative stress which could lead to an unsettled mind.

An unsettled mind is difficult to control. A mind that is uncontrollable will have difficulty in concentrating. Poor concentration will not allow for reflection. Reflection is necessary to make sense of one's situation and to gain intellectual understanding. A non-reflective, confused or "wrong thinking" mind will have difficulty meditating. A non- meditating mind will have difficulty in transcending the world of apparent dualities. One will be endlessly pulled into the "world" and the apparent thoughts going on in the mind.

As the mind will be caught up in the endless waves of joys and sorrows, it will be unable to find peace. A mind filled with too much joy or too much sorrow due to its experiences in the world will be equally agitated and one will have difficulty concentrating and calming down. One extreme (ex. Joy) leads to another (ex. Pain).

The concept of the *"Miserable Asiatic"* became known in Egypt as the concept of *"The Land of Heru and the Land of Set"*. Since Set is the god of the desert, the Asiatics, who dwelt in the desert lands (Asia Minor), became identified with Set and therefore, Setian behavior (impulsive, selfish, brute force, etc.). The teaching about the miserable Asiatic is of paramount importance because it provides an understanding of how the human mind becomes degraded and violent. A human being who is not nurtured and who is constantly experiencing stress will develop a distracted, negative character. The pressures due to lack of security, not knowing where the next meal is coming from, how to acquire the secure the needs of life and then how to hold onto them, etc., etc., does not allow the inner peace and expansiveness of the inner self to manifest. All of these worries and anxieties cause a degradation in the human mind wherein the concern is not about working with others but competing with them for food, material wealth, mates, etc. The purpose of human existence is to provide a means for the soul to experience and grow in awareness of itself as being one with Creation. This feeling is blissful, supremely satisfying and universal. When the soul in a human being is not allowed to express itself in this manner, the ego in a human being is in control, and this egoism fosters feelings of personal desire, separation, and animosity to anything which prevents the ego from getting what it wants. This is the source of animosity, enmity, anger, hatred and violence in the human experience. Spiritual practice leads a human being to discover a deeper essence of life. True spiritual understanding allows a person to understand where true happiness and peace are to be found. It shows

MEDITATION

a person that security cannot be found in the world but in that which sustains it.

The Ancient Egyptian teachings presented above are echoed in the ancient Hindu scripture known as "The Bhagavad Gita" in which Lord Krishna instructs his disciple Arjuna. This particular verse comes from the Chapter on the practice of meditation.

> 32. O Arjuna! The Yogi who sees the likeness of himself in all and thus maintains equal vision in pleasure and pain, he is considered the highest Yogi.

Arjuna then asked about the way in which the mind can be controlled.

> 33. Arjuna asked: O Krishna, I do not see how it is possible to maintain the steady state of Yogic equanimity which you have taught. This mind is ever so restless!

> 34. Verily, O Krishna, the mind is fickle, impetuous and turbulent. To me it seems more difficult to control the mind than it is to control the wind.

> 35. Bhagavan (Lord) Krishna said: Indeed the mind is restless and difficult to control, but can be brought under control by the exercise of Abhyasa (repeated effort) and Vairagya (dispassion).
> 36. It is my opinion that Yoga is difficult for anyone who is lacking self-control. But it can be attained by one who has mastered his lower self if he adopts the proper means.

These instructions bring out important teachings in reference to understanding and controlling the mind. Many people become discouraged early in their spiritual practice because they do not obtain discernible results within a short time. Sometimes they try many different techniques without giving any one sufficient time to work. In essence it is like digging for water by making a well but without going deep enough. What would happen if a person was to dig a hole, and after one or two feet stop and begin another hole? He or she would not find any water.

In spiritual practice as in any other human endeavor, sustained practice (repeated effort) is a key to success. In spiritual practice every single time you turn your mind towards the Divine you are actually creating a higher mental impression. Eventually, these positive impressions overpower the negative impressions of ignorance, anger, hatred, greed, etc. This occurs even when there is no discernible benefit. Therefore, even though you may not see immediate results you should continue practicing your spiritual discipline regularly and with faith. Also it is important to practice dispassion and detachment from worldly objects and worldly desires. If these points are not practiced along with your formal meditation efforts you will have little success or very slow success in meditation.

The Ancient Egyptian Path to Enlightenment
Witnessing Consciousness and Mindfulness in Ancient Egypt

In Ancient Egypt, the level of consciousness known as the mystical experience or cosmic awareness (Spiritual Enlightenment) was also called *Amun*, "the witness" or "watcher". The understanding of the "witnessing consciousness" achieved a high level of expression in the Ancient Egyptian *Hymns of Amun* and in the teaching of the Ancient Egyptian Trinity of Amun-Ra-Ptah. The line below from the *Hymns of Amun* explains the nature of the witnessing consciousness:

"He the One Watcher who neither slumbers nor sleeps."

The Trinity, Nebertcher: Amun-Ra-Ptah of Ancient Egypt refers to the three states of consciousness and that which transcends them. Amun, the Self, is the "hidden" essence of all things. The Sun, Ra, is the radiant and dynamic outward appearance made manifest in the light of cosmic consciousness. In this aspect, Ptah represents the physical world, the solidification of the projection of consciousness (Amun) made manifest. The Triad also has a reference to the states of consciousness in the human being. The Triad refers to the subject or seer, the object or that which is seen and interaction between the two. In all human experience there is a subject-object-interaction relationship occurring all the time. This is true in the waking as well as the dream states. The seer is Amun, that which is seen is Ptah and the interacting medium or sight is represented by Ra. They are in reality projections or emanations of the transcendental underlying consciousness or Nebertcher.

Just as the subject-object-interaction consciousness of a dream is "unreal", the subject-object-interaction consciousness of the waking state is also unreal and illusory. Even though the phenomenal world experienced in the waking state appears to be abiding and solid, modern science has proven that it is not. These new findings of science confirm the teachings of Ancient Egyptian Yoga philosophy, Vedanta and Yoga philosophy of India, Buddhism of India and Taoism of China as well as other mystical philosophies from around the world.

PART III: Formal Meditation Practice and its Effects on the Mind

The Ancient Egyptian Path to Enlightenment
INTRODUCTION

A human being can be likened to a bird. Meditation is like the wings of a bird. There are some birds in nature which have lost the ability to fly. However, with some effort and training they can fly if necessary. There are two ways in which meditation is to be practiced. One is the Formal Meditation and the other is the Meditative Lifestyle. These are the wings upon which the mind can soar to unimaginable heights of expansion and infinity. So each aspect of meditation must be well understood and correctly practiced, otherwise there can be no leaving the confinement of ordinary human existence. The formal meditation is when you set aside a particular time, a particular place and sit down to practice the three steps of meditation which lead to transcendental awareness or cosmic consciousness. The formal meditation practice involves three basic steps. These are: **Concentration, Extended Concentration and Transcendental or Cosmic Consciousness.**

Thus, meditation is to be understood not only as an exercise but as a lifestyle. As you practice living according to the teachings and serving humanity (MAAT) you are purifying yourself by removing gross impurities such as anger, hatred, greed, jealousy, etc., from your mind. As you practice studying and reflecting upon the teachings you are removing ignorance, worry, anxiety, etc. from the mind. As you practice exercise and a healthy diet you are purifying the physical constitution and removing toxins which affect your reasoning and emotions. As you practice devotion towards the Divine you are removing subtle egoistic impurities from your mind. Thus the disciplines for spiritual evolution are to be practiced in an integral manner and this method will yield the most effective results.

The usual manner of progress in formal meditation involves concentration exercises in the beginning. As progress is achieved the concentration practice focuses on concrete objects and then moves to abstract objects and ideas in the advanced stages. You may practice concentrating on any object. However your success towards spiritual enlightenment will be enhanced if you use a spiritual icon such as the image of a deity. There is no danger in using a name and form as a representation of the Divine as long as it is understood that it is only a symbol which does not capture the totality of the Divine. A name and form is useful because in the beginning the mind is too weak to sustain concentration on that which is abstract. As you progress in your spiritual practice you will eventually move towards abstract ideas and finally to the absence of all thought. Then you will move beyond time and space as well as the ego itself. When you reach this level you will discover that you are a separate entity from your ego (body, senses, feelings) as well as its adversities and prosperities. Here you will discover a heretofore unknown peace which you will learn to relish. This is the peace of the Self.

The concentration exercises in the beginning of the *Slowness Meditation* as well as the practice of chanting and watching the breath are three good exercises for beginning to control the mind. Eventually you will not need to practice concentration because you will gain the ability to focus the mind at will. Also don't forget that the more harmony and peace you foster in your life the closer you will be to discovering the Self. If you live in such a manner which reduces worry you will hasten your steps in spiritual practice. Therefore, do not become involved in situations which lead to wasting mental energy. Do not argue with others over trifles. Do not engage in idle talk. Do not gossip or engage in entertainment which engenders restlessness and agitation in the mind. To the best of your ability watch your thoughts, words and deeds. Keep busy working on worthwhile goals which will promote your success as well as harmony in the world. Seek the company of righteous individuals and if possible, the company of authentic spiritual teachers

MEDITATION

(Sages and Saints). This is known as the *Initiatic Way of Education* and it is the most effective way to promote spiritual knowledge and spiritual evolution. (see *Initiation Into Egyptian Yoga: The Secrets of Sheti* and Audio: *The Initiatic Way of Education* by Muata Ashby for more on the initiatic process)

As you begin your practices in meditation you should not put pressure on yourself to achieve results by a certain time. This attitude will be just another mental thought which will block your progress because it will cause mental agitation. You should hold the attitude that you will practice meditation indefinitely because you know that somehow it will benefit you and lead you further along the path to attain Enlightenment. So let us begin with the concentration practice.

Concentration

Have you ever tried to hold a single thought in your mind? Most people cannot hold one thought in their mind or stop the thinking process for even 4 seconds. In order to have success in controlling and going beyond the mind it is necessary to control the mind. Therefore, concentration of mind is the first level of meditation. It involves training the mind so as to develop the ability to hold attention on one object or idea. Concentration also consists of curbing the stray thoughts so as to cause a convergence of mental energy on a single object or thought. The object may be a flower or a divine icon (symbol). At this level, the practice of virtuous living is a great help because it allows you to conserve energy that would be otherwise wasted on the endless pursuit of desires and the indulgence in negative behaviors which agitate the mind and prevent concentration.

In short, the mind in an ordinary human being is like an ocean with a myriad of waves of all shapes and sizes. Through the practice of meditation the mind becomes like an ocean without waves. Have you noticed that when there are waves it is difficult to see the bottom of the water no matter how shallow it is? Have you also noticed that when the water is calm there is visibility because the sand and other objects in the water have settled to the bottom?

In the same way you cannot see the depths of your mind because it is constantly in movement. The sediment of unconscious impressions is constantly being stirred up and the foam, sprays and whirlpools of thoughts and emotions in the mind do not allow a vision of what lies beyond these. So a person who is untrained in the art of meditation and Yoga is constantly thinking about objects and how to acquire them, about the past, present or future, about how to satisfy the desires which are constantly arising, and so on. You must learn to ignore the constant stream of input from the senses. This process of withdrawal will allow you to achieve true introspection.

Many people practice concentration in the world. The big difference in the idea of concentration as it is presented here from that of the world is that worldly minded people concentrate on any means through which they feel they can achieve the object of their desires. Some want to get rich, others concentrate on creating inventions, others on becoming wealthy enough so they can spend their time on the various distractions of life which money can buy and still others concentrate on evil activities. In spiritual life the objective of concentration is to control the mind in order to promote purity of heart and strength of will. In the *Ancient Egyptian Book of Coming Forth By Day* as well as the *Ancient Egyptian Wisdom Texts* (5,000 B.C.E.) the sole objective of all spiritual practice is explicitly stated to be the attainment of *Maak-heru* (purity of heart, harmony, righteousness) which will lead to spiritual realization.

The Ancient Egyptian Path to Enlightenment

The reason for leading a meditative lifestyle which involves detachment, dispassion, righteousness and harmony is so that you may be able to reduce the distractions and wastage of mental energy which is squandered away on things which are not needed and which, upon closer reflection, are not even real anyway. Many times people are so involved with the world of human experience that they cannot stop thinking about objects, people or situations which they desire, hate or wish to acquire. As long as this condition exists it will be extremely difficult, if not impossible, to achieve success in meditation.

Aids to Concentration

Many people feel that their efforts in the practice of concentration only need to be emphasized during their formal concentration exercises. This is a limited understanding which will slow down one's progress towards effective meditation practice. In order to succeed in your formal meditation practice you need to practice concentration not only when trying to meditate, but also during your daily activities. Many people feel that it is good to be involved with many projects at once. Some people even thrive on this way of being. When there is nothing going on they must somehow find something to get into, otherwise they become restless and frustrated. In reality this way of life is like a distraction which forms restless currents in the mind. Thus, when there is no exterior activity, the person inwardly still feels the need for movement and activity. Since life is not all active or all passive, there will inevitably be periods of inactivity. A person who wants to be in harmony needs to learn how to balance these two aspects of human life.

In daily activities one should make an effort to accomplish one goal at a time, concentrating on that task before moving onto others. This will prevent the mind from being scattered in different directions and it will also have the effect of making one's actions more qualitative and effective. There should be an effort toward one-pointedness in all activities. This practice will help when it comes time to practice one-pointedness during the formal sit-down practice of meditation.

Another important point is that you need to learn how to go deep within yourself. This is accomplished by paying attention to your Self instead of outside stimulus from your mind and senses. This is simple but not easy. You need to develop the ability to tune out or ignore your senses as well as the thoughts in your mind and this process will occur if you follow the instructions given in this volume. The key to success in this practice is that your efforts must be put forth daily and regularly. You cannot expect to turn around the currents of your mind in one day nor can you expect to progress if your efforts are intermittent or without proper guidance.

There is a beautiful parable which conveys the teaching expressed above. Once there was a businessman who needed help at his establishment. One day he went to the forest and while eating, poured some water on a tree. Nearby there was a spirit who liked that tree and the spirit thought that the man was offering him some libation. So the spirit appeared to the businessman and gave him a boon that he would give him anything he asked. The man was pleased and told the spirit that he needed some help at his establishment. The spirit said that he would help him with one condition, that if he ran out of work he would eat the businessman. The businessman agreed, thinking that he had enough work to keep the spirit busy for a long time.

The next day the spirit showed up to work and he completed every task that the businessman gave him in a flash, as if by magic. The businessman became concerned and went to his spiritual preceptor who told him to have the spirit create a long pole and to plant it firmly in the ground,

MEDITATION

then that he should grease it and climb up and down until there was another task to perform in the store. This would effectively keep him busy until needed. The plan succeeded and the businessman survived with his new help.

The mystical interpretation is that the spirit is the mind of a human being. Its nature is to be involved with the world, in constant movement. If this movement is not controlled the mind will lead a human being into situations of grief and sorrow which will devour peace, happiness and prosperity, both material and spiritual. Therefore, what is needed is to keep the mind occupied with divine thoughts and feelings. Thus the movement up and down the pole symbolizes the practice of chanting the divine name (words of power) as well as the development of the inner Life Force energy and the psycho-spiritual centers of consciousness (Arat-Sekhem). These practices should be maintained when the mind is not engaged in the duties of life. When you need to perform some task then you can go to it and concentrate on it fully. This practice will not allow negativity and illusions to build up in the mind. You will develop the ability to purify your mind and to discover peace and bliss in all of your activities along with achieving success in your meditation practice.

Many people have a misguided notion of spiritual life. They feel that a spiritual person must be a priest or priestess living at a temple away from the world. Otherwise life must be lived by giving into the longings and desires as they appear in the mind. For some people the secluded lifestyle may be a correct path, but they will already have done extensive spiritual work on themselves throughout many lifetimes. Sometimes people think they are ready so they leave everything to join a temple, only to find that they couldn't leave their mental complexes and worries behind. They built up the illusion that if they were segregated from the world they could meditate and find peace. This is the wrong idea.

There should not be a contradiction between your formal meditative experience and your day-to-day life. People who do not think in this way may experience peace in meditation but when in the world they are irritable, querulous, distracted and restless. You will achieve greater success in your meditation practice if you seek to promote harmony at all times. For example, let us say that you have practiced meditation early in the morning and developed a harmonious feeling. However, at the end of your spiritual practice you begin to dread the fact that you have to go out into the world and when you do, you experience anger over something your boss did or a driver who cut you off or the fact of not getting enough pay or a myriad of other problems. You are defeating the purpose of your meditation practices. You are promoting positive spiritual movement in one area, you are nullifying it in the other. The correct path can be accomplished through a keen understanding of spiritual practice which comes from the continuous study of the teachings under the proper guidance.

The teaching of contentment figures prominently here. Contentment does not mean stopping your efforts to improve yourself. It does not mean giving up the struggle of life and letting God do all the work. The teaching of contentment is a profound mystical philosophy which must be understood thoroughly. The feeling of discontent arises when a person continuously compares themselves to others or engages in one desire after another. In this form of thinking there is always something to be dissatisfied with. There is always someone with more money, a bigger house, more possessions, etc. Therefore if you compare yourself to others or constantly crave for what you do not have, you will insure that your life will be miserable and unfulfillilled.

The Ancient Egyptian Path to Enlightenment

Contentment means that you must realize that the Self (God) has placed you exactly where you need to be, with exactly the right resources to gain the experiences you will need which will lead you to spiritual enlightenment. With this profound faith and understanding you must develop the feeling that your inner Self is guiding you, in a mysterious way, towards what which is good and right. With this understanding you can accept all situations in life with equal vision and furthermore, you can see all situations, whether or not they are prosperous or adverse, as favorable for your spiritual evolution, because the ups as well as the downs are divinely inspired events which will lead you to spiritual enlightenment. Many people who have not studied mystical philosophy live their lives in a state of perpetual contradiction. If there is peace, they complain that there is no excitement, that things are boring. If there is a lot of excitement and movement, they complain that there should be peace and calm. If it is raining, they complain that there should be sunshine. If there is sunshine they complain that it is too hot and the sun is making conditions uncomfortable, and so on. You should look at the world with an objective eye and accept it as it is and not try to impose your own egoistic notion of what it should be. A power far beyond your capacity to comprehend (through an egoistic mind set) is controlling every aspect of nature and has created just the right conditions that are necessary at the right time. Contradictions arise due to a lack of understanding. Therefore, if you become well-versed in the mystical philosophy you will be able to reduce the mental agitation which is caused by contradictions, and you will have the possibility to lead a peaceful life and to enjoy life more fully. Further you will develop a solid basis of inner harmony which will make it possible for you to succeed in the practice of formal meditation.

The world of human experience is like the testing place for all of the teachings you have learned. You can learn about controlling your emotions and understanding that the world is an expression of the Divine, but how will you react when you are confronted with ignorance, hatred and desire? The world gives you opportunities to test yourself and to practice taking the highroad. Every time you do this you will be as if placing another brick on the inner temple of peace, harmony, contentment and enlightenment, which you are building. Your problem is not with the world but with ignorance, restlessness, anxiety, anger, hatred and desire within yourself. Therefore, you can practice spirituality anywhere in the world and achieve the highest goals of spirituality if you have true aspiration, self-effort and proper guidance.

Your job is to make every effort, within your capacity, to act in a righteous manner and to use the gifts which you have been given. The gifts of the inner Self are misused or squandered when a human being is guided by *covetousness, discontent, greed, agitation, discontent, disbelief, impatience, pessimism, depression and cynicism* in the heart. This is why the spiritual scriptures of all traditions emphasize the development of virtue as part of a viable spiritual discipline. Much importance is given to *self-control, fortitude, balance, contentment, faith, hope, and patience* among others. These teachings are prominent among the Ancient Egyptian hieroglyphic texts which date back more than ten thousand years.

In general, a mental atmosphere of peacefulness and contentment is necessary for sublime thoughts and aspirations to emerge in the mind. Otherwise, through a life which is based on pursuing the satisfaction of the senses, there is constant desire and agitation of the mind, and the individual will always be occupied with the petty thoughts and disturbances of day-to-day life. Therefore, the maintenance of serenity and contentment should be the primary goal of a spiritual aspirant. The following Ancient Egyptian proverbs from the teachings of MAAT were available to Plato and to the early Christian theologians who studied philosophy and mysticism in Egypt. These would have been the first teachings that initiates would receive. MAAT itself, as discussed

MEDITATION

earlier, implies *virtue, justice, righteousness and order.*

"They who revere *MAAT* are *long lived*; **they who are covetous have no tomb.**"

"**Do not be greedy** in the division of things. **Do not covet** more than your share. Don't be greedy toward your relatives. A mild person has a greater claim than a harsh one. Poor is the person who forgets their relatives; they are deprived of their company. Even a little bit of what is wanted will turn a quarreler into a friendly person."

"MAAT is great and its effectiveness lasting; it has not been disturbed since the time of Asar. **There is punishment for those who pass over it's laws, but this is unfamiliar to the covetous one**....When the end is nigh, *MAAT* lasts."

"As a camel beareth labor, and heat, and hunger, and thirst, through deserts of sand, and fainteth not; so **the fortitude of a man shall sustain him through perils.**"
"Do not conspire against others. God will punish accordingly. **Schemes do not prevail**; only the laws of God do. **Live in peace**, since what God gives comes by itself."

"To be satisfied with little is the greatest wisdom; and they that increaseth their riches, increaseth their cares; but a **contented mind is a hidden treasure, and trouble findeth it not**."

"**Control your thoughts**, control your actions, have devotion of purpose, have faith in your master's ability to lead you along the path of truth, have faith in your own ability to accept the truth, have **faith** in your ability to **act with wisdom**, **be free from resentment** under the experience of persecution, **be free from resentment** under experience of wrong, learn how to distinguish between right and wrong, learn to distinguish the real from the unreal."

"**See that prosperity elate not thine heart above measure, neither adversity depress thine mind unto the depths***, because fortune beareth hard against thee. Their smiles are not stable, therefore build not thy confidence upon them; their frowns endureth not forever, therefore, **let hope teach thee patience.**"

*This last proverb implies the development of equal vision or equanimity. Through this practice the aspirant is able to develop a balanced state of mind in any condition, and thereby be able to practice continuous reflection on God at all times.

Thus develop the understanding that the day-to-day situations you encounter are in reality challenges which, if met with the proper understanding, will lead you to greater inner and outer fulfillment. Many times that person who spoke to you harshly will be changed when he or she does not receive a negative remark in return. In many ways you will be able to discover that anger and hatred do not promote what you want, but patience, forbearance and good will are sources of spiritual strength which can move worlds.

The Ancient Egyptian Path to Enlightenment
Extended Concentration (Meditation)

What most people call meditation is in reality only the second step in the process of Yoga Meditation. When you are successful in concentrating the mind for a certain period of time you will discover that the concentration becomes easier to hold. When this concentration occurs it is like a magnifying glass which is placed in the sun and used to focus the sun's rays on a piece of paper. When the rays are focused just right the paper begins to burn. This burning process is the goal of Extended Concentration.

The practice of concentration leads to a state of mind wherein one's ego merges with the object being concentrated upon. Since concentration on one object is psychologically equal to having "no thoughts" in the mind, the ego-consciousness is freed from the stimulation of the senses and of thinking of itself as an individual entity. Thus, one may concentrate on any *"one object"* or on *"no object"* and obtain the same results. Through concentration, the act of "focusing the psychic energy of the mind", the ego opens up and experiences expansion. Psychic energy of one's consciousness is therefore focused on the perception of itself instead of dissipating into the various thoughts and objects which attract the senses. In this manner, one's true identity is revealed, uncovered from the veil of the ego-consciousness. The expansion may feel as a loss of body consciousness and identity. One may forget one's existence as an individual and may feel the sensations of floating or falling. Often fear is experienced at this point since one's ego-consciousness may have a strong grip on one's psyche, however, if this state is mastered and explored, one will reach the stage of expansion wherein one will experience *"Enlightenment Experiences"*.

Cosmic Consciousness

Cosmic Consciousness is the stage which is reached when the meditator transcends all thoughts through the process of extended concentration. At this level there is an awareness of expansion beyond time and space. The meditator goes beyond the object of meditation, beyond words of power and beyond consciousness as an individual. There is awareness of vastness, infinity, immortality and universality. This new realm of experience creates new mental impressions which burn away the negative impressions based on ignorance and egoism. They are impressions of communion with the Absolute Self, the Higher Self. This is the goal of the meditative process and it is the potential experience for all human beings. This is the true essence of who you really are. As you gain greater knowledge of this realm you will gradually lose all traces of ignorance and egoism (Meskhenet-Ari) and become one with your essential nature as the transcendental Divine Self.

MEDITATION
Objects of Meditation

"O behold with thine eye God's plans. Devote thyself to adore God's name. It is God who giveth Souls to millions of forms, and God magnifyeth whosoever magnifieth God."

-From The Ancient Egyptian Wisdom Texts

In the practice of meditation it is important to develop mental concentration. One can concentrate on subtle objects such as the breath or thoughts or gross objects such as physical objects. Concentration assists in the program of spiritual evolution by allowing the power of the mind to be focused towards the project of spiritual enlightenment and this allows the aspirant to break the veil of illusion that binds people to mortal and limited existence. The sages have enjoined that one should concentrate on the divine images and on the name of the Divine. These objects will yield the greatest results most efficiently. The names are concentrated upon through Hessi and Shmai (Chant and Divine Singing). The image is concentrated upon through ritual and sustained visualizing of the images (iconographies) of the Divine (pictures, sculptures, etc. depicting the Divine in all its forms – i.e. male and female Divinities as well as abstract forms). The divinities emerged from the one Supreme Being through the act of Creation. By concentrating upon the lesser divinities insight is gained into the nature of the Supreme Divinity. The Creation myths allow the aspirant to understand the nature of the divinities and thereby develop a devotional feeling towards them that develops into esteem and love for the Divine, leading to spiritual enlightenment and ultimate unions with the Divine.

THE CREATION

The process of creation is explained in the form of a cosmological system for better understanding. Cosmology is a branch of philosophy dealing with the origin, processes, and structure of the universe. Cosmogony is the astrophysical study of the creation and evolution of the universe. Both of these disciplines are inherent facets of Egyptian philosophy through the main religious systems or Companies of the Gods and Goddesses. A company of gods and goddesses is a group of deities which symbolize a particular cosmic force or principle which emanates from the all-encompassing Supreme Being, from which they have emerged. The Self or Supreme Being manifests creation through the properties and principles represented by the *Pautti* Company of gods and goddesses-cosmic laws of nature. The system or company of gods and goddesses of Anu is regarded as the oldest, and forms the basis of the Osirian Trinity. It is expressed in the diagram below.

The Ancient Egyptian Path to Enlightenment

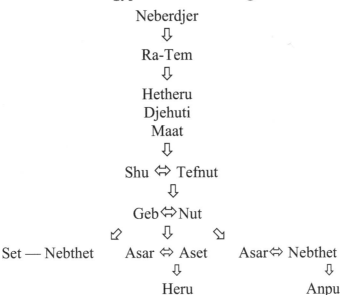

The diagram above shows that *Psedjet* (Ennead), or the creative principles which are embodied in the primordial gods and goddesses of creation, emanated from the Supreme Being. Ra or Ra-Tem arose out of the *"Nu"*, the Primeval waters, the hidden essence, and began sailing the *"Boat of Millions of Years"* which included the company of gods and goddesses. On his boat emerged the "Neters" or cosmic principles of creation. The Neters of the Ennead are Ra-Atum, Shu, Tefnut, Geb, Nut, Asar, Aset, Set, and Nebthet. Hetheru, Djehuti and Maat represent attributes of the Supreme Being as the very *stuff* or *substratum* which makes up creation. Shu, Tefnut, Geb, Nut, Asar, Aset, Set, and Nebthet represent the principles upon which creation manifests. Anpu is not part of the Ennead. He represents the feature of intellectual discrimination in the Osirian myth. "Sailing" signifies the beginning of motion in creation. Motion implies that events occur in the realm of time and space, thus, the phenomenal universe comes into existence as a mass of moving essence we call the elements. Prior to this motion, there was the primeval state of being without any form and without existence in time or space.

MEDITATION

CONCENTRATION EXERCISES

On the following pages and throughout this volume we have provided several images based on the Ancient Egyptian myth presented in this volume. Mythology is a language which is relating you back to your innermost reality, the Higher Self within. In order to draw the greatest benefit from mythology it must be lived and practiced, and not just read about for entertainment purposes. The images may be used for concentration and meditation exercises as follows.

Prior to your practice of formal meditation, sit quietly and stare at a picture or statue of the deity. At regular intervals close your eyes and retain the form in your mind for as long as you can. Open your eyes when your vision fades and repeat the exercise. You may also practice visualizing the image while recalling the attributes as described in the myth. See these attributes as facets of your own life and see how you too are experiencing the trials and tribulations of the characters as well as their triumphs and growth into spiritual awareness.

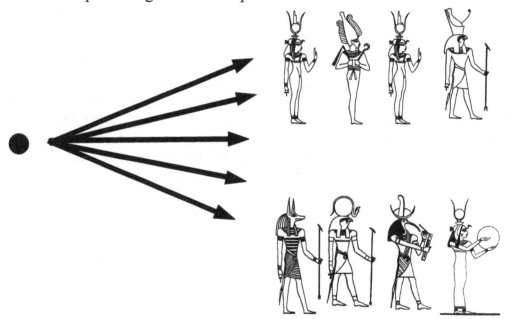

Above: The Supreme Being, Nebertcher, manifests as the various gods and goddesses as well as human beings, nature and the elements. Thus, from The One arise many, however, all objects are in reality a reflection of The one. Since a reflection is not real, only The One is real. Therefore, even though there appears to be multiplicity and duality in creation, these are only illusions based on human ignorance. All is one and the one is God.

The Ancient Egyptian Path to Enlightenment
The Neteru and Their Interrelationships

Diagram : The Primary Kamitan Neteru and their Interrelationships

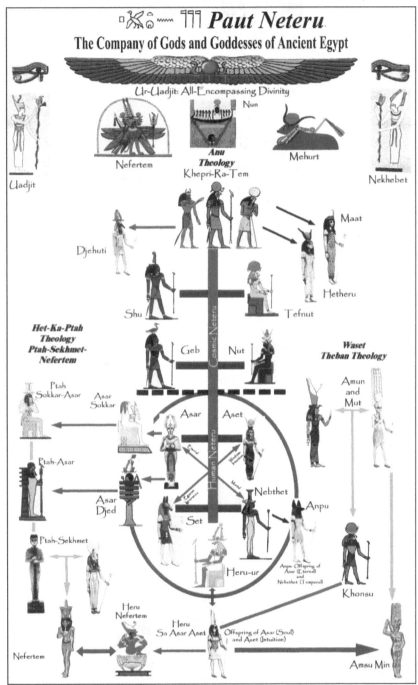

The diagram above provides insight into the divine images and also the relationships between the varied divinities. (for more see the book *The Book of Shetaut Neter* by Muata Ashby)

In the meditation system enjoined in the Ancient Egyptian Story of Hetheru and Djehuti The divine forms of the Goddess Hetheru and the God Djehuti are to be adored.

MEDITATION

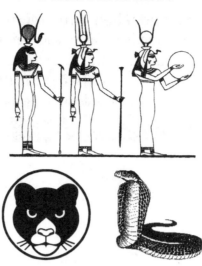

The Forms of Hetheru: The Goddess of passion, love and Life in Ancient Egyptian Mythology

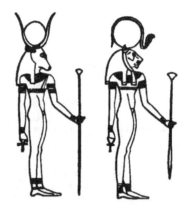

Above left: Hetheru as the Cow-headed goddess of Creation.
At right: The goddess form of Ancient Egypt as the lioness, exemplifying the power of nature.

The Forms of Djehuti

The Ancient Egyptian Path to Enlightenment

The Ancient Egyptian God Djehuti appears in the form of a baboon and in the form of an Ibis bird. He is the transmitter of Divine Wisdom. He is known as the mind of God (Ra).

The Mystical Circle

For thousands of years the symbol of the circle has signified eternity. It is a line which meets itself continuously. The sundisk is the prominent symbol of Ra, because just as the sun emanates rays which engender life in the solar system, the Supreme Self, Ra, emanates rays of consciousness which engender life in every human being and every object in Creation.

The sundisk symbol consists of an outer circle with a dot in the center. The dot represents the Self and the outer circle represents creation which has emanated from the source. In Indian mythology it is called the Bindu. The same Ancient Egyptian symbol may be seen in the Yantras (mystical symbols) of Indian Yoga.

Thus, the Ancient Egyptian Text (*Destruction of Humankind*) is instructing the practitioner of meditation to sit within this circle, i.e. to be established in the Eternal Self.

Abstract Meditation

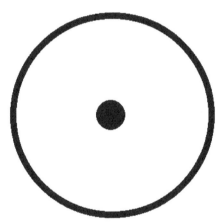

The circle may also be used as an abstract meditation on the Self, which is beyond name and form. As you concentrate on the circle, focus on its all-encompassing eternal nature, instead of associating it with a deity form. This is abstract meditation.

MEDITATION

Meditation In Life: How to Develop a Meditative Lifestyle

Meditation is not just an exercise that is to be practiced only at a certain time or at a certain place. In order for your meditative efforts to be successful, the philosophy of meditation must become an integral part of your life. This means that the meditative way of life, the yoga lifestyle, must become the focus of your life no matter what else is going on in your life. Most people who do not practice yoga cannot control the clamoring thoughts of the mind and because of this, do not experience inner peace or clarity of purpose in life. Others, beset by intensely negative thoughts, succumb to these and commit acts against their conscience and suffer the consequences of a self-defeating way of life wherein painful situations and disappointments in life are increased while happiness and contentment are decreased. The mind is weakened due to the mental energy being wasted in useless endeavors which only serve to further entangle one in complex relationships and commitments. Another source of weakening one's will to act correctly to promote situations of advancement and happiness is caused by the susceptibility to negative emotions. Negative emotions such as anger, hatred, greed, gloom, sorrow, and depression as well as excessive positive emotions such as elation serve to create mental agitation and desire which in turn cloud the intellectual capacity to make correct decisions in life.

When life seems unbearable due to the intensification of negative emotions and the obscuring of one's intellectual capacity, some people commit suicide in an attempt to escape or end the painful onslaught of uncontrollable thoughts. Still others prefer to ignore the messages from the deeper Self which are beckoning them to move toward introspection. Situations of stress in life are motivators whose purpose is to turn you away from the outer world because you have lost your balance. There is a place for material wealth and sensual experience (outer experiences of the senses), however, when the inner reality is ignored or when inner needs and inner development is impaired due to excess concentration on worldly goals and desires, then experiences of frustration and disappointment occur. If these situations are understood as messages from nature to pull back and find the inner balance, then personality integration and harmony can be discovered. However, if these times are faced with lack of inner strength, then they lead to suffering. Sometimes there are moments of clarity wherein the Higher Self is perceived in an intuitive flash, but people usually tend to discount the occurrence as a coincidence or other curious event while others in bewilderment believe they are going mad. Others prefer to ignore the issue of spirituality altogether and simply shun any thoughts about death or the afterlife. This is a reverse-yogic movement that stunts spiritual evolution. Its root-cause is fear, fear of the unknown and fear of letting go. The practice of yogic meditation techniques can serve to counteract any and all negative developments in the mind if the correct techniques are used and the correct understanding is adopted.

There are four main components of meditation. These are: *posture, breath-life force control, sound and visualization.* In the beginning stages of practice, these components may be somewhat difficult to perform with consistency and coordination, but with continued effort they become a pleasurable experience which will bring you closer to your awareness of your Self. It is difficult to control the mind in the beginning. Many aspirants loose heart because they have not obtained the results they had anticipated. They either quit prematurely or jump to different techniques without giving sufficient time for the exercises to work. They do not understand that although on occasion, profound changes will occur in a short time, for the most part it's a gradual process.

A meditative lifestyle should be developed along with one's formal meditation practices. This means acting in such a way that there is greater and greater detachment from objects and situations and greater independence and peace within. This can only occur when there is a keen understanding of one's deeper Self and the nature of the world of human experience, along with formal meditation practices and other activities which promote physical health (diet and exercise). Ordinarily, people "do" things in order to gain some objective or to derive some pleasure or reward. From a yogic or Buddhist perspective they are "doers of action". They act out of the unconscious and subconscious desires arising in the mind at any given time, and are thus beset with a perpetual state of unrest and agitation. The meditative way of life means that your actions are always affirmations of your higher knowledge and awareness and not based on the unconscious desires and emotions of the mind. The perfection in this discipline only comes with practice. When this art is perfected the practitioner is referred to as a "non-doer". This is because even though they may be doing many things in their life, in reality they have discovered that the true rewards of life do not depend on the outcome of an activity, its fruit or reward.

The main difference between a doer and a non-doer is that the doer is driven by desires while the non-doer is indifferent to the desires of the mind and the fruits of the action they are performing. The non-doer acts out of wakefulness while the doer acts out of a desire filled mind. Thus, the non-doer can never be disappointed or made unhappy because of a situation in life while the doer is always engaged in a roller coaster ride of elation or depression, happiness or sorrow, pain or pleasure, etc., never finding an abiding peace The non-doer acts out of necessity and is primarily concerned with experiencing the moment fully while carrying out the present task to perfection, not worrying about the rewards for the task. Thus, it may be said that for the non-doer there is an immediate reward of peace and joy whereas the doer is always looking to the future or the past. Their (non-doers) peace and happiness do not come from expectations of the future nor do they experience sorrow due to some negative situation which occurred in the past. They have discovered a deep experience in the present which transcends both past and future. Thus, they experience a unique form of peace and happiness in an eternal present which is not affected by the various ups and downs of life. Adversity and prosperity are an integral part of human existence. The belief that life can or should only be composed of happy or positive situations is a factor of philosophical ignorance and a lack of reflection on history. A wise person

MEDITATION

realizes that life is full of adverse as well as prosperous situation. While trying to promote the prosperous situations there must be expectation of adversity as well. This wisdom leads to the understanding that the world and worldly situations cannot be relied upon as a source of happiness. There will always arise some situation which will bring any form of worldly prosperity to an end. Therefore, a wise person does not become attached to worldly objects, people or situations, even while being involved with them during the normal course of a lifetime.

General society believes that actions are to be performed for the goal of attaining some objective which will yield a reward. The socialization process teaches the individual to seek to perform actions because this is the way to attain something which will cause happiness. This is the predicament of the masses of people who have not studied Yoga or Mystical Philosophies such as Buddhism, Shetaut Neter or Vedanta. The following line from the Declaration of Independence illustrates this point succinctly.

> We hold these truths to be self-evident, that all men are created equal, that they are endowed by their Creator with certain unalienable Rights, that among these are Life, Liberty and the **pursuit of Happiness**.

Yoga philosophy is not against the pursuit of happiness in the world of time and space, however, it does teach that the pursuit of happiness with a sense of attachment and dependence on objects and situations in the world of human experience will not fulfill the deeper need of the Soul. If at all, they should be pursued with an attitude of detachment and dispassion. In reality, happiness does not and cannot come from objects that can be acquired or from activities that are performed. It can only come from within. Even actions that seem to be pleasurable in life cannot be considered as sources of happiness from a philosophical point of view because all activities are relative. This means that while one activity is pleasurable for one person, it is painful for another. This leads to the realization that it is not the activity itself that holds the happiness, but the individual doer who is performing the action and assigning a value to it which she or he has learned from society to assign. Therefore, if it was learned that going out to a party is supposed to be fun, then that activity will be pursued as a source of happiness. Here action is performed in pursuit of the fruit of the action in the form happiness; a result is desired from the action. However, there are several negative psychological factors which arise that will not allow true happiness to manifest. The first is that the relentless pursuit of the action renders the mind restless and agitated. The second is that if the activity is not possible there will be depression in the mind. If the activity is thwarted by some outside force, meaning that something or someone prevented you from achieving the object or activity you saw as the "source of happiness," you develop anger towards it or them. If by chance you succeed in achieving the object or activity you become elated, and this will cause greed in the mind. You will want more and more of it. When you are not able to get more at any particular time you will become depressed and disappointed. Under these conditions a constant dependence on outside activities and worldly objects develops in the mind which will not allow for peace and contentment. Even though it is illogical to pursue activities which cause pain in life, people are constantly acting against their own interests as they engage in actions in an effort to gain happiness while in reality they are enhancing the probability of encountering pain later on. People often act and shortly regret what they have done. Sometimes people know even at the time of their actions that they are wrong, yet they are unable to stop themselves. This is because when the mind is controlled by desires and expectations the intellect, the light of reason, is *clouded* and *dull*. However, when the mind is controlled by the intellect, then it is not possible to be led astray due to the *fantasies* and *illusions* of the mind. When the individual is guided by their intellect, then only right actions can be performed, no matter what negative ideas arise in the mind. Such a person cannot be deluded into negative actions and when negative actions (actions which lead to future pain and disappointments) are not performed, then unhappiness cannot exist. Thus, a person who lives according to the teachings of non-doership (without desire or expectations for the future results of their actions) lives a life of perpetual peace and happiness in the present.

Thus, true peace and inner fulfillment will never come through the pursuit of actions when there is an expectation or desire for the fruits of those actions. The belief in objects or worldly activities as sources of happiness is therefore seen as a state known as *ignorance,* wherein the individual is caught up in the *illusions, fantasies* and *fanciful notions* of the mind. However, happiness and peace can arise spontaneously when there is an attitude of detachment and dispassion towards objects and situations in life. If actions are performed with the idea of discovering peace within, based on the understanding of the philosophy outlined above, and for the sake of the betterment of society, then these actions will have the effect of purifying the heart of the individual. The desires and expectations will dwindle while the inner fulfillment and awareness of the present moment will increase. There will be greater and greater discovery of peace within, a discovery of what is truly stable and changeless within as opposed to the mind and outer world which are constantly changing and unpredictable. Along with this there is greater effectiveness and perfection in one's actions.

Actions of any type will always lead to some result. However, this result is not as predictable as people have come to believe. In reality, the only thing a human being can control is the action itself and not the fruits of the action. If there is concentration on the action without desire or expectation of the fruits of the action, then there can be peace and contentment even while the action is being performed. This is the way of the non-doer. Actions performed with expectations and desire are the way of the doer. The non-doer is free from the fruits because he/she is free from desires and expectations while the doer is dependent on the actions and is bound to the results be they positive or negative. When desires and expectation in the mind are resolved, the mind becomes calm and peaceful. Under these conditions the non-doer is free from elation or depression because his/her pleasure is coming from the present action in the present moment and is not based on memories of the past of pleasurable situations which are impelling a movement to repeat those activities or on expectations for the future activities which will somehow bring happiness. The non-doer, not being bound to the memories or to the expectations, is not bound by either the past nor the future, and thereby discovers an eternal present. The doer is always caught up in the past or the future and thereby loses the opportunity to discover peace and true happiness. This is the condition of most people in the world. Before they realize it their entire life has gone by without their being aware of the passage of time. The art of true spiritual life leads one to detach from the world even while continuing to live in it, and thereby to discover the hidden inner spiritual dimensions of the unconscious mind and what lies beyond. The doer is always bound to a form of experience which is determined by and linked to the world of time and space, because only in time and space can there manifest the memories of the past and the expectations for the future. The non-doer eventually discovers a transcendental experience of expanding consciousness in the present moment.

MEDITATION

The philosophy of meditation may seem foreign to you at first but if you reflect upon it you will discover that it holds great truth as well as a great potential to assist you in discovering abiding peace and harmony in your life. When you begin to practice and discover how wonderful it is to be in control of your mind instead of being prey to the positive or negative emotions and desires, you will discover an incomparable feeling which goes beyond the ordinary concept of happiness. As with other human endeavors, in order to gain success you need to study the philosophy intensively with great concentration and then practice it in your day-to-day life. Treat it as an experiment. The world and your life will not go away. Just ask yourself: What would happen if I were to become less attached and more in control of my mind? Follow the teachings and discover the inner resources you have to experience true happiness and to overcome the obstacles of life.

The practice of meditation requires regular and sustained effort. Failure is assured if there is no effort. Likewise, success is assured if there is sustained, regular effort. Further, you cannot expect to succeed in meditation if you do not work towards controlling your thoughts, emotions and actions in the normal course of life. Your actions, thoughts and speech are closely related to your unconscious mind. It is like a register which records all as karmic impressions. Any unresolved desires or feelings become lodged there and later cause agitation and restlessness. Therefore, you must keep a close watch on your mind, speech and deeds. Take care to act righteously, speak the truth and think positive thoughts. The Ancient Egyptian Texts state that one cannot expect to obtain results unless one is:

"mentally pure and physically pure."

These are the keys to accomplishing any goal in life and, enlightenment is a goal like any other, albeit the highest goal. With respect to attaining the goal of enlightenment, all other goals are like dust blowing in the wind. The following instruction will serve as guidelines for meditation and is not intended to be a substitute for a competent instructor. There are many techniques of meditation. Here we will focus on basic techniques of "moving" meditations for initially calming the mind of the beginning practitioner.

Another important factor of meditation is that health of the body must be maintained through proper diet and proper exercise. This means that the diet should be composed of fresh whole foods and it should be exclusively vegetarian. You cannot expect to have success in meditation if you have a weak constitution or if your are constantly craving foods which heighten the body consciousness and negative emotions (meats) or those which have drug-like effects on the body (sugars). The mind is affected by these in the same manner that it is affected by other mind altering drugs. Therefore, a spiritual aspirant must cleanse the mind and body in order to climb the ladder of spiritual evolution. (see *Initiation Into Egyptian Yoga: The Secrets of Sheti* by Muata Ashby)

The Ancient Egyptian Path to Enlightenment
The Diet

"Strive to prevent fatness so as that the weight on thy body will not
weigh down thy Soul"

Ancient Egyptian Proverb
from the Temple of Aset (Aset)

Many people do not realize that what they consume has a strong effect on their psyche. This implies not only foods but all manner of consumption. Just as there are three major states of relative consciousness, there are three basic kinds of foods. The first group is composed of those foods which engender restlessness and distraction.

Ex. sugars, salty foods, dry foods, hot spices, coffee, fish, poultry, eggs, etc.

These foods promote passion, stimulate the emotions and excite the body. Also eating in a hurry promotes restlessness and distraction. The second group is composed of foods which promote dullness. This group includes:

meats, tobacco, alcohol, fermented foods, processed foods, stale or overripe foods.

These foods promote dullness of intellect, anger, hatred, greed, volatility, negative thoughts, disease and clouded reasoning ability. These foods are filled with negativity due to the way in which they are handled in the food processing system. The addition of unnatural chemicals to food in and of itself is reason enough to classify them as tainted with poison. The killing of animals effectively poisons the food with negative hormones as well as fear vibrations from the animals. Also the human digestive tract is not designed to handle meat so the food rots as it passes through the intestinal system, causing diseases such as cancer. Is there any wonder why medical doctors admonish those who contract cancer or experience heart trouble to stop eating meat and to stop smoking? Shouldn't they begin promoting a meat free diet for everyone (including themselves) at an early age? If smoking is known to produce cancer shouldn't it be outlawed as are other addictive drugs? Poisons are sold out of greed and ignorance. Also, such poisons are consumed due to ignorance and addictive desire.

Dull foods are not good for the body or for the mind, but much like the stimulating foods, they create an addictive form of dependency wherein even when the person has a full understanding of the deleterious effects of the foods, he or she continues to consume them anyway using the excuse "well I want to enjoy my life even if I shorten it". The weakened will disables a person's reasoning capacity as well as their willpower to resist the urge for the foods.

Lucid foods are those which promote harmony, inner mental peace, bright intellect, willpower, etc. They foster purity of the mind as well as the body. They are nutritious and enhance the body's ability to fight off disease. Lucid foods include:

whole foods, cereals, fresh vegetables and fruits, legumes, seeds, nuts, sprouted seeds,
herb teas, honey.

MEDITATION

A serious spiritual aspirant must learn about the nature of food as he or she climbs the ladder of mystical spirituality. In so doing, a healthy constitution can be created which will allow for a positive and fruitful spiritual movement towards self-discovery. Since every human being is not exactly the same as another, the exact diet which is optimal for each individual will be slightly different. Therefore each individual should experiment with their diet within the broad guidelines given above in order to discover the right combination within the Lucid Diet category which is best suited for him or her.

Tips for Formal Meditation Practice

Begin by meditating for 5 minutes each day, gradually building up the time. The key is consistency in time and place. Nature inspires us to establish a set routine to perform our activities; the sun rises in the east and sets in the west every day; the moon's cycle is every 28 days and the seasons change approximately at the same times of the year, every year. It is better to practice for 5 minutes each day than 20 minutes one day and 0 minutes the next. Do a formal sit down meditation whenever the feeling comes to you but try to do it at least once a day, preferably between 4-6 am or 6-8 pm. Do not eat for at least 2 hours before meditation. It is even more preferable to not eat 12 hours before. For example: eat nothing (except only water or tea) after 6 p.m. until after meditation at 6 a.m. the following morning. Do not meditate within 24 hours of having sexual intercourse. Meditate alone in a quiet area, in a dimly lit room (candle light is adequate). Do light exercise (example: Chi Kung or Hatha Yoga) before meditating, then say Hekau (affirmations, prayers, mantras, etc.) for a few minutes to set up positive vibrations in the mind. Burning your favorite incense is a good way to set the mood. Keep a ritualistic procedure about the meditation time. Do things in a slow, deliberate manner, concentrating on every motion and every thought you perform.

When ready, try to focus the mind on one object, symbol or idea such as the heart or Hetep (Supreme Peace). If the mind strays, bring it back gently. Patience, self-love and self-forgiveness are the keys here. Gradually, the mind will not drift towards thoughts or objects of the world. It will move towards subtler levels of consciousness until it reaches the source of the thoughts and there commune with that source, The Self. This is the desired positive movement of the practice of meditation because it is from The Self that all inspiration, creativity and altruistic feelings of love come. The Self is the source of peace and love and is who you really are.

Rituals Associated With Meditation Practice

In the beginning the mind may be difficult to control. What is needed here is perseverance and the application of the techniques described here. Another important aid to meditation is ritualism. You should observe a set of rituals whenever you intend to practice meditation. These will gradually help to settle the mind even before you actually sit to practice the meditation. They are especially useful if you are a busy person or if you have many thoughts or worries on the mind. First take a bath. Water is the greatest cleanser of impurities. In ancient times the practitioners of yoga would bathe before entering the temples and engaging in the mystery rituals. This practice has been kept alive in the Christian practice of baptism and the prayers using the Holy Water.

The Ancient Egyptian Path to Enlightenment

Once you have bathed, put on clothing which you have specifically reserved for the practice of meditation. This will have a strong effect on your mind and will bring meditative vibrations to you because the clothing will retain some of the subtle essence of the meditation experience each time you use them. The clothing should be loose and comfortable. It is recommend that you wear 100% Cotton or Silk because these are natural materials which will allow the skin to breath and feel comfortable. Keep the clothing clean and use the same style of clothing for your meditation practice.

When you are ready, go to your special room or corner which you have set aside for meditation. Take the phone off the hook or turn off the ringer and close the door behind you, leaving instructions not to be disturbed for the period of time you have chosen. When you sit for meditation, light a candle and some incense of your choice and then choose a comfortable position maintaining the back straight either sitting on the floor in the cross-legged posture (Lotus), or sitting in a chair with feet on the floor or lying on your back on the floor in the corpse-mummy pose (without falling asleep). First, locate an area of your home where you can perform spiritual practices such as yoga exercises, prayers and meditations and not be disturbed. This area will be used only for yoga practice.

Now gather the basic materials needed to create your own meditation area. An altar is a place of worship which contains certain artifacts which hold specific spiritual symbolism that lead to spiritual awareness. They do not need to have a specific religious affiliation. However, they should have spiritual significance. This will help to draw the mind away from worldly thoughts and lead it toward concentration on higher (spiritual) thoughts. The following items are to be considered as a basic listing of items. You are free to choose other items which resonate with your spiritual consciousness.

1- Small **table**

2- **Candle** - The candle holds deep mystical symbolism. It contains within itself all of the four elements of creation: fire, earth (wax in solid form), water (wax in liquefied form), and air. All are consumed in the burning process and all of them come together to produce light. This singular light represents the singular consciousness which shines throughout the entire universe. This light is the illumination which causes life to exist and it is the reason and source of the human mind. This light is life itself and life is God. Therefore, God is ever-present in the candle, in the universe (nature) and in your heart and mind.

3- **Incense** - Incense invokes divine awareness through the sense of smell. When you perform spiritual practices and use a special incense consistently, every time that you smell the incense you will have divine thoughts and feelings even if you are not in the regular area of meditation. Therefore, select a fragrance which appeals to you and reflect within yourself that this is the fragrance of God in the same way as a flower emanates fragrance. Visualize that you are

MEDITATION

smelling divinity itself.

4- **Ankh** - The Ankh is one of the most universal symbols expressing eternal life, the union of opposites and it was, and is used by the world religious traditions (Ancient Egyptian religion, early Christianity, Indian religion and others.

5- **Icon-** picture, sculpture or other symbol of a Deity (as a symbol of the Supreme Being). This may be an Ancient Egyptian Deity such as Heru, Aset, etc., or a Christian Icon such as Jesus or Mary, an Eastern icon such as Buddha (Buddhist), or Krishna, Rama or Saraswati of the Vedantic-Hindu tradition, etc. Choose an icon according to your spiritual inclination. This will help you to develop devotion toward the Divine and will hasten your progress in yoga. This is called worship of God with name and form. As you progress you will be instructed on how to worship the Divine in an abstract way without using any names or forms.

The Development of Devotional Feeling

Many people have been soured on the idea of a "Supreme Being" or a "God" due to their experiences with religion and their experiences with the world. Some people even believe that talks of religion and God are the basis for the maladies of the world and the fanatical violence which humanity has seen throughout history. They feel "If there was a God or Supreme Being why would he allow the world to go on as it does with all the violence and negativity?" This statement is backed up by ignorance because while this world is supported by Divine Will, the events which occur are inspired by human greed and desire. Therefore, God cannot be blamed for the negativity of the world. Rather it is human ignorance and egoism which are to blame. When a human being is able to rise above the pettiness and sentimentality of egoistic human thinking, the higher divine vision emerges in the mind. This is the central goal of spiritual practice, and of meditation in particular. When you become reconciled to the understanding that you are the one who has caused any pain and sorrow in your life and that you have the means to rise above all obstacles, you can begin to see that God or the ultimate reality, which is the innermost Self within you, has been waiting all the time with open arms to receive your love and to give it in return, one thousand fold. Therefore, you should allow your mind to flow towards the Divine. Devotional feeling enhances all spiritual practices and hastens the dissolution of egoism, which is the primary obstacle to spiritual realization. Thus meditation is supported by wisdom and devotion.

"Seekest thou God, thou seekest for the Beautiful. One is the Path that leadeth unto It: Devotion joined with Wisdom."

-Ancient Egyptian Proverb

Many people shy away from sentimentality saying I am not emotional or sentimental. Yet even intellectuals are sentimental about their particular form of philosophy. So every one is sentimental in one way or another. Furthermore, deep within the heart of every human being there lies an innate desire to love. This desire is often expressed in limited ways, loving individuals, objects, jobs, etc. What is really desired by the soul is to express unlimited love. Therefore, any limitation of love constitutes a falling short of the possibility to achieve emotional fulfillment. Therefore, one should understand that if the emotional aspect of oneself is harnessed and channeled, it can be a formidable force toward self-discovery. The Self is the true objective of all love. When you love a person you are really loving the Soul (God) which is the sustaining reality of that person. When you love an object you are really loving the Soul which is the sustaining reality of that object. This is the basis of the discipline known as Devotional Yoga. It involves developing greater and greater attachment to God first by learning about God through the spiritual scriptures (wisdom teachings) and from here developing faith that there truly is an entity which transcends all. Ordinary love for objects is limited. If you love a car or a house it cannot reciprocate and you could even lose it. Similarly if you love a human being sometimes they cannot reciprocate either due to their own egoism or impairment or death. They may someday even hate you. When you discover love for God who is within you there can be no separation and no reduction in the feeling; it goes on increasing and expanding. This is the glory of true Devotion to God. It is like a perpetual feeling of joy and bliss not unlike the feeling of young lovers or a mother for her child. In both of these cases there is a constant awareness of the loved one no matter what activity one may be engaged in. Love for God is more exalted and more magnanimous because it is infinite and eternal.

Choosing a Word(s) of Power

After reading this manual completely, select a **Hekau** - Mantra (words of power) which resonates with you. If you do not feel a special connection to a particular hekau or if you would prefer to wait for a period of time to allow yourself to become acquainted with the philosophy and the presiding deities of the hekau, simply use "Om" for now. Om is a universal word of power which was used in Ancient Egypt and is used extensively in India by yogis. Om or AUM is related to the word Amun from Ancient Egypt and Amun is related to the Amen of Christianity. Therefore, Om is generally useful for spiritual practice. Om is also not related to a particular deity but is common to all and is seen as a name of the Divine Self. It is also the hekau-mantra of the 6th energy center at the point between the eyebrows known as the Ancient Egyptian Udjat or Eye of Heru, *Arat* or Uraeus serpent and the *Third eye of Shiva* in India. You will use hekau for chanting during your worship periods, and at idle times during the day. You will use it from now on to dig deeply into the unconscious regions of your mind as a miner uses a pick to cut into a mountain in search of gold.

Sometimes the meditative mood is promoted by listening to music, sounds of nature, etc. You may use these but you should keep in mind that your objective is to reach a state of mind which does not depend upon externalities. Many times the mind with its endless desires will become fickle about the type of music or the type of incense or the type of position, etc. These are all distractions which can become excuses for failure. You must keep in view that you are working with your mind by trying to facilitate the beginning stages of meditation practice. However, if suddenly you cannot turn on the music because the power went off what will you do? If you ran out of incense and forgot to get some on the way home what will you do? You must gradually learn to withdraw from all externalities by training the mind to be one pointed towards your object of meditation.

A Yogi (one who practices Yoga) should abide in solitude...

Gita: Chapter 6
Adhyadma Yogah--The Yoga of Meditation

Another factor which is important to promoting an atmosphere which is conducive for meditation is to be alone. Many people think of meditation as a practice which is performed by hermits or people who live a solitary life up on a mountain and so on. This form of lifestyle can be conducive for spiritual life but only if you are truly prepared to live in this manner. Many

MEDITATION

people dream about how it would be so wonderful to get away from it all. When they finally take a vacation or move to some other place where they thought they would be more at peace, they find that they are plagued by the same worries and anxieties. If you reflect upon this honestly you will understand that there is no escaping the world. This is because the world is within you or rather you are creating your vision of the world with your thoughts, desires, worries and cares. Therefore, you carry the world around with you wherever you go. So running away will not work. This is why the authentic mystical philosophers from ancient times have taught that a spiritual aspirant must not run away from the adversities of life, but must learn to understand them while at the same time developing spiritual wisdom and strength in order to overcome them. This is the only way to truly succeed in life. Overcoming them implies gaining the ability to remain at peace and abiding in the awareness of Divine communion at all times, even under the most adverse conditions. This ability is more important and more valuable that all the riches in the world. Thus, a geographical location does not insure peace and tranquillity.

So what is the best way to be alone even when living in the middle of a bustling city? If you plan your day properly you can create silence and time alone. In the morning hours no one is around and there is silence, therefore you are essentially alone. During your work you can take breaks and you may even be able to come home so as to practice silence time and meditation.

Prior to beginning your meditation practice you can practice yoga exercises but if you are pressed for time you can practice breathing and relaxation exercises. These will be useful especially if you have just come from a dynamic activity and the entire process should take no more than five minutes. Simply sit or lay quietly and focus attention on one part of your body after another. Begin tensing the muscles in that particular area and then release them. Feel the tension and stress leaving the body.

The Daily Schedule for Yoga Practice

A practitioner of Yoga must be able to integrate the main practices of yoga into daily life. This means that you need to begin adding small amounts of time for Prayer, Repetition of the Divine Name (Hekau), Exercise (includes proper breathing exercise), Study of the Teachings, Silence, Selfless Service, Meditation, and Daily Reflection. This also means that you will gradually reduce the practices which go against yogic movement as you gain more time for Sheti.

Below you will find an outline of a schedule for the beginning practice of Yoga. The times given here are a suggested minimum time for beginners. You may spend more time according to your capacity and personal situation, however, try to be consistent in the amount of time and location you choose to practice your discipline as well as in the time of day you choose to perform each of the different practices. This will enable your body and mind to develop a rhythm which will develop into the driving force of your day. When this occurs you will develop stamina and fortitude when dealing with any situation of life. You will have a stable center which will anchor you to a higher purpose in life whether you are experiencing prosperous times or adverse times. In the advanced stages, spiritual practice will become continuous. Try to do the best you can according to your capacity, meaning your circumstances. If your family members are not interested or do not understand what you are trying to do simply maintain your practices privately and try to keep the interruptions to a minimum. As you develop, you may feel drawn toward some forms of practice over others. The important thing to remember is to practice them all in an integrated fashion. Do not neglect any of the practices even though you may spend additional time on some versus others.

Practicing spirituality only during times of adversity is the mistake of those who are spiritually immature. Any form of spiritual practice, ritualistic or otherwise is a positive development, however, you will not derive the optimal spiritual benefits by simply becoming religious when you are in trouble. The masses of people only pray when they are in trouble...then they ask for assistance to get out of trouble. What they do not realize is that if they were to turn their minds to God at all times, not just in times of misfortune, adversity would not befall them. As you progress through your studies you will learn that adversities in life are meant to turn you toward the Divine. In this sense they are messages from the Divine to awaken spiritual aspiration. However, if you do not listen to the message and hearken to the Divine intent behind it, you will be in a position to experience more miseries of life and miseries of a more intense nature.

Basic Schedule of Spiritual Practice

1a-Deep breathing, using the *proper breathing technique.*
1b-Alternate Breathing exercise (10 minutes in am and in pm),
2-Prayer (10-30 minutes in am* and in pm),
3-Exercise (10 minutes in am and before study time),
4-Repetition of the Divine Name in the form of your chosen hekau-mantra (10 minutes in am and in pm),
5-Meditation practice (10 minutes in am, should be practiced after exercise, prayer and repetition of the Divine Name),
6-Study of the teachings (reading 30 minutes per day),
7-Silence time (30 minutes per day),
8-Listening to the teachings: Choose an audio recording of a yogic spiritual preceptor and listen for a minimum of 30 minutes per day without any distractions if possible. If possible, go to a yogic spiritual center (Ashram, Wat, Temple) where teachings are presented by a qualified teacher of yoga wisdom. If this is not possible, form a study group wherein the teachings may be discussed and explored.
9-Selfless service (as required whenever the opportunity presents itself),
10-Daily reflection: Remembering the teachings during the ordinary course of the day and applying them in daily living situations- to be practiced as much as possible.

The suggested times given above are the minimum amount you should spend on daily spiritual practices each day. Whenever possible you should increase the times according to your capacity and ability. You should train your mind so that it rejoices in hearing about and practicing the teachings of yoga instead of the useless worldly activities. Follow this path gradually but steadily.

Once you have established a schedule of minimal time to devote to practices, even if you do 5-10 minutes of meditation time per day and nothing else, keep your schedule if at all possible. Many people feel that they do not have the time to incorporate even ordinary activities into their lives. They feel overwhelmed with life and feel they have no control. If there is no control it is because there is no discipline. If you make a schedule for all of your activities (spiritual and non-spiritual) and keep to it tenaciously, you will discover that you can control your time and your life. As you discover the glory of spiritual practice, you will find even more time to expand your spiritual program. Ultimately, you will create a lifestyle which is entirely spiritualized. This

MEDITATION

means that every act in your life will be based on the wisdom teachings (MAAT) and therefore you will not only spend a particular time of day devoted to spiritual practices, but every facet of your life will become a spontaneous worship of the divine.

Proper Breathing

Most people in the modern world do not know how to breathe properly. Most people (especially males) have learned to breathe by pushing out the chest in a "manly" or "macho" fashion. This mode of breathing is harmful for many reasons. The amount of air taken in is less and vital cosmic energy is reduced and becomes stagnant in the subtle vital energy channels, resulting in physical and mental diseases. The stagnation of the flow of energy through the body has the effect of grounding one's consciousness to the physical realities rather than allowing the mind and body to operate with lightness and subtlety.

"Belly breathing" or abdominal breathing massages the internal organs and develops Life Force energy (Ra, Chi or Kundalini). It will be noticed that it is our natural breathing pattern when we lie down on our back. Instruction is as follows:
A- Breathe in and push the stomach out. B- Breathe out and pull the stomach in. This form of breathing is to be practiced at all times, not just during meditation. It allows the natural Life Force in the air to be rhythmically supplied to the body and nervous system. This process is indispensable in the achievement of physical health and mental-spiritual power to control the mind (meditation).

The Ancient Egyptian Path to Enlightenment

Proper Breathing Diagram

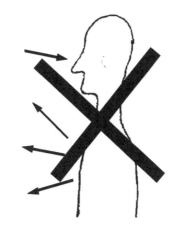

Above: Chest breathing.
Below: Abdominal breathing.

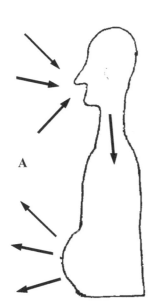

A

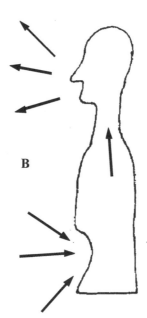

B

MEDITATION
Meditation Postures

The following postures are used for the practice of meditation.

At left: The Lotus posture

At left: The seated position with arms resting on the thighs.

Below: the Corpse pose.

Above left- Amunhotep, son of Hapu, Ancient Egyptian philosopher, priest and Sage at 80 years old in a meditative posture.

The Ancient Egyptian Path to Enlightenment
WORDS OF POWER IN MEDITATION:

"Devote yourself to adore God's name."

Ancient Egyptian Proverb

Chanting the Divine Name:

The word *"mantra"* in Indian Yoga signifies any sound which steadies the mind. Its roots are: "man" which means "mind" and "tra" which means "steady". In Ancient Egyptian terminology, "hekau" or word formulas are recited with meaning and feeling to achieve the desired end.

Hekau-mantra recitation, (called *Japa* in India), is especially useful in changing the mental state. The sounds coupled with ideas or meditations can have the effect of calming the mind by directing its energy toward sublime thoughts rather than toward degrading, pain filled ones. This allows the vibrations of the mind to be changed. There are three types of recitations that can be used with the words of power: 1- Mental, 2- Recitation employing a soft humming sound and 3- loud or audible reciting. The main purpose of reciting the words of power is somewhat different than prayer. Prayer involves you as a subject, "talking" to God, while words of power - hekau - mantras, are used to carry your consciousness to divine levels by changing the vibrations in your mind and allowing it to transcend the awareness of the senses, body and ordinary thought processes.

The recitation of words of power has been explored to such a degree that it constitutes an important form of yoga practice. Two of the most comprehensive books written on this subject by Sri Swami Sivananda were *Japa Yoga* and *Sadhana*. Swami Sivananda told his pupils to repeat their mantras as many as 50,000 per day. If this level of practice is maintained, it is possible to achieve specific changes in a short time. Otherwise, changes in your level of mental awareness, self-control, mental peace and spiritual realization occur according to your level of practice. You should not rush nor suppress your spiritual development, rather allow it to gradually grow into a fire which engulfs the mind as your spiritual aspiration grows in a natural way.

Hekau-mantras can be directed toward worldly attainments or toward spiritual attainment in the form of enlightenment. There are words of power for gaining wealth or control over others. We will present Egyptian, Indian and Christian words of power which are directed to self-control and mental peace leading to spiritual realization of the Higher Self. You may choose from the list according to your level of understanding and practice. If you were initiated into a particular hekau or mantra by an authentic spiritual preceptor, we recommend that you use that one as your main meditative sound formula. You may use others for singing according to your inclination in your leisure or idle time. Also you may use shortened versions for chanting or singing when not engaged in formal practice. For example, if you choose "Om Amun Ra Ptah", you may also use "Om Amun".

Reciting words of power is like making a well. If a well is made deep enough, it yields water. If the words of power are used long enough and with consistency, they yield spiritual vibrations which reach deep into the unconscious mind to cut through the distracting thoughts and then reveal the deeper you. If they are not used with consistency, they are like shallow puddles which get filled easily by rain, not having had a chance to go deeply enough to reveal what lies within.

MEDITATION

Don't forget that your movement in yoga should be balanced and integrated. Therefore, continue your practice of the other major disciplines we have described along with your practice of reciting the hekau-mantras. Mental recitation is considered to be the most powerful. However, in the beginning you may need to start with recitation aloud until you are able to control the mind's wandering. If it wanders, simply return to the words of power (hekau-mantras). Eventually the words of power will develop their own staying power. You will even hear them when you are not consciously reciting. They will begin to replace the negative thought patterns of the mind and lead the mind toward serenity and from here to spiritual realization. When this occurs you should allow yourself to feel the sweetness of reciting the divine names.

As discussed earlier, HEKAU may be used to achieve control over the mind and to develop the latent forces that are within you. Hekau or mantras are mystic formulas which an aspirant uses in a process of self-alchemy. The chosen words of power may be in the form of a letter, word or a combination of words which hold a specific mystical meaning to lead the mind to deeper levels of concentration and to deeper levels of understanding of the teaching behind the words. You may choose one for yourself or you my use one that you were initiated into by a spiritual preceptor. Also, you may have a special hekau for meditation and you may still use other hekau, prayers, hymns or songs of praise according to your devotional feeling. Once you choose a hekau, the practice involves its repetition with meaning and feeling to the point of becoming one with it. You will experience that the words of power drop from your mind and there are no thoughts but just awareness. This is the soul level where you begin to transcend thoughts and body identification. You may begin practicing it out loud (verbally) and later practice in silence (mentally). At some point your level of concentration will deepen. You may use a rosary or "mala" (beads on a string) to keep track of your recitation. At that point your mind will disengage from all external exercises and take flight into the unknown, uncharted waters of the subconscious, the unconscious, and beyond. Simply remain as a detached witness and allow yourself to grow in peace. Listed below are several hekau taken from Ancient Egyptian texts. They may be used in English or in ancient Kemetic according to your choice.

If you feel a certain affinity toward a particular energy expressed through a particular deity, use that inclination to your advantage by aligning yourself with that energy and then directing it toward the divine within your heart. Never forget that while you are working with a particular deity in the beginning stages, your objective is to delve into the deeper mystical implications of the symbolic form and characteristics of the deity. These always refer to the transcendental Self which is beyond all deities. According to your level of advancement you may construct your own Hekau according to your own feeling and understanding. As a rule, in meditations such as those being discussed now, the shorter the size of the hekau the more effective it will be since you will be able repeat it more often. However, the shorter the hekau, the more concentration it requires so as not to get lost in thoughts. You may wish to begin with a longer hekau and shorten it as your concentration builds. Words of power have no power in and of themselves. It is the user who gives them power through understanding and feeling.

When practicing the devout ritual identification form of meditation, the recitation of hymns, the wearing of costumes and elaborate amulets and other artifacts may be used. Ritual identification with the divine may be practiced by studying and repeatedly reading the various hymns to the divine such as those which have been provided in this volume, while gradually absorbing and becoming one with the teachings as they relate to you. When a creation hymn is being studied, you should reflect upon it as your true Self being the Creator, as your true Self being the hero(heroine), and that you (your true essence) are the one being spoken about in all

The Ancient Egyptian Path to Enlightenment

the teachings. It is all about you. "You" are the Creator. "You" are the sustainer of the universe. "You" are the only one who can achieve transcendence through enlightenment according to your own will. When you feel, think and act this way, you are using the highest form of worship and meditation toward the divine by constantly bringing the mind back to the idea that all is the Self and that you essentially are that Self. This form of practice is higher than any ritual or any other kind of offering. Here you are concentrating on the idea that your limited personality is only an expression of the divine. You are laying down your ego on the offering mat.

In *Sadhana*, Swami Sivananda gives the following outline for the frequency of possible recitations. We have included two types of words of power: short, containing one or two syllables, medium length, containing two to three and average, containing six to eight. They are presented as guidelines for practice of hekau-mantra repetition practice.

Generally, when the words of power are used over a sustained period of time, the benefits or *Siddhis* (psychic powers) arise. The most important psychic powers you can attain to facilitate your spiritual program are peace, serenity of mind, and concentration of the mental vibrations. Concentration opens the door to transcendental awareness and spiritual realization. Various estimates are given as to when you may expect to feel results; these vary from 500,000 repetitions to 1,200,000 or more. The number should not be your focus. Sustained practice, understanding the teachings about the Self and practicing of the virtues and self-control in an integral, balanced fashion are the most important factors determining your eventual success.

While *Om* is most commonly known as a *Sanskrit* mantra (word of power from India), it also appears in the Ancient Egyptian texts and is closely related to the Kemetic *Amun* in sound and Amen of Christianity. More importantly, it has the same meaning as Amun and is therefore completely compatible with the energy pattern of the entire group. According to the Egyptian Leyden papyrus, the name of the "Hidden God", referring to Amun, may be pronounced as *Om*, or *Am*.

Om is a powerful sound; it represents the primordial sound of creation. Thus it appears in Ancient Egypt as Om, in modern day India as Om, and in Christianity as Amen, being derived from Amun. Om may also be used for engendering mental calm prior to beginning recitation of a longer set of words of power or it may be used alone as described above. One Indian Tantric scripture (*Tattva Prakash*) states that Om or AUM can be used to achieve the mental state free of physical identification and can bring union with *Brahman* (the Absolute transcendental Supreme Being - God) if it is repeated 300,000 times. In this sense, mantras such as Om, Soham, Sivoham, Aham Brahmasmi are called *Moksha Mantras* or mantras which lead to union with the Absolute Self. Their shortness promotes greater concentration and force toward the primordial level of consciousness.

There is one more important divine name which is common to both Indian as well as Ancient Egyptian mystical philosophy. The sanskrit mantra **Hari* Om** is composed of Om preceded by the word Hari. In Hinduism, *Hari* means: "He who is Tawny". The definition of tawny is: "A light golden brown". This is a reference to the dark colored skin of Vishnu and Krishna. Vishnu is usually depicted with a deep blue and Krishna is depicted with a deep blue or black hue symbolizing infinity and transcendence. Hari is one of Krishna's or Vishnu's many divine names. It also means "hail" as in "hail to the great one" or it may be used as "The Great One". In the Ancient Egyptian magical texts used to promote spiritual development (words of power or HEKA - mantras) the word Haari also appears as one of the divine names. Thus, the hekau-

MEDITATION

mantra Hari Om was also known and used in Ancient Egypt and constitutes a most powerful formula for mystical spiritual practice. *(the spelling may be Hari or Hare)

Simply choose a hekau which you feel comfortable with and sit quietly to recite it continuously for a set amount of time. Allow it to gradually become part of your free time when you are not concentrating on anything specific or when you are being distracted by worldly thoughts. This will serve to counteract the worldly or subconscious vibrations that may emerge from the your own unconscious mind. When you feel anger or other negative qualities, recite the hekau and visualize its energy and the deity associated with it destroying the negativity within you.

For example, you may choose **Amun-Ra-Ptah.** When you repeat this hekau, you are automatically including the entire system of all gods and goddesses. Amun-Ra-Ptah is known as **Nebertcher,** the "All-encompassing Divinity". You may begin by uttering it aloud. When you become more advanced in controlling your mind, you may begin to use shorter words. For example simply utter: *Amun, Amun, Amun...* always striving to get to the source of the sound. Eventually you will utter these silently and this practice will carry your consciousness to the source of the sound itself where the very mental instruction to utter is given. Hekau-mantras are also related to the spiritual energy centers of the subtle spiritual body (Uraeus-Kundalini).

The Ancient Egyptian Path to Enlightenment

The following Ancient Egyptian selections come from the *"Book of Coming Forth by Day"* and other Ancient Egyptian scriptures:

Nuk pu NETER
I am the Supreme Divinity.

Nuk pu Ast
I am ASET

nuk neter aa kheper tchesef
I am the great God, self created,

Ba ar pet sat ar ta.
Soul is of heaven, body belongs to the earth.

Nuk uab-k uab ka-k uab ba-k uab sekhem.
My mind has pure thoughts, so my soul and life forces are pure.

Nuk ast au neheh ertai-nef tetta.
Behold I am the heir of eternity, everlastingness has been given to me.

Sekhem - a em mu ma aua Set.
I have gained power in the water as I conquered Set (greed, lust, ignorance).

Rex - a em Ab - a sekhem - a em hati - a.
I know my heart, I have gained power over my heart.

Un - na uat neb am pet am ta.
The power is within me to open all doors in heaven and earth.

Nuk sah em ba - f.
I am a spirit, with my soul.

amma su en pa neter sauu - k su emment en
pa neter au tuanu ma qeti pa haru
Give thyself to GOD; keep thou thyself daily for God; and let tomorrow be as today.

Haari Om
The Divine Self, Om

Om Asar Aset Heru
The Divine Self (Om) expressing as the Trinity Asar, Aset and Heru.

MEDITATION

Recitation of the name of the divine can be performed as a means to control the mind and direct it toward the divine.

Nebertcher
All encompassing existence
(The Absolute)

Om Amun-Ra-Ptah
The Divine Self (Om) expressing as the holy
Trinity Amun (witnessing consciousness), Ra (mind) and Ptah (physical universe). The following are Indian mantras:

Thus assert:

I love my neighbor as myself.

"I am the embodiment of service; I care for all human beings and all living beings in the universe as I care for my very self; I care for all of nature, as I care for my very own body."

Assert within yourself:

I am Divine.

"I am not this mind and body with their negative thoughts and desires"; "I am the Self, who is like a bird that is free to roam the vast expanse of the sky"; "I am not this perishable body that is a conglomeration of earthly elements that will some day return to the earth; I am the spirit which is subtle and free of all associations of the body"; "I am free from all associations of the body, be they of family, country, etc.; these associations of the body may have a practical value in the world of time and space but they do not in any way affect or hamper the real me."

Thus assert:

The Kingdom of God is within me.

I have nowhere to go, nowhere to seek, nowhere to search for the greatest treasure of all existence because it is within me already and it always was"; "Within my heart lies the source of all happiness. I am the abode of all fulfillment!"; "All I need to do in order to discover this treasure is to open my heart by discarding the illusions and ignorance which cloud my mind"; "I look not to the world of time and space but to the eternity and infinity which is within me"; "I look not to the vanity of my body but to the peace of my innermost self: I am That I am!

I and the Father are one.

This statement has a most ancient origin and it is one of the highest spiritual teachings. It exists in the Ancient Egyptian Mysteries and in the Indian Vedantic teachings and is used as a *hekau* or *mantra* to be repeated with deep understanding and feeling by those aspirants who want to direct their minds toward their essential nature.

The Ancient Egyptian Path to Enlightenment

You must, by now, realize that you are the focus of the Christian movement. Not you, your ego-personality, body, name, family, etc., but the innermost Self within you. When Jesus stated that he and the Father are one, he was not referring to his personality. He was referring to his innermost Self. He was also not referring to God as the "Creator-Father", sitting on the throne in heaven somewhere, because these are mental concepts that human beings have created. The terms "The Father" and "God" are metaphors to explain that which transcends all human conceptions. When we think of God using this new understanding, we should begin to think about that which is without name or form, that which is all pervasive and eternal and that which is not personal. Look within yourself; your soul is all of these things also. When you sleep your ego is not there. You do not have a name or form and yet you continue to exist, therefore, you are not the ego. Reflect constantly on this relationship between your innermost Self and the innermost Self of all creation (God) because they are one and the same. This ecstatic union with the divine was beautifully described by Teresa de Jesus also popularly known as Teresa of Avila:

> "The soul neither sees, hears, nor understands while she is united to God - God establishes himself in the interior of this soul in such a way that when she comes to herself, it is impossible for her to doubt that she has been in God and God in her. So does that Beauty and Majesty stamped on the soul that nothing can drive it from her memory. The soul is no longer the same, always enraptured."

Thus assert: "I, the innermost Self, not the ego, am one with the innermost reality of all that exists which transcends all outer manifestations, all names and all forms!" This is the internal realization of Divinity within you.

Assert boldly:

"The Kingdom of the Father is spread upon the earth, and I see it!"

"This world, this universe, my body, my loved ones, all human beings are manifestations of Divine consciousness!"; "All this is a reflection of the innermost Self who is eternal and infinite!"; "I (the innermost Self) am the sustainer of this reality as I sustain my dreams in the vastness of the mind"; "All that I see is a reflection of the innermost self."; "All this is the Kingdom/Queendom of Heaven!"; "Therefore, both internally and externally I have discovered the transcendental reality!"; "I am all this!" This is the external realization of Divinity in all creation."

MEDITATION
Meditation Technique #1: Simple Meditation Technique

Modern scientific research has proven that one of the most effective things anyone can do to promote mental and physical health is to sit quietly for 20 minutes twice each day. This is more effective than a change in diet, vitamins, food supplements, medicines, etc. It is not necessary to possess any special skill or training. All that is required is that one achieves a relaxed state of mind, unburdened by the duties of the day. You may sit from a few minutes up to an hour in the morning and in the late afternoon.

This simple practice, if followed each day, will promote above average physical health and spiritual evolution. One's mental and emotional health will be maintained in a healthy state as well. The most important thing to remember during this meditation time is to just relax and not try to stop the mind from pursuing a particular idea but also not trying to actively make the mind pursue a particular thought or idea. If a Hekau or Mantra (Prayer) is recited, or if a special hieroglyph is meditated upon, the mind should not be forced to hold it. Rather, one should direct the mind and when one realizes that one has been carried away with a particular thought, bring the mind gently back to the original object of meditation, in this way, it will eventually settle where it feels most comfortable and at peace.

Sometimes one will know that one has been carried away into thoughts about what one needs to do, or who needs to be called, or is something burning in the kitchen?, etc. These thoughts are worldly thoughts. Simply bring the mind back to the original object of meditation or the hekau. With more practice, the awareness of the hekau or object of meditation (candle, mandala, etc.) will dissipate as you go deeper. This is the positive, meditative movement that is desired. The goal is to relax to such a degree that the mind drifts to deeper and deeper levels of consciousness, finally reaching the source of consciousness, the source of all thought; then the mind transcends even this level of consciousness and there, communes with the Absolute Reality, Neter. This is the state of "Cosmic Consciousness", the state of enlightenment. After a while, the mental process will remain at the Soul level all the time. This is the Enlightened Sage Level.

The Ancient Egyptian Path to Enlightenment
Meditation Technique #2: The Integrated Meditation

As stated in the beginning of this section, there are four main components of meditation: posture, breath-life force control, sound and visualization. The previous meditation exercises have touched upon these areas but here we will use them all in an integrated fashion to achieve maximum concentration.

Before you begin, practice some light physical exercises (yoga, tai chi, etc.) for several minutes. This will serve to free up any energy blockages and wake up the mind by stimulating the circulation of the vital forces within the body.

Now choose a comfortable posture. If you consistently practice meditation, you will gradually be able to stay in one position for longer periods of time. If you practice regularly, you will discover that your body will develop a daily rhythm which will be conducive to your meditation time.

Next practice alternate nostril breathing so as to balance the positive and negative charges within the body and open up the central channel of vital energy as we discussed in the last section. Choose a particular visualization exercise or hekau. This will serve the purpose of helping to occupy the attention of the mind and prevent it from straying. It will also help you to develop sensitivity and control over the vital energy so that eventually you will be able to direct it according to your will.

A meditation on the energy centers will be used here (Uraeus Serpent Power Tape) or you may use the format presented in the audio tape (Morning Worship and Meditation). Inhale and visualize the energy flowing up from the first energy center, through the second, and then through the third, fourth, fifth and sixth up to the seventh, the highest energy center and then as you exhale, visualize the energy flowing back through the centers from the highest to the first center at the base of the spine.[21] As you visualize the energy flowing from center to center, you are controlling the Life Force energy and the direction of the mind at the same time. Now we will add sound to the meditation. You may choose a hekau of your choice, one you feel especially drawn to and one that you understand the deeper meaning of, to some degree, or the one suggested by your spiritual preceptor. Repeat it with meaning and feeling as you breathe, visualize and remain steady in your pose. You can link your breath and hekau repetition by reciting the first part of your hekau upon inhalation as the energy is moving up and the second part upon exhalation as the energy is moving back down.

In the beginning it may seem as though not much is happening, but within a short time, you will begin to notice changes within yourself. Your level of relaxation will improve immediately and your awareness of yourself will increase gradually. Eventually, you will begin to perceive various new sensations and psychic expansion. You will hear your heart beat. A feeling of peacefulness will develop. When you succeed in transcending your body consciousness you will be going beyond the exercises. You will not feel your arms or legs. This is an initial stage of transcendence. Your inner vision will open and you will perceive reality beyond the mind and body. At this point, do not worry about the components of the meditation. Simply relax and remain a witness to all you perceive. Do not try to run away from or to anything you notice.

---

[21] For more specific instructions listen to the Serpent Power audio tapes.

MEDITATION

Gradually allow yourself to go deeper and deeper until you become one with the source of all thoughts. This is the real you. Continue practicing this "communion" exercise with the divine until you are fully established in this level of being at all times. This is the state of Enlightenment.

The Ancient Egyptian Path to Enlightenment
Meditation Technique #3: The Basic Serpent Power Meditation based on Ancient Egyptian Wisdom Teachings

The subject of life force energy and the sublimation of sexual energy into spiritual energy existed many thousands of years in Egypt prior to its development in modern India under the name *Kundalini Yoga*. It later appears in many parts of the world but it did not find extensive documentation until the Sages of India composed the voluminous scriptures in relation to Kundalini Yoga. Since the topic of the Serpent Power Yoga is so vast, a full treatment of it would be beyond the scope of this work.

As in the Indian Chakra System, the Ancient Egyptian Sefech Ba Ra (Seven Spheres) are related to the seven energy centers of the subtle body which are not visible to the ordinary eye and are in the same space as the physical spine though not in the same plane as the physical body. They are linked to the awakening of one's spiritual powers and consciousness. As one progresses on their spiritual path of evolution, while either purposely employing a yogic spiritual discipline (study and application of spiritual and philosophic scriptures, reflection and meditation) or learning through the process of trial and error, these centers will automatically open, allowing one to experience increasing communion with the higher self: GOD. The process of raising one's spiritual power may be aided by specific exercises such as concentration, proper breathing, meditation on the meanings of the spiritual symbols and surrendering to the will of the Higher Self (GOD). These techniques allow one to transform one's waking personality so that one may discover their innermost self: GOD. This should be done under the guidance of a qualified teacher (spiritual master).

The energy centers of the subtle body are likened to a tree which the aspirant climbs through personality integration, which leads to intuitional realization of the transcendental Self. In the process of creation, the creative energy manifests in the form of six planes of consciousness. This is the realm of phenomenal reality including physical, astral and mental existence. Most people exist on the level of the first three energy-consciousness levels. The goal of this Yoga is to unite the six phenomenal consciousness centers with the seventh or transcendental realm of consciousness, the Absolute. This Absolute is what various religions refer to by different names such as the Kingdom of Heaven, Asar, Krishna, Brahman, the Tao, etc.

The Serpent Power energy flows throughout thousands of energy channels. If any of the energy channels are blocked or over-sensitized, a dis-balance can arise, causing illness in the mind and physical body. There are three most important channels through which the Serpentine Life Force flows. These are: *Asar (also Amun-Ra), Aset and Nebethet.*[22] These are represented by the Egyptian Caduceus of Djehuti which is composed of a staff which has two serpents wrapped around it.

The two opposing forces in the Life Force energy of a human being are balanced by the various practices of yoga in an integral fashion. Increasing wisdom, reflection, practice of virtues, purification of the diet, exercise and specific serpent power breathing exercises eventually cause the opposites to balance and then they rise through the central subtle channel up the spine and into the head where they eventually become established, providing a continuous shower of bliss to the practitioner.

---

[22] See the books *The Serpent Power* and *The Book of the Dead*

MEDITATION

There are two stages of practice in the YOGA of life force energy development. The first stage of practice is the cleansing stage. Here the concentration is on cleansing the mind and body and on balancing the energy flow of the body. The mind is purified by practicing the wisdom teachings. The body is purified by purifying the diet and regular practice of physical exercise. The energy flow is balanced by alternate nostril breathing. In order for your consciousness to unfold your mind needs to be cleansed of gross impurities such as anger-hate-greed-selfishness, etc. and the physical body needs to be cleansed of mind altering chemicals and elements of lower vibratory rate which will cause the mind and body to be agitated and preoccupied with the desires of worldly concerns.

After the cleansing stage of Serpent Power Yoga wherein the elements of the body are cleansed and the subtle energy channels of the body are cleansed, which may take months or years, the attention turns to the three main channels wherein spiritual realization unfolds. This is accomplished by manipulating the energy in the subtle mental planes and directing it towards the divine.

The Psychic Energy Centers in the spiritual or etheric body are distributed throughout the spine going up from the base of the spine to the Crown of the head: *The Uraeus.* Each one of these centers are called *Ba Ra* or vortexes of energy of Ra. In Egyptian symbolism they are depicted as circles or links in a chain in the Karmic scales of the initiate. In Indian symbolism they are portrayed as *padmas* or "Lotuses", symbolizing psycho-spiritual principles of human consciousness. By understanding these and removing obstacles to them, Arat Sekhem (Life Force) energy is freed. When your consciousness is freed you can move toward the divine essence of your being.

Mental and emotional complexes and sentiments constitute the main obstacles and blocks to Arat Sekhem, one's own spiritual consciousness. Through physical exercises, physical cleansing through diet and lifestyle changes and meditation on the psycho-spiritual implications of each center, Serpent Power Yoga is effected.[23]

The Serpent Power

The latent spiritual energy lies dormant, coiled up as it were, at the base of the spine and when awakened, spirals upward, awakening the spiritual energy centers in the subtle spiritual body.

This is the same depiction used in Ancient Egyptian iconography (A) with the staff of the god Djehuti which later became known as the Caduceus of Hermes Trismegistus.

(B) Artistic rendition of the Ancient Egyptian psycho-spiritual energy centers.

In Indian iconography (C), the three main *nadis* or astral channels through which the Serpent Power travels are depicted as one straight channel or central shaft which runs vertically, and two intertwining channels representing the two opposite poles of the same Serpent Power energy. This is the same depiction used in Ancient Egyptian iconography (A) with the staff of the god Djehuti which later became known as the Caduceus of Hermes Trismegistus.

---

[23] Note: For more on the Serpent Power Yoga see the book *The Serpent Power* by Dr. Muata Ashby.

The Ancient Egyptian Path to Enlightenment

A

The Energy Centers of the Subtle Body

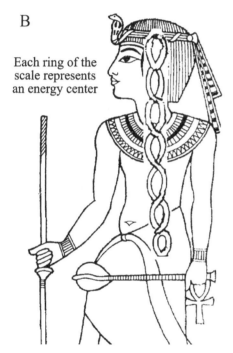

B

Each ring of the scale represents an energy center

C- A Yogi in the Lotus Pose Meditating on the Energy Centers

MEDITATION

Below: Diagram of the Psycho-Spiritual Energy Centers of Human consciousness also known as the Serpent Power for concentration and meditation exercises. .

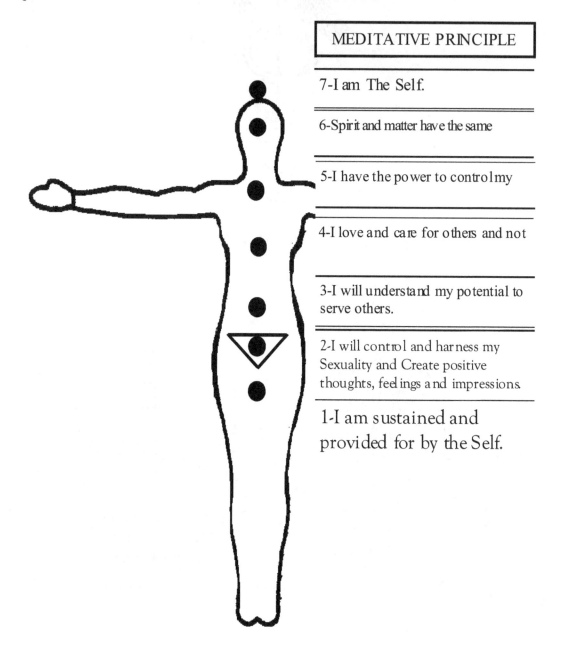

MEDITATIVE PRINCIPLE
7-I am The Self.
6-Spirit and matter have the same
5-I have the power to control my
4-I love and care for others and not
3-I will understand my potential to serve others.
2-I will control and harness my Sexuality and Create positive thoughts, feelings and impressions.

1-I am sustained and provided for by the Self.

The Ancient Egyptian Path to Enlightenment

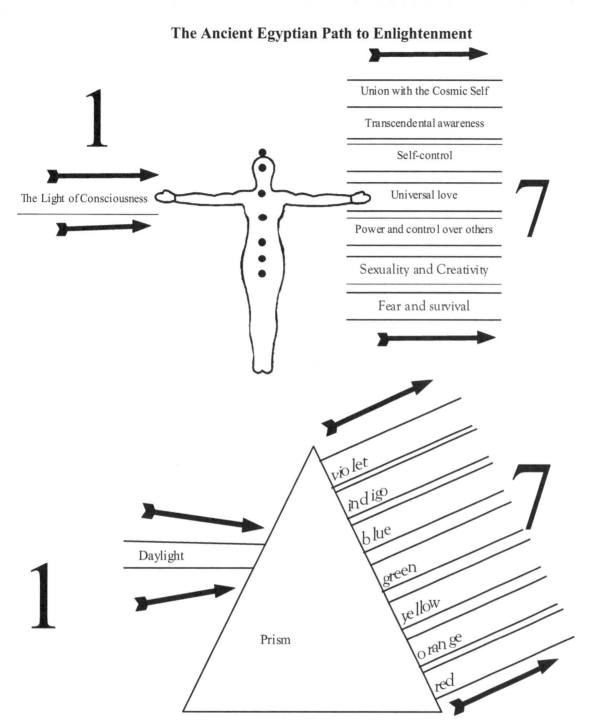

169

MEDITATION

Instruction:

Practice concentrating on one meditative principle each month. As you reflect on each meditative principle chant the words of power of your choice and direct your heart and mind toward one-pointedness on that principle. Then remain in silence and allow the Divine feeling to rise within you, lifting you above all weakness and difficulty (ignorance, obstruction) in each particular center. Allow yourself to be cleansed and the Serpent Power will rise within you normally.

Arat: The Serpent Power Goddess of Ancient Egypt.

The Ancient Egyptian Path to Enlightenment
Meditation Technique #4: The Supreme Self Meditation: Based on the hieroglyphic text of the "Destruction of Humankind"

To Begin: Be seated or lie down in a relaxed pose. See the diagram provided for the location of the energy centers. VISUALIZE yourself gaining cosmic energy. See it accumulating in the body. Place your concentration on the first energy center at the base of the spine as you inhale. See the energy tapping that spot, then see it rising through the other energy centers going up to the sixth center where the pineal gland is situated (The Uraeus). Exhale and see the energy go back down to the first center. Inhale and repeat the exercise. Feel the increasing levels of PEACE *(htp)* develop.

MEDITATION

Meditation Technique #5: The Highest Form of Meditation: Identification With the Divine

Nuk pu Ra
(I am God)

Nuk pu Nuk
(I am the Self)

This meditation appears in the Ancient Egyptian Myth of the *Destruction of Evil Men and Women* which was presented in Part II. The highest form of meditation is maintaining an awareness of the supreme truth which transcends all other realities. This truth is that God is the underlying reality behind all things and most importantly, that the innermost reality of your own heart is none other than the Absolute Supreme Self which transcends time, space, thought and the ego. The meditation presented below outlines a format for a formal sit-down meditation in which the meditator is directed to see himself or herself as the Supreme Being (Ra). This is a most powerful visualization for meditation practice.

As stated earlier, the oldest known formal meditation instruction comes from the Ancient Egyptian story of "The Destruction of Evil Men and Women". The following lines of scripture are from the original text translations. The meditation is to be practiced after listening to and having gained an understanding of the teachings presented in the myth.

Whosoever shall recite the words, here written, shall perform the ceremonies which are to be performed when this book is being read.1 And they shall make their position in a circle which is beyond them, and their two eyes shall be fixed upon themselves, all their members shall be composed, [relaxed, motionless] *and their steps shall not carry them away* [from the place of meditation].*2 Whoever among men shall recite* [these] *words shall visualize themselves as Ra on the day of his birth; and his possessions shall not become fewer, and his house shall never fall into decay, but shall endure for a million eternities.3*

1-Posture and Focus of Attention

Posture is one of the main components of the meditation practice. This text prescribes a sitting position within a circle. Then it instructs that there should be a focusing of the mind between the eye brows. This area is also known as the sixth energy-consciousness center where the Uraeus serpent, the Eye of Ra and the Udjat, the Eye of Heru, are located. All the members of the body, the arms, legs, etc. should be motionless.

Posture: Be seated in a comfortable posture. You may create a circle figure in which to sit or simply visualize that you are seated within a circle. See yourself at the center of the circle which comprises the Sundisk of Ra, ☉, and see yourself as the source of all that is.

The Ancient Egyptian Path to Enlightenment

2- Words of power

The papyrus instructs that after having read and recited the story one should assume a specific posture and adopt a specific visualization. The story in the papyrus (Destruction of Humankind) is as follows.

> Ra (Supreme Being) created the world and human beings. After many years they became arrogant and spoke evilly about him. They forgot about his greatness and about their own origins. Ra decided to punish them for their egoism and sinful behavior and so he sent out his eye of destruction in the form of Hetheru to kill all sinners. He then recalled his eye before it could kill all human beings and then He retreated to heaven where he traverses in the form of the sun and installed his vicar to watch over the world during the night in the form of the moon.*

Thus, Ra is the creator of this entire universe and it is sustained by him at all times. This Supreme Self, Ra, is the same essence which abides in the heart of every human being. This is confirmed by the *Ancient Egyptian Book of Coming Forth By Day* in Chapter 17. Therefore, having this knowledge, one should understand that one's Higher Self is in reality not the limited and transient human personality but the Supreme Self.

Therefore, one who understands this teaching should see himself or herself as that very same Self. The words of power which affirm this understanding are:

Nuk pu Ra
I am Ra (the Supreme Divinity).

*for a complete version of the story see *The Asarian Resurrection* by Muata Ashby.

3- Visualization

Visualization is the next important element in this meditation instruction. The form of visualization to be practiced here is called: *Ritual Identification with the Divine Self.* Ritual Identification falls under the category of Yoga of Devotion. As explained throughout this text, the ordinary form of identification people have, that is, their idea of who they are, is an egoistic notion based on ignorance of the deeper Self within. This form of visualization should be practiced at all times as a perpetual mindfulness exercise, as well as when practicing a formal meditation session.

In this meditation the aspirant is directed to identify himself/herself with the Supreme Being in the form of birth. This form is known as *Khepri,* and symbolizes the emerging spiritual birth of the Divine within the human heart. Therefore, after performing the necessary ablutions of mind and body, meditate thus:

Visualization: See yourself as the transformative power which gives life to all things. See yourself as the sustainer of creation. See yourself as the being into which the creation dissolves in order to give way to a new cycle of creation. You are not just the body, but you encompass the entire universe. This is your true possession. Even though the world may come into existence, decay and die, you do not decay, or die, and neither are you born. You are the immortal, transcendental Self. You are the beginning, middle and end. You have

MEDITATION

existed from immeasurable time and will exist for eternity. You are one with the Absolute!

MEDITATION AS MEDICINE: For Peace, Health and Spiritual Enlightenment

"Feed the Ba With What Endures"

Ancient Egyptian Proverb

Many people in modern society have learned to look toward modern science for healing. Also, many people rely not only on man made drugs, but also on herbs and natural extracts for promoting health. It must be clearly understood that physical health is a product of mental health. The diseases of the body, including cancer and the common cold, are caused by a person's karmic basis or the thoughts, feelings, sentiments, anxieties and worries of their unconscious mind which they have accumulated over thousands of lifetimes. This is because over a period of time, which may include several lifetimes, a person has intensified the feelings of negativity, and these have restricted or blocked the flow of spiritual energy which comes from the Soul (Ba) and then passes into the mental plane, and then to the physical. Thus, mental illness arises when negativity is intensified in the mind. Each form of negativity distorts a human being's spiritual energy, and this distortion leads to mental and physical disease. Negative feelings and emotions block and distort spiritual energy while positive, harmonious thoughts and emotions promote the harmonious flow of spiritual energy throughout the mind and body. Therefore, those people who experience more stress, anger, hatred, tension, worry and anxiety will experience more illness. So it is important to promote mental health first and foremost.

Insanity is in reality more common than people realize. Most people have come to believe that giving vent to emotions and allowing anger to be expressed is a healthy way of living. Indeed, emotions such as anger can cause dire effects when suppressed but the answer is not to allow it free expression whenever one is at the boiling point. This philosophy has developed as a way for modern society to cope with the increased stress and tension of modern society. Instead of realizing that this stress is unnatural and undesirable, psychologists and other leaders of society seek to rationalize it and accept it as a normal factor of human life. From a yogic perspective, extremes of emotion are signs of severe ignorance and mental dullness. Extremes of emotion and ignorance lead to a degraded state of human experience. Examples of this are people who express anger, hatred and greed towards others, and in a more degraded state, these people will do violence against others. In an even more degraded state these people will be unable to sustain the "normal" realities of life and will be homeless or need to be institutionalized. Mental health degenerates the more a person engages in negativity which draws the mind down to the Dull State. The ideal of a personality who has integrated all aspects (emotional, intellectual, action and will) should be kept in view. Such a personality will not be affected by the curses of others nor by inner anxieties and fears. This is the ideal which we have been promoting throughout this volume. It is attainable by anyone who sincerely applies themselves to the teachings and practice of Yoga. Therefore, one should try to rise above anger, hatred, greed, fear, anxiety, etc., through the teachings of yoga presented in this volume. So the problems of human existence can be alleviated and even eradicated through the perfection of yoga practice. This means that as you cleanse your heart and become more mentally lucid, pure and harmonious, you will be clearing up mental complexes and in turn, you will be promoting physical health.

The Ancient Egyptian Path to Enlightenment

Reflect on the following. You say that you want peace and harmony in the world and yet you cannot maintain peace in your own life. Do you engage in extremes of emotion? Do you express anger and hatred towards others? Do you eat meat, a product of the violent killing of animals, and other negative substances which deteriorate your physical and mental state? Do you show contempt for others and refuse to acknowledge your kinship to them? Do you engage in racism or sexism? Do you engage in gossiping or participate in forms of entertainment which agitate the mind, such as violent shows, or denigrate others, like pornography or political propaganda? Do you turn away from people when they are trying to tell you something about yourself in order to help you? In order to experience true peace and harmony you must promote purity in your life at all levels. You cannot simply talk about it and not try to practice it.

The idea that a human being is supposed to grow senile and feeble as he or she grows old is backed up by ignorance and the Distracted and Dull lifestyles. If you have lived properly, taking care to reduce anxiety and practicing the art of harmonious living, you will increase in wisdom, mental clarity and spiritual awareness even as the body deteriorates as you approach the time of death. Therefore, the meditative lifestyle should be promoted in society as a means for improving mental and physical health, harmony in society and spiritual evolution for all. Meditation is the best medicine to reduce stress, anxiety, restlessness and dullness, and to increase inner peace, harmony and spiritual awareness. Therefore, you can substitute the mental and physical dependencies on drugs, parties, and other addictions for what truly endures and brings abiding happiness and bliss. Meditation is the path which allows you to not simply release tension, but also to overcome and transcend all that is negative, base and painful in life. Thus, anger, hatred, greed, ignorance, vanity, jealousy, covetousness, lust, longings, urges, cravings and all forms of tension and stress are to be considered as mental diseases. These diseases of the mind keep the mind at a low state (in dullness). Such a human being leads himself or herself to negative experiences. Meditation and the meditative lifestyle are the preferred treatment to eradicate all ills.

MEDITATION
Weathering the Storm of Uncontrolled Thoughts: How to Handle the Restless Mind

"I remove the thunder-cloud from the sky when there is a storm with thunder and lightning therein."
From the Ancient Egyptian
Book of Coming Forth By Day
Ch. 17:69-70

In the *Book of Coming Forth by Day* there is specific reference made to a storm. This is a special utterance or words of power which bear much importance in the control of the mind. As stated earlier, the mind is likened to an ocean and when there is agitation in that ocean, the waves can be seen but the bottom cannot. Likewise when the mind is overpowered by anger, hatred, greed, etc., the transcendental truth cannot be seen. Even when you have made an effort to control your negative psychological traits they will sometimes come out and overpower you because of the past habits and customs which the mind has developed over time. Therefore, a spiritual aspirant must learn to practice detachment even when the mind cannot be controlled to perfection. You must learn to objectively stand back and observe the mind. You may reflect: "Yes I feel anger rising and I am taking note of how I am acting." Do not develop anguish or regret over what you have done but seek to understand what has happened so as to remove that negative behavior. Thank the Self for providing you with an opportunity to bring out the negative because it is this negative behavior and others like it which are obstructing your vision of the Self. Thus, just as the most powerful storm seems hellish and is the cause of sorrow and pain but eventually passes away, so too the storms of mental agitation must be endured with patience and faith until they finally pass away when the state of Enlightenment has been attained.

There should be understanding for yourself as well as for others. Not all people get upset at the same time. Sometimes people who are not upset look down on others not realizing that they too have their times of emotional tumult. You should not allow yourself to become conceited when you see others in distress because you have been in that position in the past.

Many times in human relations mental upset is accepted as normal behavior. How many times have you heard "don't talk to him now, wait until he calms down" or "wait until she comes to her senses, then you can ask her permission to go out."

This form of behavior is not normal and should not be accepted. You should strive to control your emotions and eventually you should be able to control yourself to the extent of not allowing emotions to distract you or cause you to lose even a moment of life due to mental turbulence or disquietude. The following are diagrams showing the mental process and how it affects the conscious awareness of the deeper spiritual being and how that in turn affects ones outlook on life and ones concept of Self.

The Ancient Egyptian Path to Enlightenment

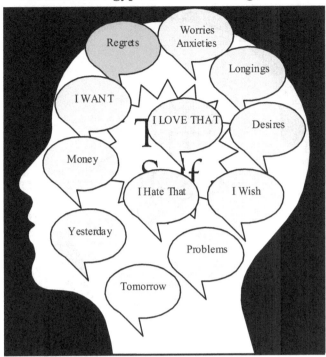

The thoughts of the unenlightened mind are concerned with the perceived realities which the person has learned and experienced. They are all centered around the individual ego and its desires. These thoughts are like clouds which clutter the mind, obstructing one's perception of the transcendental reality. They constantly agitate the ocean of the mind, and this agitation makes the thoughts seem real. They are like dust particles on a mirror which prevent a clear view of the image being reflected. Thoughts cloud a person from discovering the innermost reality: The Self. The agitation causes the normally clear mental substance to take on various shapes and sizes. These shapes and sizes are called thoughts. When the mind is in this state it is referred to as being "conditioned." Consciousness has assumed the form of opposites (positive and negative, male and female, light and dark, here and there, etc.) known as *duality*. There are names and forms, opposites, conflict, memories, desires, etc., in the mind which are accepted as absolute realities. When there is conditioning of the mental substance, there is time and space or relative awareness composed of desires, ideas, memories, past, present and future, etc. When there is conditioning (duality) there is always limitation, because the mind cannot hold all of reality (the universe) and view it in a conditioned form at once.

MEDITATION

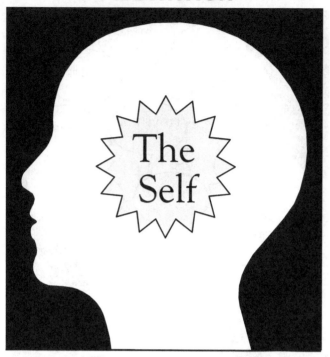

When the thoughts and desires subside through understanding, detachment and dispassion, lucidity and meditation, the thoughts fade and the Innermost Self which was there all the time becomes the sole and resplendent reality. This state is likened to sleeping when there are no dreams. There is no ego, no subject who is thinking, only pure consciousness, pure existence, pure bliss and pure peace. When you are in the dreamless sleep state there are no problems, worries or ego notions. You have transcended ordinary ego-consciousness. This is what brings about the feelings of rest and rejuvenation you experience upon waking up in the morning. However, when you wake, the thoughts and concerns of your individual ego existence rush into the mind again, and these constitute your day-to-day life. In meditation you can also transcend ego-consciousness, but intentionally day-to-day. When the mind is in this state it is referred to as "unconditioned" because the mental substance is devoid of names, forms, as well as egoism, the notion that "I am an individual." Instead there is awareness of infinity, eternity and immortality. Now there is an awareness that "I am the Self who is the source of all." There is no awareness of time and space, past, present or future, only of the eternal present. Duality has been transcended.

The Ancient Egyptian Path to Enlightenment

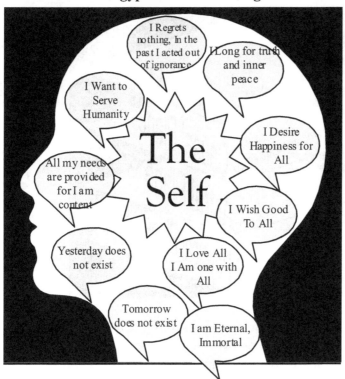

Having transcended the ego through yoga and meditation you now see the world not as an individual ego-personality, but as the Self who is all powerful, majestic, unlimited, supremely blissful and confident. You can deal with all problems of life with the awareness that you are being led and sustained by the Divine Self and that all situations of life have a divine purpose, to give you the opportunity to grow in self-knowledge and to serve humanity. Therefore, your desires and concerns are no longer ego-based selfish concerns, but are permeated with a vision of universality, peace and contentment. Now there is true willing; this state is known as *Maakheru* or "true of speech." Maakheru is the Ancient Egyptian mystical term signifying that the unconscious is cleansed and that the desires, thoughts, and impulses are true emanations of the Self and not of the ego. The faculty of speech is tied directly into the unconscious. This is why people sometimes speak and something comes out which they did not intend. What came out was backed up by their deep-rooted impressions, the clouds of negativity, ignorance and delusion. When the unconscious is cleansed through meditation the light of the Self shines forth and goodness, sweetness, and harmonious words come forth spontaneously. This is the basis of all spiritual scriptures and it is the reason why, when an enlightened Sage speaks, his or her words are considered to be Divinely inspired words of wisdom.

MEDITATION

Below: A three dimensional drawing representing Creation. The four tiers of the Ancient Egyptian Djed symbol refer to states of psycho-spiritual consciousness as well as the nature of the universe. Thus, The Self is the origin and sustainer of Creation.

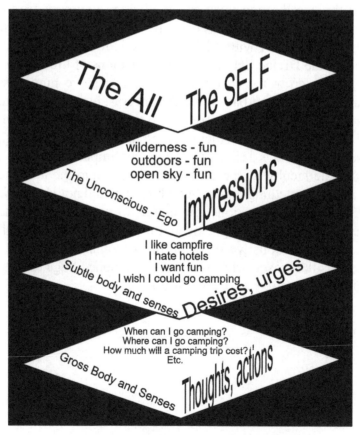

Above: A three dimensional drawing representing the human mind.

The Ancient Egyptian Path to Enlightenment

The unconscious level of the mind is like a filing cabinet which stores memories in the form of impressions and events. These impressions form the basis which impels the soul forward after the death of the physical body. They are carried over after death and they impel the soul to have experiences in the astral plane and also lead it to reincarnate after a period of time. A child seems to be unburdened and happy-go-lucky. However as the process of growth ensues, the desires, urges, preferences, etc., emerge. These are a factor of the dormant or latent, deep impressions which are sprouting up from the unconscious level of mind. If there are no impressions based on ignorance and egoism the soul does not reincarnate, but experiences union with the Absolute. This is termed Nirvana, Liberation, Resurrection, Freedom, etc.

When an intense event is experienced, the impression is stored in the unconscious. When a situation occurs which relates to that impression, the impression will come forth and emerge in the form of an urge or feeling of desire in the subconscious level, and then the urge emerges as a thought in the conscious level. When intensified they become cravings or uncontrollable yearnings or longings. If the longings are not fulfilled there arises anger and hatred toward whatever is seen as the object or person which is preventing the fulfillment of the desire. For example, if you had an experience in your youth which you found positive, you will store a positive feeling about it. For instance, if you enjoyed a camping trip you will feel positive about doing it again. If you had a bad experience camping you will develop a dislike, and if an opportunity arises to go camping, you will refuse. This principle works for all desires whether they be positive or negative. For example, if you have developed impressions of criminality and enjoyment from stealing, you will be stimulated when situations arise which afford you the opportunity to steal or you will think, plot and finally act in certain ways which will lead you to criminal activities and to meet other criminals.

In this manner, a human being reflects both positive and negative thoughts and feelings on outside objects and personalities. If you have karmic impressions which make you desire hot-dogs for instance, whenever you see or smell them you will be drawn to them, and you will feel elation. When intensified, the elation will cloud your judgment (intellect) and you will not consider if you should eat it or not, is it healthy, or if you are hungry or not. You have projected your inner happiness on to the object (hot-dog) and thus you see it as a source of happiness and fulfillment. You have developed the habit of feeling hungry when you see even a picture of a hot-dog and will not be able to restrain yourself when you pass by a hot-dog stand. You have given them the control over you. They decide when you are happy. Like all other objects, they are not true sources of fulfillment because the feeling of satisfaction wears off and the desire rises again in a short time. A human being who is led by his or her desires is like a slave. This is a pathetic state of Dullness which every human being needs to grow out of through the teachings of the meditative lifestyle.

Regret, sorrow and guilt work the same way. If you had an experience which you felt was your fault and you felt bad, you will store impressions of guilt. For example, say that you were married and got divorced, and your children were angry with you. You may eventually not remember the exact situation which caused the negative feelings but the impression remains. Whenever you have another experience of someone putting down your parenting skills you will develop feelings and thoughts of guilt. If people sense these feelings in you they can exploit them for their own negative purposes.

The important thing to understand is that the mind is a bundle of impressions of past experiences and the feelings and desires which they engender. If they are based on ignorance and delusion, the desires, thoughts and feelings will also be based on ignorance and delusion. The project of spiritual practice is to gain an understanding of where these desires and feelings come from, and then to control them.

The impressions of the mind are like clouds which block a person from viewing the sky (the Self). The only way to rise above the clouds of negative mental impressions is to promote positive impressions. These will lead to inner peace and harmony. Inner calm will allow the mind to reflect the presence of the Self like a

MEDITATION

mirror which is free of dust. Positive impressions are developed through spiritual practice. As you gain knowledge of your *Self* you become less restless. You will forgive yourself and cleanse all guilt, regrets and fears, while you develop more insight into human nature and the cause of your errors which led to negative situations. As you discover greater and greater inner fulfillment you have less need for external sources of "fun," such as hot-dogs or camping. Therefore, there is less mental agitation and distraction. As you progress further you will rise above the positive impressions* as well and you will discover that both positive and negative are relative experiences which apply only to human existence and not to the absolute transcendental Self which, in reality, is who you are. *see page 95

Meditation has the effect of focusing the light of the Self on the unconscious the impressions, and this illumination nullifies them because it allows you to see the impressions from a transcendental plane. From there they are like match lights as compared to the sun. What need does the sun have for match lights? The sun is effulgent and overpowering. In the same manner you are the Self and your true nature towers over all impressions. What are a lifetime worth of impressions compared to eternity? Your individual existence is a minuscule expression of your true Self. In this manner, ignorance and negativity is purged from the unconscious level of the mind, and when this occurs, the transformation in personality becomes expressed visible at the conscious level of the mind as compassion, tranquillity, contentment, inner peace, universal love, self-control, selfless service to humanity, etc.

Consider the desires and preferences which people exhibit in their life. Preferences seem to be arbitrary. Some people like this and others like that, but if you look more deeply you will discover that there is an underlying basis for desires. Suppose that you had a bad experience in the outdoors and you died with this impression in your deep unconscious mind. In your next lifetime you may experience anxiety at the mention of camping without knowing why. This is how karmic impressions of the past can have an effect on the present lifetime. If these fears and mental complexes are not cleansed from the mind they can cause untold pain and anguish as well as limitation in the present lifetime. Ancient mystical philosophy has presented extensive teachings in reference to this phenomenon. In recent times parapsychologists have uncovered proof of these through past life regression therapy. However, past life regression therapy cannot fully cleanse past impressions. This is because the deep seeded cause for the impressions are not to be found in past lives. These are only the effects. What needs occur is a complete process of self-discovery wherein the root-cause of all karmic desires, needs and urges are discovered and uprooted from the unconscious mind. In order for this to happen a person must develop completely in all areas of the psycho-spiritual and psycho-physical personality, i.e. emotion, action, will and intellectual (wisdom). This is the plan of Integral Yoga.

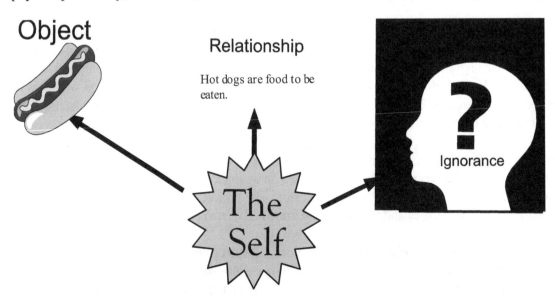

The Ancient Egyptian Path to Enlightenment

The diagram on this page is an illustration of the triad of consciousness which a human being experiences in the waking and dream states. The light of the one Self refracts as it were and assumes the form of objects, subjects and the relationships between these two. When the mind operates with egoism (ignorance) there is awareness of oneself as a subject in a world of objects, and there is interest in anything that one perceives will bring happiness. This is an illusory relationship based on ignorance. When there is enlightenment in the mind, there is an understanding that the underlying basis of all subjects, objects and relationships is the same Supreme Self. With this understanding, desires to possess and interact with objects to be happy are eradicated and the feeling of universality, the awareness that the Self underlies all, increases. A human being comes to understand that he or she is not a limited individual personality, but one with all objects. Here the term *objects* implies people, plants, minerals, elements, animals, planets, stars, etc.

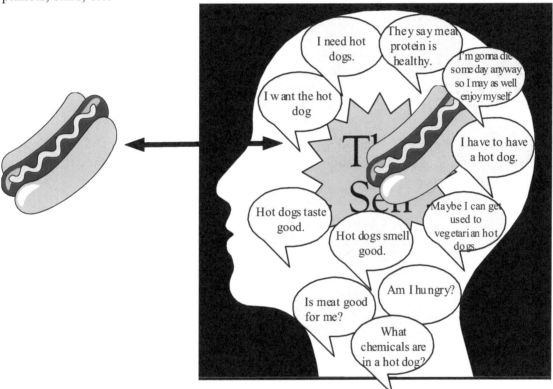

The Image above has been included for the purpose of illustrating how the mind reacts to stimulus based on the contents of the mind or its karmic conditioning (egoism).

If there is an impression in the mind which the mind has learned to think of as desirable, it will seek to act on that impression when evoked to do so. The impulses and thoughts which arise in a person occur without their knowing and without their control. A person who has practiced reflectiveness and who has been taught mystical psychology will begin to notice the subtle processes which go on in the mind.

When the mind is overwhelmed by thoughts of impressions of egoistic desire, the thoughts of truth, righteousness, correctness, logic and reason as well as the vision of the Self are drowned out. Examples of the correct thoughts might be: "Am I hungry?", "Is meat good for me?", "What chemicals are in a hot dog?" and "Maybe I can get used to the vegetarian hot dogs."

MEDITATION

Using the example of the hot dog, a person will feel compelled to acquire and consume the hot dog even though they have thoughts which contradict the desire. Even if they have heard that human beings do not require animal meat in order to be healthy, that hot dogs have cancer causing chemicals and are produced with fecal matter from rodents and other substances, the mind will not have the will to resist. The mind begins to rationalize several thoughts which will enable a person to do whatever it is that they desire. Examples of the rationalizing thoughts are: "They say meat protein is healthy." and "I'm gonna die some day anyway so I may as well enjoy myself."

This process works the same way for all activities in life. Some of the most prominent areas which most people may recognize are smoking, adultery, stealing, hurting the feelings of others and sex. The key factor here is acting on impulse based on the desires in the mind rather than on the basis of truth and righteousness. This is a factor of ignorance of course, but also of a weak will.

Through the practice of Yoga and Meditation, the light of the Self increases and as it illuminates the mind it allows a person to discover increasing wisdom, devotion to truth and the will to act righteously.

The first task in the project of controlling the mind is to control the senses. The following section is devoted to bringing an understanding of what the senses are and how they relate to the mind and to human experience.

The Ancient Egyptian Path to Enlightenment

Controlling the Senses

Bottom right: The Gods of the senses.

Maa: Sight

Saa: Understanding, Knowledge and Feeling/Touch

Hu: Taste, Pure food and Godly food.

Setem: Hearing

The subject of controlling the senses is very important in the process of meditation. In the Yoga system of Sage Patanjali of India (200 B.C.E.) the process of withdrawing the senses was termed as *Pratyahara*. It means withdrawing the senses from the objects of the world so as to enable the mind to have an unhampered experience of consciousness when there is no awareness of objects. In Indian Yoga this experience is called *Samadhi* or super-consciousness. In Ancient Egypt the word *Seeh* (*Sihu*) or religious ecstasy was used. When the senses are controlled and the mind begins to rise above them a unique form of peace and happiness arises in the mind which is termed "bliss." Most people do not ever have this experience in their lifetime except in brief moments after they have fulfilled a longing or desire. They associate objects with sources of happiness because when they acquire objects of desire there is a brief period of relaxation and expansion because the tension of desiring has subsided so they strive to acquire more and more objects not realizing that objects and the idea of possessing them are sources of worry, distraction and burden for the mind. In this condition the mind degrades itself and wastes its energy looking after objects, longing for objects and it never finds peace. It must be understood that as far as an individual person is concerned other people are also "objects". In fact, everything outside of yourself is an object in reference to your individual point of view. Thus, a mind in this condition is considered to be a slave to objects rather than being their controller and master. A person under the control of their senses will not be able to control the movements of the senses even if their mind tells them not to look at a certain object or listen, etc. Coupled with the desires of the body, the senses are always searching for objects which are of interest to the desires of the body and of the ignorant mind which does not understand that objects cannot satisfy any desire but only multiply them to infinity. This is the plight of the *Distracted* mind.

The Ancient Egyptian relief on the previous page from Edfu (Egypt - Africa) denotes the mystical understanding of the senses in relation to the Self. The boat of Ra depicts the sundisk with an image of the winged scarab (*Khepri* - the morning sun) in the center. Notice that there are certain gods inside and others outside. The ones inside are those which denote qualities

MEDITATION

which are innate to the Self. That is, those cosmic forces which are expressions of the Divine itself. These are *Heru-merti* (Heru of the two eyes), *Apuat, Maat, Hetheru, Djehuti, Net,* and *Heru-khent-khathet* (The unborn Heru). The ones outside are, Heru-pa-khart (Heru the child - rising sun) directly in front of the boat, in front of him is king Ptolemy IV offering *Maat* (truth and righteousness) to the Divine Company. Behind the King, outside of the boat, stand the gods of the senses of *Hu* (Taste and divine sustenance) and *Saa* (Touch, feeling and understanding). At the other end, also outside of the boat, stand the gods of the senses of *Maa* (Sight) and *Setem* (Hearing). *Hu* and *Saa* were known to serve as bearers of the Eye of Heru (enlightened consciousness). They were also considered to be the tongue and heart of *Asar-Ptah* (the Self). Thus, they represent the vehicles through which human beings can understand and espouse the teachings of moral and spiritual wisdom.

The positioning of the gods and goddesses is of paramount importance, because it points to the understanding that the neters within the boat itself are emanations of the Divine, while those outside of the boat are effects or reflections of the creative principles. Therefore, the occupants of the boat may be understood as *absolute attributes* of the Divine, while the characters outside of the boat may be understood as *relative manifestations* of the Divine in time and space. This is significant because it means that the senses are not real and abiding but conditional and transient. Also their depiction in the *Ushet* (praise - worship) posture with upraised arms towards the Divine conveys the understanding that the senses are subservient. So just as the Self has senses the human body has senses and these should be under the control of the soul and not the other way around.

There are two most effective methods of controlling and transcending the senses. First through the use of mystical philosophy the mind is to be rendered subtle. Through Saa, the faculty of understanding, the mind can realize at every moment that the objects which the senses are aware of are not absolute realities and that they are emanations from the Divine and nothing to desire. This can occur even as the mind is perceiving the objects as a person practices daily reflection on the spiritual teachings. As this movement occurs in the mind it becomes easier and easier to let go of the objects of the minds interest which are not in line with Maat (correctness, truth, etc.). Secondly, through the practice of concentration, the senses can be controlled whether or not there is awareness of objects. Concentration increases will power. So the senses can be controlled through understanding or through willpower. However, the integral practice of all of the disciplines of yoga will assist in the movement to control and transcend the mind and senses.

The senses can be transcended through any of the paths of yoga (Wisdom, Devotion, Action, and Meditation). However, the Yoga of Meditation specializes in this art and all yogas enhance the practice of meditation. When the control and transcendence of the senses occurs the person may experience various kinds of psychic phenomena. This is the lower form of transcendence. In the advanced form one goes beyond all concepts, thoughts and feelings and encounters a region within wherein there is no being or un-being, no life or death, no desires and no absence of desires. This region transcends all and it is called *Nrutef.* This is Asar (Asar), the transcendental Self from which all souls (seer-subject), all objects (seen) and the awareness of objects (sight-senses) arises from. Thus, having had this experience over larger and larger periods of time a human being discovers that he or she is that same transcendental, immortal, infinite, formless, objectless, genderless, etc. Supreme Self and thereby merges with his/her own nature. When this occurs a human being is said to have reached spiritual enlightenment or in Ancient Egyptian terminology, *Nehast,* or to have achieved "resurrection."

The Ancient Egyptian Path to Enlightenment
SPIRITUAL EXPERIENCES

Through the practices of mystical spirituality you will encounter many forms of experience. You will discover a growing peace within you as well as increased willpower and moral strength. In the beginning however, you may encounter pain and negative feelings. Some people blame their spiritual practices for causing them to become aware of their inner negativity, and then quit their practices. This is an immature and ignorant attitude. As you advance in your spiritual practices you will encounter feelings, and sometimes memories and thoughts which seem to arise out of nowhere. These thoughts cause you pain because they force you to face the untoward feelings you were not aware of that were buried (dormant) in your unconscious. Spiritual practice is not about escaping the world or your problems. It is the most effective way to face and transcend them.

If you persevere with faith you will discover that you are gradually cleansing your heart. You are purging the negativity away but this process occurs in its own time and it depends on the individual, because all people have had different experiences throughout many lifetimes. Therefore, your experiences in spiritual practice as well as in meditation will be unique.

As you progress in meditation you will dive deeper and deeper within yourself. You may have experiences with deities and these will appear to you in accordance with the nature of your religious faith. You may see lights. You may experience sensations you never thought possible. The possibilities are infinite.

The bodiless state is an important experience to achieve. It is important because it will, in no uncertain terms, give you a direct experience of your own essence beyond the physical body. This means that you are going beyond ordinary consciousness and this "going beyond" will engender a new feeling of expansion and inner awareness in a way that no book or instruction can. The spiritual experiences, such as the bodiless state, will allow you to seriously begin to understand that your physical self is only a part of your true Self. You will begin to experience the truth about which the Sages and Saints from time immemorial have spoken, that the body is evanescent while the Soul is immortal and eternal. Thus you will begin to discover your own immortality. However, there is one obstacle which stands in your way, FEAR.

If you progress in your spiritual practices you will encounter all manner of situations and experiences which, in the beginning, may frighten you. The bodiless state is one of these. This is the fear of letting go of the body and the familiar sensations of the body. It is due to the conditioning of your mind in which you have learned to identify yourself with your body as your "true Self". Body identification is the feeling that this is you and that when the body is no more, that you are no more. Of course this is an erroneous understanding which you begin to lose when you experience the bodiless state.

The way to overcome this fear is to maintain sustained practice and to move forward gradually. You should not rush into spiritual practices or various exercises without proper guidance and counseling. You should gradually allow yourself to integrate these experiences into your personality. Eventually you will come to enjoy the spiritual experiences, so much so that you may expect and even look forward to them. However you should not get caught up in these because they are just another form of experience, and all experiences are relative. Your true goal is to discover what lies beyond all experience while at the same time encompassing all experiences. This is the absolute, transcendental Supreme Self which is your innermost reality.

MEDITATION

Therefore, become the witness, Amun, and behold the majesty of the Self within as well as without.

A meditator and practitioner of the yogic lifestyle explained how the meditative lifestyle changed their ability to cope with the challenges of life:

"Before I began to practice meditation I would become angry very easily. I would sometimes start arguments with my family members and looking back on it, the reasons were because I could not get what I wanted. I expected them to act in certain ways and when they did not, I would become irritated. Now that I have practiced Yoga and Meditation for some time I have learned not to expect anything of others but to look at my own reasons for wanting the things I want. I realized that I was acting as a hypocrite and doing things because I wanted something from others. I have discovered that the things which I thought were so important are not more important than peace and harmony. The inner peace I have discovered is more important to me than trying to get others to act the way I want. I make an effort to work with others and I allow them space, but when things don't go my way I can still remain at peace. I would not trade this peace for all the money in the world..."

A meditator and practitioner of the yogic lifestyle described meditation experiences:

"I had been practicing formal meditation and reducing the tension and stress in my life for a year, and one day during meditation I experienced something wondrous, though frightening at first. After an hour or so I lost awareness of the surroundings and felt that I was lifting out of my body. The sensation was like no other. I felt as if I was being ripped away from my body. I suddenly realized that I was still me but not the body or the personality that was there meditating. It was just as the teachings describe, like the dream world but this had an important difference. I was aware of this new world and I was not caught up in it or lost in it like in a dream. At first it was frightening, the feeling of dropping away from my physical body which I was so accustomed to. After a short time I found myself in my body again and I felt as if a brand new world had opened up for me. Looking back, I realize now that over the past several years a similar feeling had been happening when I was asleep. The difference is that when this feeling would come over me I would wake up immediately out of fear. My Yoga counselor told me that this was my soul which had been trying to push me toward expansion in consciousness and spiritual enlightenment. Now that I have understood what is going on and have allowed the feeling to come whenever it is ready, the transition is natural from one state of consciousness to another, and I have even come to enjoy the experience deeply as I discover more about who I am. In a strange way, the bodiless state feels more natural and comfortable than the regular state. The regular state of everyday awareness seems almost alien to my true being. That is the best way that I can explain it in words..."

The Ancient Egyptian Path to Enlightenment

A meditator and practitioner of the yogic lifestyle described the following meditative experiences:

"One day as I practiced meditation I experienced something I can barely describe. I transcended normal body consciousness as I had done several times before, but this time I had a fantastic experience. I was in what I believe was the astral plane and I was aware of myself in my astral body, and I could see other beings carrying on various activities. In an instant I could feel a searing sensation in my head and I gave into it. I did not fight it. Then I felt myself falling to the ground of this astral world. I could hear the loudest sound I have ever heard, a bright light consuming all and then power beyond imagining. I felt a most powerful vibration coursing though me like a lightning strike and then I was that supreme power. I then began to dissolve into that essence and later found myself back in the physical body. Who am I? I know now that I am more than this mortal self. I am transcendental. Strangely, the more I experience this all-encompassing energy the more peaceful I feel and the more I feel connected to all things..."

A meditator and practitioner of the yogic lifestyle explained the mystical experience in the following manner:

"I had been practicing yoga and meditation for some time. One day I was reading as I usually do before bed time and all of a sudden, in a split second, I was transported into a transcendental form of awareness. I knew that there is only one consciousness that exists, mine. I discovered that all that exists depends on my consciousness. As I looked at the ceiling of the room I knew it was my creation, some form of projection which emanated from me. I knew that my consciousness is the same one which underlies and supports all other human beings. My soul is the same as the soul of every other human being. All at once I thought of my spouse and suddenly I knew that our consciousness, not our personalities, are one. I knew that this consciousness is distinct from the ego-personality of others, that it is their true inner self, their soul, of which even they are unaware, and that my Soul is one with every other soul! Immortality, I felt at once immortal, infinite, boundless.

These realizations came and the whole experience lasted only a few seconds. The actual experience of oneness seemed to occur in the first instant and then afterward my mind made sense of the meanings. For weeks afterward I felt a new feeling of kinship with others. I could somehow see myself in the place of others since I knew our consciousness is one. I understand this experience as a brief encounter of cosmic consciousness, a mystical experience. The experience was overwhelming, beyond anything else I have known before or since, and every aspect of my life has been transformed even though the memory has faded somewhat since that time. Somehow the memory has given way to a divine feeling or awareness which I cannot put into words. It is as if the Divine presence itself, the Supreme Being, the Self, is with me at all times. More and more it is as if I myself am that same Self, the innermost reality which I experienced. It is like losing myself and finding my greater Self. I am joyous, peaceful and more loving to my family, friends and even to strangers, though in a detached manner. I have discovered a deeper feeling for them than that which can be expressed in any physical way. I am often asked if I am some kind of minister or member of a religious order because my calmness and patience seem to make me stand out when ordinary people have become burdened with tension and stress. I feel exalted and full of goodwill towards all."

MEDITATION

Mystical experiences are like windows which open up for you through your spiritual efforts. They are events which the spirit uses to encourage you to move towards self-discovery. They are like confirmations of your inner discovery which allow you to believe that there is something beyond the mundane realities of life. Through your meditation practice you will have many experiences based on your religious education. This means that you may have experiences with Jesus or with Angels if you are Christian, Krishna if you are Hindu or Heru if you are Kemetic. If you do not have a specific affiliation your experience my be of a more abstract nature, not in the form of a deity or religious symbol. In any case you will begin to experience an expansion in your consciousness and you will eventually feel a oneness with the universe, bliss and a peace which you cannot understand or express with the rational mind. These experiences are not normal. They are supernormal glimpses into the Divine within you. They will not remain as the everyday forms of consciousness because if you were in that state all the time you would not be able to support the practical realities of life. They will fade as experiences of the conscious mind but their effect will remain as an unexplained feeling of Divine presence. You will be always aware of the Supreme Self which is with you at all times in your innermost heart. Also, you will begin to understand that that same Self is the same reality within everyone and everything, and thus, you will glorify every activity you engage in and revere the Divine in all human beings and in every speck of dust in the universe.

The entire philosophy of meditation brings up many important points. We have spoken about developing intuitional awareness or knowledge of the inner Self but what is intuitional knowledge like. Consider that there are two forms of knowledge. The first is indirect and the second is direct, through experience. However, some knowledge which is intuitional cannot be put into words. When you begin to gaze into the depths of your inner Self you will begin to discover intuitional realization. You will begin to "realize" the reality of your Higher Self. It may be likened to the knowledge which you have when you remember some feeling or understanding you had forgotten. Imagine if you could remember the knowledge you had, with clear insight. It is something that you "know" but cannot put into words or explain to anyone, but it is real. It may also be likened to remembering your identity when you wake up in the morning. During the dream you had certain situations and circumstances which seemed perfectly real and correct. You had a different personality, relations and circumstances in the dream but upon waking up you left all of that behind in favor of your waking identity.

The pains and sorrows of human life are due to misunderstanding, mental illusions and learned negative habits. If you reflect you will realize that even when something painful occurs in your life it is only painful as long as you remember it. Think about it. If you lost a loved one, or some other tragedy just transpired, you are not miserable one hundred percent (100%) of the time. You may forget for some time as you carry on the activities of life and then, all of a sudden, you remember what caused you grief. This means that the cause of pain as well as the cause of pleasure is in the mind and the way in which it responds to the situations of life. Meditation will lead you to have a transcendental outlook on life in which you transcend your ego existence and see it as you would an actor in a play. This detachment will allow you to see things objectively and not to be shaken by the adversities of life. Your true Self cannot be affected by the events which will occur to the body. Therefore, having transcended body consciousness through meditation, you will gaze on life with amusement and an internal sense of peace. This is a state in which the full enjoyment of life can be experienced. This is only possible when you see the world through the eyes of the Higher Self and not through the eyes of the Ego.

The Ancient Egyptian Path to Enlightenment

The intensity of spiritual experiences is much greater than those experiences at the physical plane. This is because the body acts as a safety valve in a manner of speaking. If there is too much pain the body faints or swoons. If there is too much elation the body also faints or swoons. When the mind and soul are freed from the body there is no such safety valve. Therefore, the experiences are more intense. This is why in the dream state the objects and situations seem as real as those in the day-to-day waking state even though there is less physicality in the dream. After the death of the physical body the soul continues to have experiences through the subtle body composed of the mind and body. The experiences are caused by the impressions lodged in the deep unconscious levels of mind. If the impressions are positive there will be positive experiences. These are sometimes referred to as heavenly conditions. If there are negative impressions then there will be hellish experiences generated. Thus, the soul of a person leads itself to have experiences of "punishment" or "reward" after death for the actions while alive on earth. This is all possible because all experiences, in the dream as well as in the waking state, are in reality mental experiences.

The body and senses are only instruments for perceiving objects. In the lower state of meditation where the relative spiritual experiences occur (astral plane) there is conscious awareness that the experiences are mental and have no reality of their own. Thus the meditator develops mental control and the soul discovers expansion and freedom while reducing fear and extremes of delusion which lead to intense relative experiences based on the triad of consciousness (subject, object and relationship between the two). When there is discovery of the Absolute Transcendental Self there is complete release of egoism and this release eradicates all possibility of experiencing intense relative emotions. In this sense, meditation is like a controlled exploration and cleansing process of the unconscious mind as well as of the after death experience. Also the intensity of emotions is an important factor which causes a person to believe in the reality of an experience.

"See that prosperity elate not thine heart above measure; neither adversity depress thine mind unto the depths, because fortune beareth hard against you. Their smiles are not stable, therefore build not thy confidence upon them; their frowns endure not forever, therefore let hope teach you patience."

-Ancient Egyptian Proverb

When you are dreaming, the dream seems intensely real but upon waking is is understood to be "unreal". This is why the spiritual scriptures admonish a spiritual aspirant to practice contentment, control of emotions and harmony in day-to-day activities in adverse situations as well as in prosperous situations. Harmony is practiced by keeping balance in all activities. So don't become upset and begin ranting and raving if a fly lands on your bowl of soup or if a television program was pre-empted or if you cannot go out to a party because you had to stay home and take care of your younger sibling, etc. Also don't become elated when there is some apparent gain in your life. See these as tests which are only temporary conditions to help you build endurance, patience, forbearance and inner strength. Some day your adverse conditions as well as your prosperous conditions will fade away. Therefore do not depend on these. Rather, seek inner peace and do not be shaken by the conditions of life whatever they may be. As you practice the principles of the meditative lifestyle you will generate and store new mental impressions of peace and harmony, and these lead to positive experiences in life on earth and in the afterlife.

MEDITATION

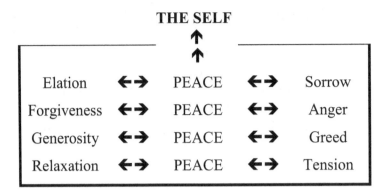

Those who lead agitated lives live in the realm of relativity and distraction born of the opposites. People are caught in the endless and enticing issues of right or wrong, you and me, male and female, here and there, and so on. Everything in creation exists in the form of opposites and in a human being these opposites create the need to constantly make choices. The main cause of human trouble is not understanding that all opposites emanate from oneness, the Self, and that since the innermost Self is the reality within, all that a person can ever want is already within them. The key to going beyond the opposites which agitate the mind and keep a human being involved in a futile search for fulfillment, is to discover inner peace. In Ancient Egypt this concept was called *Hetep,* Supreme Peace - Transcendence beyond the opposites of Creation. Peace transcends all opposites, and there is no peace like the peace which comes from spiritual realization through the meditative lifestyle. As you practice meditation and achieve success in leading a meditative lifestyle you will accomplish the task of developing new positive impressions in your mind. These impressions of peace, communion with spiritual beings (as described above) and Divine feeling will begin to replace the impressions of negativity (anger, hatred, jealousy, lust, greed, restlessness, loneliness, depression, etc.) You will discover fulfillment and inner happiness and your outer personality will be transformed in time. This is the process of spiritual enlightenment which occurs in degrees, and which can be yours as you practice concentration and meditation on the Divine.

May you discover the peace, bliss and joy of
Self-Discovery through the
path of Meditation.

Index

Ab, 159
Abdu, 44, 72
Abhyasa, 124
Absolute, 18, 35, 58, 67, 99, 101, 119, 133, 157, 162, 165, 172, 174, 181, 191
Absolute XE "Absolute" Reality, 67
Africa, 13, 16, 21, 22, 32, 54, 94, 185
Air, 77
Akhenaton, 14, 20
Akhnaton, 45
Akhus, 48
Amen, 149, 157
Amenta, 77, 114, 210
Amentet, 213
Amma, 219, 221
Amun, 14, 19, 20, 22, 24, 30, 34, 39, 42, 77, 125, 149, 155, 157, 158, 160, 165, 187, 204, 219, 221
Amunhotep, 154
Amun-Ra-Ptah, 125, 158, 160, 204, 221
Ancient Egypt, 1, 2, 3, 4, 10, 11, 13, 14, 16, 17, 20, 21, 22, 24, 32, 33, 35, 36, 49, 51, 52, 53, 54, 55, 56, 57, 58, 62, 63, 68, 71, 72, 73, 74, 77, 90, 94, 95, 99, 101, 103, 106, 109, 111, 112, 115, 116, 117, 120, 121, 122, 124, 125, 128, 131, 134, 136, 137, 138, 139, 144, 145, 148, 149, 154, 155, 156, 157, 159, 160, 165, 166, 170, 172, 173, 174, 176, 179, 180, 185, 186, 191, 192, 197, 200, 201, 203, 204, 205, 206, 207, 208, 209, 210, 211, 212, 214, 215, 216, 217, 218, 219, 221, 222, 223, 224, 225
Ancient Egyptian Wisdom Texts, 128, 134, 219
Ancient mystical philosophy, 182
Angels, 190
Anger, 192
Ankh, 52, 148
Anu, 30, 39, 40, 212
Anu (Greek Heliopolis), 14, 30, 39, 40, 134, 212
Anubis, 24, 135
Anunian Theology, 34, 37, 40
Apep serpent, 47
Apophis, 47
Ari, 30
Arjuna, 113, 124
Aryan, 203
Asar, 14, 19, 21, 22, 24, 30, 34, 39, 40, 44, 53, 54, 55, 68, 69, 70, 72, 77, 110, 112, 114, 132, 135, 159, 165, 186, 214, 215, 219, 221, 224, 225
Asarian Resurrection, 34, 62, 214, 216
Aset, 14, 19, 22, 24, 34, 40, 43, 44, 53, 55, 57, 58, 68, 69, 72, 94, 99, 112, 113, 120, 135, 145, 148, 159, 165, 213, 214, 215, 218, 219, 221, 224
Aset (Isis), 34, 40, 43, 44, 53, 55, 57, 58, 68, 213, 214, 215
Asia, 54, 67
Asia Minor, 20, 123
Asiatic, 122, 123
Aspirant, 120, 218
Assyrians, 20
Astral, 64, 77, 84, 86, 210
Astral Plane, 64, 210
Aton, 14, 30, 39, 45
Atonism, 45
Augustus, 21
Awareness, 102, 121
Ba (also see Soul), 69, 73, 159, 165, 166, 174
Balance, 120
Being, 11, 18, 22, 29, 31, 35, 36, 37, 39, 49, 54, 69, 112, 115, 134, 135, 136, 148
Bhagavad Gita, 49, 113, 115
Bible, 214, 218
Big Bang, 22
Bindu (see also Black Dot), 139
Black, 114
Book of Coming Forth By Day, 19, 120, 128, 173, 176, 211, 218
Book of Enlightenment, 73
Book of the Dead, see also Rau Nu Prt M Hru, 34, 38, 211
Brahman, 58, 77, 99, 157, 165
Buddha, 69, 103, 148
Buddhist, 69, 103, 141, 148
Caduceus, 165, 166
Carl Jung, 102
Catholic, 214
Chanting, 58, 155, 219, 221
Chi, 146, 152
Chi Kung, 146
China, 51, 67, 106, 125
Christian Yoga, 219
Christianity, 55, 77, 148, 149, 157, 201, 214
Church, 214, 219
Civilization, 51
Coffin Texts, 34
Company of gods and goddesses, 134
Concentration, 127, 128, 129, 133, 134, 157, 186, 218, 219
Conception, 68
Consciousness, 21, 50, 54, 55, 95, 100, 102, 112, 115, 116, 125, 127, 133, 162, 177, 218
Contentment (see also Hetep), 8, 32, 130, 131
Coptic, 33, 210
Cosmic consciousness, 49
Cosmogony, 134
Cosmos, 67
Cow, 43
Creation, 18, 32, 34, 35, 38, 40, 41, 42, 43, 44, 45, 55, 64, 67, 68, 69, 106, 109, 112, 123, 134, 138, 139, 180, 192, 204, 209, 212, 219
Crete, 67
Culture, 32, 203, 208, 216
Cymbals, 223, 225
Death, 218
December, 213
Denderah, 210
Detachment, 197
Dharmakaya, 69
Diet, 145, 146, 202
Diodorus, 21, 23
Discipline, 4, 57, 60
Divine Consciousness, 48
Djehuti, 19, 24, 53, 55, 109, 111, 112, 113, 114, 115, 120, 135, 137, 138, 139, 165, 166, 186, 197, 218
Dream, 100
Duality, 178
Dynastic period, 19
Earth, 116
Eastern religions, 106
Edfu, 44, 59, 210
Egoism, 47, 218
Egyptian Book of Coming Forth By Day, 19, 95, 113, 114, 210
Egyptian civilization, 56
Egyptian magic, 157
Egyptian Mysteries, 55, 203
Egyptian Physics, 212
Egyptian proverbs, 53, 206
Egyptian religion, 21, 54
Egyptian Yoga, 4, 21, 25, 42, 49, 51, 52, 53, 54, 55, 63, 70, 95, 121, 128, 144, 200, 201, 203, 204, 209, 210, 218, 219, 221, 222, 223, 224, 225
Egyptian Yoga see also Kamitan Yoga, 42, 49, 51, 52, 53, 54, 55, 63, 70, 201, 203, 204, 209, 210
Egyptologists, 47, 54
Enlightened Sages, 8
Enlightenment, 2, 8, 21, 32, 46, 50, 54, 55, 73, 81, 85, 96, 125, 128, 133, 164, 174, 176, 203, 204, 205, 206, 207, 217, 219

Ennead, 135
Ethics, 59
Ethiopia, 16, 21, 22, 23
Ethiopian priests, 21
Eucharist, 210
Eudoxus, 216
Evil, 106, 109, 172
Exercise, 96, 150, 151, 209, 219, 221
Eye of Heru, 48, 113, 114, 149, 172, 186
Eye of Ra, 109, 115, 172
Fear, 219
Feuerstein, Georg, 62, 63
Forgiveness, 192
Geb, 24, 40, 62, 63, 68, 69, 106, 135, 209
Gnostic, 113
Gnostic Christianity, 113
God, 31, 32, 35, 48, 49, 53, 54, 55, 56, 58, 60, 67, 68, 73, 77, 102, 106, 108, 109, 114, 115, 116, 120, 121, 130, 131, 132, 134, 136, 137, 139, 147, 148, 151, 155, 157, 159, 160, 161, 172, 205, 211, 212, 221, 225
Goddess, 19, 30, 34, 35, 39, 43, 68, 137, 170, 213, 222, 225
Goddesses, 29, 35, 40, 42, 43, 64, 134, 209
Gods, 21, 29, 35, 40, 42, 64, 114, 134, 221
Good, 8, 218
Good Association, 8, 218
Gospels, 214
Great Truths, 29, 30, 31
Greece, 23, 51, 203, 216
Greed, 192
Greek philosophy, 201
Greeks, 20, 216
Grimaldi, 22
Guru, 112, 113
Harmony, 120, 191
Hatha Yoga, 62, 63
Hathor, 19, 24, 135, 209, 210, 213, 217
Health, 106, 174, 201, 218, 219
Hearing, 186
Heart, 30, 215
Heart (also see Ab, mind, conscience), 30, 215
Heaven, 78, 116, 161
Hekau, 73, 96, 113, 122, 146, 149, 150, 155, 156, 158, 162, 219, 225
Heliopolis, 216
Hell, 78
Hermes, 24, 166
Hermes (see also Tehuti, Thoth), 24, 166
Herodotus, 23
Heru, 14, 18, 19, 22, 24, 34, 37, 40, 44, 51, 53, 55, 59, 63, 68, 69, 94, 112, 113, 114, 120, 122, 123, 135, 148, 159, 186, 190, 210, 211, 213, 214, 215, 218, 219, 221, 224, 225
Heru (see Horus), 14, 18, 19, 22, 24, 34, 37, 40, 44, 51, 53, 55, 59, 63, 68, 69, 94, 112, 113, 114, 120, 122, 123, 135, 148, 159, 186, 190, 210, 211, 213, 214, 215, 218, 219, 221, 224, 225
Hetep, 52, 146, 192
Hetheru, 14, 19, 24, 34, 37, 43, 53, 55, 62, 63, 107, 108, 109, 111, 114, 115, 116, 119, 120, 121, 135, 137, 138, 173, 186, 197, 217, 223
Hetheru (Hetheru, Hathor), 34, 37, 43, 53, 55, 62, 63, 217
Het-Ka-Ptah, see also Men-nefer, Memphis, 37
Hidden God, 157
Hieroglyphic Writing, language, 207
Hindu, 73, 124, 148, 190
Hinduism, 113, 157
Horus, 18, 19, 24, 34, 44, 68, 69, 224
Hymns of Amun, 22, 125
Ibis, 109, 139
Ice Age, 22
Identification, 50, 95, 172, 173
Illusion, 219
India, 23, 49, 51, 54, 57, 58, 62, 63, 67, 69, 71, 94, 99, 103, 106, 115, 122, 125, 149, 155, 157, 165, 185, 203, 207, 221, 224
Indian Yoga, 49, 120, 139, 155, 185, 200, 203, 225
Indus, 51, 203, 218, 221
Indus Valley, 51, 203
Initiate, 202
Isis, 19, 24, 34, 43, 44, 57, 58, 68, 69, 209, 210, 213, 224
Isis, See also Aset, 43, 44, 57, 58, 68, 69, 209, 210, 213
Islam, 201
Japa, 155
Jesus, 113, 120, 148, 161, 190, 210, 214
Jesus Christ, 210
Jewish, 11
Jnana Yoga, 57, 58, 99
John the Baptist, 120
Joy, 32, 123
Judaism, 201
Jyotirmayananda, Swami, 73
Ka, 37
Kabbalah, 201
Kali, 69
Kali XE "Kali" position, 69
Kali Position, 69
Kamit, 11, 13, 16, 24, 29, 32, 35, 36, 43, 44, 218, 221
Kamit (Egypt), 11, 13, 16, 24, 29, 32, 35, 36, 43, 44, 218, 221
Kamitan, 29, 33, 34, 35, 37, 46, 50, 60, 63, 65, 68, 69, 137, 203, 213, 216
Karma, 23, 50, 88, 94, 207, 219
Kemetic, 18, 24, 65, 68, 69, 156, 157, 190, 222, 224, 225
Khepra, 219
Khepri, 173, 185
Kingdom, 22, 55, 63, 160, 161, 165, 214
Kingdom of Heaven, 165, 214
Kingdom of the Father, 161
KMT (Ancient Egypt). See also Kamit, 22
Know thyself, 46
Know Thyself, 52
Krishna, 113, 120, 124, 148, 157, 165, 190, 214
Kundalini, 4, 23, 50, 69, 152, 158, 165
Kush, 16, 218, 221
Lake Victoria, 22
Liberation, 181
Life Force, 23, 30, 53, 130, 152, 163, 165, 166, 208
Listening, 30, 39, 57, 58, 60, 96, 99, 120, 151, 218
Lotus, 2, 53, 147, 219
Love, 3, 49, 50, 60, 95, 96, 149, 206, 218
Lower Egypt, 19, 51, 53, 123
Maakheru, 29
Maat, 11, 24, 29, 30, 34, 50, 59, 96, 106, 135, 186, 207, 213, 215, 216, 218, 219, 220, 221
MAAT, 19, 94, 95, 114, 120, 122, 127, 131, 132, 152, 205, 207
MAATI, 206
Magic, 109, 113
Mahabharata, 49
Manetho, 23
Mantras, 73, 157
Matter, 212
Meditating, 57
Meditation, 2, 30, 31, 43, 49, 50, 58, 59, 71, 72, 73, 74, 77, 80, 85, 86, 96, 97, 99, 100, 102, 103, 104, 105, 106, 111, 126, 127, 133, 134, 139, 140, 146, 150, 151, 154, 162, 163, 165, 171, 172, 175, 182, 184, 186, 188, 190, 192, 197, 199, 202, 205, 208, 218, 219, 221, 225
Mediterranean, 67
Mehurt, 43
Memphis, 216
Memphite Theology, 19, 34, 41, 43
Mental health, 174
Merikara, 121
Meskhenet, 133
Metaphysics, 212
Metu Neter, 53, 56, 112
Middle East, 201
Min, 209
Mind, 82, 84, 86, 87, 113, 126, 176

The Ancient Egyptian Path to Enlightenment

Mindfulness, 103, 125
Miserable Asiatic, 123
Moksha, 157
Mookerjee, Ajit, 67
Moon, 22, 109, 113
Morals, 216
Music, 149, 224, 225
Mysteries, 43, 55, 160, 213
Mystical experience, 190
Mysticism, 54, 60, 203, 210, 211, 212, 217
Mythology, 21, 54, 136, 138, 210
Nature, 33, 102, 146, 218, 219
Neberdjer, 29, 135, 204
Nebertcher, 125, 136, 158, 160
Nebthet, 40
Nefer, 52, 110, 223, 225
Nefertari, Queen, 63
Nefertem, 41
Nehast, 48, 186
Neolithic, 18
Nephthys, 24
Net, goddess, 34, 43
Neter, 11, 12, 13, 21, 29, 30, 32, 33, 34, 35, 36, 37, 39, 45, 48, 49, 53, 54, 56, 77, 94, 162, 219, 221
Neterian, 29, 30, 37, 39, 43, 47, 48
Neterianism, 30, 35
Neters, 54, 56, 67, 135
Neteru, 29, 31, 33, 35, 36, 37, 47, 48, 63, 67, 77, 137, 209, 221, 223, 224, 225
Netherworld, 64
New Kingdom, 42, 45, 63
Nile River, 32
Nirvana, 181
Non-violence, 220

North East Africa . See also Egypt Ethiopia Cush, 13

Nubia, 11, 16, 22, 109
Nubian, 16, 20, 110
Nubians, 32
Nun, 37, 64
Nun (primeval waters-unformed matter), 37, 64
Nun (See also Nu), 37, 64
Nut, 24, 40, 63, 64, 68, 69, 106, 108, 135, 209
Om, 149, 155, 157, 159, 160, 219, 221, 224, 225
Opposites, 19
Orion Star Constellation, 213
Osiris, 14, 24, 34, 43, 44, 68, 69, 209, 210, 224, 225
Pa Neter, 29, 219, 221
Pain, 123
Paleolithic, 18
Papyrus of Any, 34
Patanjali, 49, 185
Patience, 146
Paut, 63

Peace (see also Hetep), 32, 98, 146, 174, 192
Pert Em Heru, See also Book of the Dead, 53, 211
Philae, 14, 72, 210
Philosophy, 3, 4, 11, 12, 13, 20, 21, 24, 31, 34, 51, 52, 53, 55, 56, 67, 73, 77, 102, 103, 122, 203, 204, 205, 211, 212, 215, 218, 219
Plato, 131, 216
Plutarch, 216
Priests and Priestesses, 36, 203
Ptah, 14, 19, 24, 30, 34, 37, 39, 41, 113, 125, 155, 158, 160, 186, 212, 219, 221

PTAH, 212

Ptahotep, 2, 19, 34
Pyramid of Unas, 114
Pyramid Texts, 14, 19, 23
Pythagoras, 216
Queen of the Gods, 114
Ra, 14, 18, 24, 30, 34, 39, 40, 42, 47, 64, 73, 106, 107, 108, 109, 112, 115, 116, 119, 121, 125, 135, 139, 152, 155, 158, 160, 165, 166, 172, 173, 185, 209, 218, 219, 221, 223, 225
Rama, 113, 120, 148
Reality, 67, 162
Realization, 31
Realm of Light, 18
Reflecting, 57
Reflection, 58, 96, 99, 123, 150
Reincarnation, 88, 94
Religion, 4, 11, 12, 13, 18, 21, 33, 48, 53, 54, 55, 95, 210, 214, 215, 216, 218, 219, 224
Resurrection, 19, 34, 62, 81, 115, 120, 173, 181, 209, 210, 214, 215, 218
Righteous action, 30
Righteousness, 59
Ritual, 30, 34, 50, 60
Rituals, 146
Roman, 34
Romans, 20
Rome, 216
Saa (spiritual understanding faculty), 94, 186
Sages, 55, 96, 112, 115, 121, 128, 165, 187, 204, 210, 211, 215
Saints, 121, 128, 187, 211
Sais, 216
Salvation, 53, 54, 56
Salvation . See also resurrection, 53, 54, 56
Salvation, See also resurrection, 53, 54, 56
Samadhi (see also KiaSatori), 185
Sanskrit, 51, 157
Saraswati, 148
Sebai, 45
Sekhem, 30, 130, 159, 166
Sekhmet, 19

Self (see Ba, soul, Spirit, Universal, Ba, Neter, Heru)., 30, 47, 50, 51, 52, 53, 54, 55, 56, 57, 58, 59, 63, 68, 203, 207, 210
Self (seeBasoulSpiritUniversal BaNeterHorus)., 2, 8, 9, 30, 50, 51, 52, 53, 54, 55, 56, 57, 58, 59, 63, 68, 71, 74, 77, 85, 86, 87, 88, 94, 95, 96, 97, 98, 99, 101, 103, 109, 111, 112, 113, 116, 117, 119, 121, 122, 125, 127, 129, 131, 133, 134, 136, 139, 140, 141, 146, 148, 149, 155, 156, 157, 159, 160, 161, 165, 171, 172, 173, 176, 178, 179, 181, 182, 183, 184, 185, 186, 187, 189, 190, 192, 197, 199, 219
Selfless service, 151
Self-realization, 113
Sema, 2, 3, 4, 29, 30, 51, 52, 53, 54, 57, 59, 60, 63, 67, 71, 200, 219
Sema XE "Sema" Paut, see also Egyptian Yoga, 30, 63
Semite, 22
Senses, 86, 185
Serpent, 18, 49, 50, 72, 96, 163, 165, 166, 168, 170, 219, 221
Serpent Power, 18, 49, 50, 72, 96, 163, 165, 166, 168, 170, 219, 221
Serpent Power (see also Kundalini and Buto), 18, 49, 50, 72, 96, 163, 165, 166, 168, 170, 219, 221
Serpent Power see also Kundalini Yoga, 49, 50, 72
Set, 24, 29, 40, 47, 51, 53, 55, 112, 113, 114, 123, 135, 159, 219
Seti I, 59, 72
Sex, 22, 209
Sexuality, 219
Shakti (see also Kundalini), 69
Shetaut Neter, 32, 34, 39, 46, 49, 54, 210
Shetaut Neter See also Egyptian Religion, 11, 12, 13, 21, 32, 34, 39, 46, 49, 54, 95, 137, 142, 210
Shiva, 69, 70, 149
Shiva XE "Shiva" and Shakti, 69
Shu (air and space), 40, 64, 106, 108, 110, 135
Silence, 96, 150, 151, 219
Sirius, 19, 213
Sky, 18
Slave Trade, 118
Sleep, 100
Sma, 30, 51
Smai, 29, 49, 51, 52, 53, 63
Smai Tawi, 49, 51, 52, 63
Solon, 216
Soul, 9, 21, 53, 56, 77, 84, 86, 87, 88, 103, 111, 116, 122, 142, 145, 148, 159, 162, 174, 187, 189, 219
Sphinx, 11, 18, 56
Spinal twist, 64

Spirit, 11, 18, 29, 37, 53, 73, 115, 122
Spiritual discipline, 202
Study, 30, 55, 96, 150, 151, 218, 219
Sublimation, 209
Sudan, 13, 16
Sufi, 120
Sumer, 51
Sun, 125
Sundisk, 64, 73, 172
Supreme Being, 11, 22, 29, 31, 35, 36, 37, 39, 40, 41, 42, 43, 44, 45, 49, 54, 69, 95, 112, 113, 115, 121, 134, 135, 136, 148, 157, 172, 173, 189, 204, 213
Swami, 4, 73, 155, 157
Swami Jyotirmayananda, 4, 73
Tantra, 67, 115, 209
Tantra Yoga, 67, 72, 115, 209
Tantric Yoga, 49, 50, 95, 96
Tanzania, 22
Tao, 165
Taoism, 125, 201
Tawi, 29, 49, 52, 63
Tefnut, 40, 106, 110, 135
Tefnut (moisture), 40, 106, 110, 135
Tem, 135
Temple of Aset, 44, 57, 58, 72
Thales, 216
The Absolute, 113, 160, 204
The Bhagavad Gita, 124
The God, 19, 40, 43, 114, 138, 209, 221
The Gods, 19, 40, 209, 221
The Hymns of Amun, 22
The Pyramid Texts, 23
The Self, 77, 85, 86, 87, 89, 134, 146, 148, 177, 180
The way, 187

Theban Theology, 19, 34
Thebes, 14, 72, 204, 208
Themis, 24
Thoughts (see also Mind), 59, 176, 177
Time, 218
Tomb, 63, 73, 74, 208
Tomb of Seti I, 73, 74, 208, 225
Tradition, 30, 39, 40, 41, 42, 43, 44, 45
Transcendental Self, 191
Triad, 125, 204
Trilinga, 70
Trinity, 14, 19, 41, 42, 44, 125, 134, 159, 160, 204, 210, 221, 225
Truth, 31, 220
Unas, 114
Understanding, 218
Universal Ba, 86
Universal Consciousness, 54, 55, 209
Upanishads, 115, 120, 211
Upper Egypt, 51, 53
Ur, 40
Uraeus, 50, 109, 149, 158, 163, 166, 171, 172
Utchat, 114
Vedanta, 54, 55, 57, 58, 73, 77, 103, 125, 142
Vedantic. See also Vedanta, 113, 148, 160
Vedic, 203
Virtues, 218
Vishnu, 157
Waking, 100, 197
Waset, 30, 39, 72, 204
Water, 146
Western Culture, 47
White, 114
Will, 96, 97, 122, 148

Wisdom, 30, 31, 34, 49, 50, 57, 58, 72, 204, 205, 208
WISDOM (ALSO SEE DJEHUTI), 19, 30, 31, 34, 49, 50, 57, 58, 59, 60, 67, 72, 97, 99, 139, 148, 165, 186, 218, 219
Wisdom (also see Djehuti, Aset), 30, 31, 34, 49, 50, 57, 58, 72, 204, 205, 208
Wisdom teachings, 57, 58, 99
Words of power, 73, 156, 173
Yoga, 2, 3, 4, 9, 11, 12, 21, 25, 49, 50, 51, 52, 53, 54, 55, 57, 58, 62, 63, 67, 70, 72, 73, 77, 87, 95, 96, 97, 99, 101, 102, 103, 106, 112, 113, 115, 119, 120, 122, 124, 125, 128, 133, 142, 146, 149, 150, 155, 165, 166, 173, 174, 182, 184, 185, 186, 188, 200, 201, 202, 203, 207, 209, 211, 212, 215, 218, 219, 221, 222, 223, 224, 225
Yoga Exercise, 219, 221
Yoga of Action, 50, 95, 96
Yoga of Devotion (see Yoga of Divine Love), 49, 50, 95, 96, 173
Yoga of Divine Love (see Yoga of Devotion), 50, 96
Yoga of Meditation, 49, 50, 95, 96, 149, 186
Yoga of Selfless Action. See also Yoga of Righteous, 49, 50, 95
Yoga of Wisdom, 57
Yoga of Wisdom (see also Jnana Yoga), 49, 50, 57, 59, 60, 67, 95, 96, 99
Yoga Sutra, 49
Yoga Vasistha, 113, 115
Yogic, 49, 62, 122, 124

The Ancient Egyptian Path to Enlightenment

Audio Seminar Workshop Series
Presentation of
The Glorious Light Meditation System

Glorious Light Meditation System of Ancient Egypt

Meditation Lectures Series and Technique Directly Based on Ancient Egyptian Scriptures:

6001A Introduction to the Glorious Light Meditation Part 1
6001B Introduction to the Glorious Light Meditation Part 2
6002A Insights into the practice of Meditation Part 1
6002B Insights into the practice of Meditation Part 2
6003 Insights into the myth of Hetheru and Djehuti
6004 Insights into the myth of Hetheru and Djehuti
6005A The Steps of the Glorious Light Meditation Technique Part 1
6005B The Steps of the Glorious Light Meditation Technique Part 2
6005C The Steps of the Glorious Light Meditation Technique Part 3
6006A Waking Up to the Higher Self Through Detachment Part 1
6006B Waking Up to the Higher Self Through Detachment Part 2
6006C Waking Up to the Higher Self Through Detachment Part 3
6007A Glorious Light Meditation Session
6007B Glorious Light Meditation Session Q and A

6100 Glorious Light Meditation Session 1/30/00

Available Through
Cruzian Mystic Books
305-378-6253

MEDITATION

Other Books From C M Books
P.O.Box 570459
Miami, Florida, 33257
(305) 378-6253 Fax: (305) 378-6253

This book is part of a series on the study and practice of Ancient Egyptian Yoga and Mystical Spirituality based on the writings of Dr. Muata Abhaya Ashby. They are also part of the Egyptian Yoga Course provided by the Sema Institute of Yoga. Below you will find a listing of the other books in this series. For more information send for the Egyptian Yoga Book-Audio-Video Catalog or the Egyptian Yoga Course Catalog.

Now you can study the teachings of Egyptian and Indian Yoga wisdom and Spirituality with the Egyptian Yoga Mystical Spirituality Series. The Egyptian Yoga Series takes you through the Initiation process and lead you to understand the mysteries of the soul and the Divine and to attain the highest goal of life: ENLIGHTENMENT. The *Egyptian Yoga Series*, takes you on an in depth study of Ancient Egyptian mythology and their inner mystical meaning. Each Book is prepared for the serious student of the mystical sciences and provides a study of the teachings along with exercises, assignments and projects to make the teachings understood and effective in real life. The Series is part of the Egyptian Yoga course but may be purchased even if you are not taking the course. The series is ideal for study groups.

Prices subject to change.

The Ancient Egyptian Path to Enlightenment

1. EGYPTIAN YOGA: THE PHILOSOPHY OF ENLIGHTENMENT An original, fully illustrated work, including hieroglyphs, detailing the meaning of the Egyptian mysteries, tantric yoga, psycho-spiritual and physical exercises. Egyptian Yoga is a guide to the practice of the highest spiritual philosophy which leads to absolute freedom from human misery and to immortality. It is well known by scholars that Egyptian philosophy is the basis of Western and Middle Eastern religious philosophies such as *Christianity, Islam, Judaism,* the *Kabala,* and Greek philosophy, but what about Indian philosophy, Yoga and Taoism? What were the original teachings? How can they be practiced today? What is the source of pain and suffering in the world and what is the solution? Discover the deepest mysteries of the mind and universe within and outside of your self. 8.5" X 11" ISBN: 1-884564-01-1 Soft $19.95

2. EGYPTIAN YOGA II: The Supreme Wisdom of Enlightenment by Dr. Muata Ashby ISBN 1-884564-39-9 $23.95 U.S. In this long awaited sequel to *Egyptian Yoga: The Philosophy of Enlightenment* you will take a fascinating and enlightening journey back in time and discover the teachings which constituted the epitome of Ancient Egyptian spiritual wisdom. What are the disciplines which lead to the fulfillment of all desires? Delve into the three states of consciousness (waking, dream and deep sleep) and the fourth state which transcends them all, Neberdjer, "The Absolute." These teachings of the city of Waset (Thebes) were the crowning achievement of the Sages of Ancient Egypt. They establish the standard mystical keys for understanding the profound mystical symbolism of the Triad of human consciousness.

3. THE KEMETIC DIET: GUIDE TO HEALTH, DIET AND FASTING Health issues have always been important to human beings since the beginning of time. The earliest records of history show that the art of healing was held in high esteem since the time of Ancient Egypt. In the early 20th century, medical doctors had almost attained the status of sainthood by the promotion of the idea that they alone were "scientists" while other healing modalities and traditional healers who did not follow the "scientific method' were nothing but superstitious, ignorant charlatans who at best would take the money of their clients and at worst kill them with the unscientific "snake oils" and "irrational theories". In the late 20th century, the failure of the modern medical establishment's ability to lead the general public to good health, promoted the move by many in society towards "alternative medicine". Alternative medicine disciplines are those healing modalities which do not adhere to the philosophy of allopathic medicine. Allopathic medicine is what medical doctors practice by an large. It is the theory that disease is caused by agencies outside the body such as bacteria, viruses or physical means which affect the body. These can therefore be treated by medicines and therapies The natural healing method began in the absence of extensive technologies with the idea that all the answers for health may be found in nature or rather, the deviation from nature. Therefore, the health of the body can be restored by correcting the aberration and thereby restoring balance. This is the area that will be covered in this volume. Allopathic techniques have their place in the art of healing. However, we should not forget that the body is a grand achievement of the spirit and built into it is the capacity to maintain itself and heal itself. Ashby, Muata ISBN: 1-884564-49-6 $28.95

4. INITIATION INTO EGYPTIAN YOGA Shedy: Spiritual discipline or program, to go deeply into the mysteries, to study the mystery teachings and literature profoundly, to penetrate the mysteries. You will learn about the mysteries of initiation into the teachings and practice of Yoga and how to become an Initiate of the mystical sciences. This insightful manual is the first in a series which introduces you to the goals of daily spiritual and yoga practices: Meditation, Diet, Words of Power and the ancient wisdom teachings. 8.5" X 11" ISBN 1-884564-02-X   Soft Cover $24.95 U.S.

5. *THE AFRICAN ORIGINS OF CIVILIZATION, MYSTICAL RELIGION AND YOGA PHILOSOPHY* HARD COVER EDITION ISBN: 1-884564-50-X $80.00 U.S.   81/2" X 11" Part 1, Part 2, Part 3 in one volume 683 Pages Hard Cover First Edition Three volumes in one. Over the past several years I have been asked to put together in one volume the most important evidences showing the correlations and common teachings between Kamitan (Ancient Egyptian) culture and religion and that of India. The questions of the history of Ancient Egypt, and the latest archeological evidences showing civilization and culture in Ancient Egypt and its spread to other countries, has intrigued many scholars as well as mystics over the years. Also, the possibility that Ancient Egyptian Priests and Priestesses migrated to Greece, India and other countries to carry on the traditions of the Ancient Egyptian Mysteries, has been speculated over the years as well. In chapter 1 of the book *Egyptian Yoga The Philosophy of Enlightenment,* 1995, I first introduced the deepest

MEDITATION

comparison between Ancient Egypt and India that had been brought forth up to that time. Now, in the year 2001 this new book, *THE AFRICAN ORIGINS OF CIVILIZATION, MYSTICAL RELIGION AND YOGA PHILOSOPHY,* more fully explores the motifs, symbols and philosophical correlations between Ancient Egyptian and Indian mysticism and clearly shows not only that Ancient Egypt and India were connected culturally but also spiritually. How does this knowledge help the spiritual aspirant? This discovery has great importance for the Yogis and mystics who follow the philosophy of Ancient Egypt and the mysticism of India. It means that India has a longer history and heritage than was previously understood. It shows that the mysteries of Ancient Egypt were essentially a yoga tradition which did not die but rather developed into the modern day systems of Yoga technology of India. It further shows that African culture developed Yoga Mysticism earlier than any other civilization in history. All of this expands our understanding of the unity of culture and the deep legacy of Yoga, which stretches into the distant past, beyond the Indus Valley civilization, the earliest known high culture in India as well as the Vedic tradition of Aryan culture. Therefore, Yoga culture and mysticism is the oldest known tradition of spiritual development and Indian mysticism is an extension of the Ancient Egyptian mysticism. By understanding the legacy which Ancient Egypt gave to India the mysticism of India is better understood and by comprehending the heritage of Indian Yoga, which is rooted in Ancient Egypt the Mysticism of Ancient Egypt is also better understood. This expanded understanding allows us to prove the underlying kinship of humanity, through the common symbols, motifs and philosophies which are not disparate and confusing teachings but in reality expressions of the same study of truth through metaphysics and mystical realization of Self. (HARD COVER)

6. AFRICAN ORIGINS BOOK 1 PART 1 African Origins of African Civilization, Religion, Yoga Mysticism and Ethics Philosophy-Soft Cover $24.95 ISBN: 1-884564-55-0

7. AFRICAN ORIGINS BOOK 2 PART 2 African Origins of Western Civilization, Religion and Philosophy(Soft) -Soft Cover $24.95 ISBN: 1-884564-56-9

8. EGYPT AND INDIA (AFRICAN ORIGINS BOOK 3 PART 3) African Origins of Eastern Civilization, Religion, Yoga Mysticism and Philosophy-Soft Cover $29.95 (Soft) ISBN: 1-884564-57-7

9. THE MYSTERIES OF ISIS: The Path of Wisdom, Immortality and Enlightenment   Through the study of ancient myth and the illumination of initiatic understanding the idea of God is expanded from the mythological comprehension to the metaphysical. Then this metaphysical understanding is related to you, the student, so as to begin understanding your true divine nature. ISBN 1-884564-24-0 $24.99

10. EGYPTIAN PROVERBS: TEMT TCHAAS *Temt Tchaas* means: collection of ——Ancient Egyptian Proverbs How to live according to MAAT Philosophy. Beginning Meditation. All proverbs are indexed for easy searches. For the first time in one volume, ——Ancient Egyptian Proverbs, wisdom teachings and meditations, fully illustrated with hieroglyphic text and symbols. EGYPTIAN PROVERBS is a unique collection of knowledge and wisdom which you can put into practice today and transform your life. 5.5"x 8.5" $14.95 U.S   ISBN: 1-884564-00-3

11. THE PATH OF DIVINE LOVE The Process of Mystical Transformation and The Path of Divine Love This Volume will focus on the ancient wisdom teachings and how to use them in a scientific process for self-transformation. Also, this volume will detail the process of transformation from ordinary consciousness to cosmic consciousness through the integrated practice of the teachings and the path of Devotional Love toward the Divine. 5.5"x 8.5" ISBN 1-884564-11-9 $22.99

12. INTRODUCTION TO MAAT PHILOSOPHY: Spiritual Enlightenment Through the Path of Virtue Known as Karma Yoga in India, the teachings of MAAT for living virtuously and with orderly wisdom are explained and the student is to begin practicing the precepts of Maat in daily life so as to promote the process of purification of the heart in preparation for the judgment of the soul. This judgment will be understood not as an event that will occur at the time of death but as an event that occurs continuously, at every moment in the life of the individual. The student will learn how to become allied with the forces of the Higher Self and to thereby begin cleansing the mind (heart) of impurities so as to attain a higher vision of reality. ISBN 1-884564-20-8 $22.99

The Ancient Egyptian Path to Enlightenment

13. MEDITATION The Ancient Egyptian Path to Enlightenment   Many people do not know about the rich history of meditation practice in Ancient Egypt. This volume outlines the theory of meditation and presents the Ancient Egyptian Hieroglyphic text which give instruction as to the nature of the mind and its three modes of expression. It also presents the texts which give instruction on the practice of meditation for spiritual Enlightenment and unity with the Divine. This volume allows the reader to begin practicing meditation by explaining, in easy to understand terms, the simplest form of meditation and working up to the most advanced form which was practiced in ancient times and which is still practiced by yogis around the world in modern times. ISBN 1-884564-27-7 $24.99

14. THE GLORIOUS LIGHT MEDITATION TECHNIQUE OF ANCIENT EGYPT ISBN: 1-884564-15-1 $14.95 (PB) New for the year 2000. This volume is based on the earliest known instruction in history given for the practice of formal meditation. Discovered by Dr. Muata Ashby, it is inscribed on the walls of the Tomb of Seti I in Thebes Egypt. This volume details the philosophy and practice of this unique system of meditation originated in Ancient Egypt and the earliest practice of meditation known in the world which occurred in the most advanced African Culture.

15. THE SERPENT POWER: The Ancient Egyptian Mystical Wisdom of the Inner Life Force.   This Volume specifically deals with the latent life Force energy of the universe and in the human body, its control and sublimation. How to develop the Life Force energy of the subtle body. This Volume will introduce the esoteric wisdom of the science of how virtuous living acts in a subtle and mysterious way to cleanse the latent psychic energy conduits and vortices of the spiritual body. ISBN 1-884564-19-4 $22.95

16. EGYPTIAN YOGA MEDITATION IN MOTION Thef Neteru: *The Movement of The Gods and Goddesses* Discover the physical postures and exercises practiced thousands of years ago in Ancient Egypt which are today known as Yoga exercises. This work is based on the pictures and teachings from the Creation story of Ra, The Asarian Resurrection Myth and the carvings and reliefs from various Temples in Ancient Egypt 8.5" X 11" ISBN 1-884564-10-0 Soft Cover $18.99   Exercise video $21.99

17. EGYPTIAN TANTRA YOGA: The Art of Sex Sublimation and Universal Consciousness This Volume will expand on the male and female principles within the human body and in the universe and further detail the sublimation of sexual energy into spiritual energy. The student will study the deities Min and Hathor, Asar and Aset, Geb and Nut and discover the mystical implications for a practical spiritual discipline. This Volume will also focus on the Tantric aspects of Ancient Egyptian and Indian mysticism, the purpose of sex and the mystical teachings of sexual sublimation which lead to self-knowledge and Enlightenment. 5.5"x 8.5"   ISBN 1-884564-03-8 $24.95

18. ASARIAN RELIGION: RESURRECTING OSIRIS The path of Mystical Awakening and the Keys to Immortality NEW REVISED AND EXPANDED EDITION!   The Ancient Sages created stories based on human and superhuman beings whose struggles, aspirations, needs and desires ultimately lead them to discover their true Self. The myth of Aset, Asar and Heru is no exception in this area. While there is no one source where the entire story may be found, pieces of it are inscribed in various ancient Temples walls, tombs, steles and papyri. For the first time available, the complete myth of Asar, Aset and Heru has been compiled from original Ancient Egyptian, Greek and Coptic Texts. This epic myth has been richly illustrated with reliefs from the Temple of Heru at Edfu, the Temple of Aset at Philae, the Temple of Asar at Abydos, the Temple of Hathor at Denderah and various papyri, inscriptions and reliefs.   Discover the myth which inspired the teachings of the *Shetaut Neter* (Egyptian Mystery System - Egyptian Yoga) and the Egyptian Book of Coming Forth By Day. Also, discover the three levels of Ancient Egyptian Religion, how to understand the mysteries of the Duat or Astral World and how to discover the abode of the Supreme in the Amenta, *The Other World*   The ancient religion of Asar, Aset and Heru, if properly understood, contains all of the elements necessary to lead the sincere aspirant to attain immortality through inner self-discovery. This volume presents the entire myth and explores the main mystical themes and rituals associated with the myth for understating human existence, creation and the way to achieve spiritual emancipation - *Resurrection*. The Asarian myth is so powerful that it influenced and is still having an effect on the major world religions. Discover the origins and mystical meaning of the Christian Trinity, the

MEDITATION

Eucharist ritual and the ancient origin of the birthday of Jesus Christ. Soft Cover ISBN: 1-884564-27-5 $24.95

19. THE EGYPTIAN BOOK OF THE DEAD MYSTICISM OF THE PERT EM HERU $26.95   ISBN# 1-884564-28-3 Size: 8½" X 11" I Know myself, I know myself, I am One With God!–From the Pert Em Heru "The Ru Pert em Heru" or "Ancient Egyptian Book of The Dead," or "Book of Coming Forth By Day" as it is more popularly known, has fascinated the world since the successful translation of Ancient Egyptian hieroglyphic scripture over 150 years ago. The astonishing writings in it reveal that the Ancient Egyptians believed in life after death and in an ultimate destiny to discover the Divine. The elegance and aesthetic beauty of the hieroglyphic text itself has inspired many see it as an art form in and of itself. But is there more to it than that? Did the Ancient Egyptian wisdom contain more than just aphorisms and hopes of eternal life beyond death? In this volume Dr. Muata Ashby, the author of over 25 books on Ancient Egyptian Yoga Philosophy has produced a new translation of the original texts which uncovers a mystical teaching underlying the sayings and rituals instituted by the Ancient Egyptian Sages and Saints. "Once the philosophy of Ancient Egypt is understood as a mystical tradition instead of as a religion or primitive mythology, it reveals its secrets which if practiced today will lead anyone to discover the glory of spiritual self-discovery. The Pert em Heru is in every way comparable to the Indian Upanishads or the Tibetan Book of the Dead." - Muata Abhaya Ashby

20. ANUNIAN THEOLOGY THE MYSTERIES OF RA The Philosophy of Anu and The Mystical Teachings of The Ancient Egyptian Creation Myth Discover the mystical teachings contained in the Creation Myth and the gods and goddesses who brought creation and human beings into existence. The Creation Myth holds the key to understanding the universe and for attaining spiritual Enlightenment. ISBN: 1-884564-38-0 40 pages $14.95

21. MYSTERIES OF MIND AND MEMPHITE THEOLOGY Mysticism of Ptah, Egyptian Physics and Yoga Metaphysics and the Hidden properties of Matter This Volume will go deeper into the philosophy of God as creation and will explore the concepts of modern science and how they correlate with ancient teachings. This Volume will lay the ground work for the understanding of the philosophy of universal consciousness and the initiatic/yogic insight into who or what is God? ISBN 1-884564-07-0 $21.95

22. THE GODDESS AND THE EGYPTIAN MYSTERIESTHE PATH OF THE GODDESS THE GODDESS PATH The Secret Forms of the Goddess and the Rituals of Resurrection The Supreme Being may be worshipped as father or as mother. *Ushet Rekhat* or *Mother Worship*, is the spiritual process of worshipping the Divine in the form of the Divine Goddess. It celebrates the most important forms of the Goddess including *Nathor, Maat, Aset, Arat, Amentet and Hathor* and explores their mystical meaning as well as the rising of *Sirius*, the star of Aset (Aset) and the new birth of Hor (Heru). The end of the year is a time of reckoning, reflection and engendering a new or renewed positive movement toward attaining spiritual Enlightenment. The Mother Worship devotional meditation ritual, performed on five days during the month of December and on New Year's Eve, is based on the Ushet Rekhit. During the ceremony, the cosmic forces, symbolized by Sirius - and the constellation of Orion ---, are harnessed through the understanding and devotional attitude of the participant. This propitiation draws the light of wisdom and health to all those who share in the ritual, leading to prosperity and wisdom. $14.95 ISBN 1-884564-18-6

23. *THE MYSTICAL JOURNEY FROM JESUS TO CHRIST* $24.95   ISBN# 1-884564-05-4 size: 8½" X 11" Discover the ancient Egyptian origins of Christianity before the Catholic Church and learn the mystical teachings given by Jesus to assist all humanity in becoming Christlike. Discover the secret meaning of the Gospels that were discovered in Egypt. Also discover how and why so many Christian churches came into being. Discover that the Bible still holds the keys to mystical realization even though its original writings were changed by the church. Discover how to practice the original teachings of Christianity which leads to the Kingdom of Heaven.

24. THE STORY OF ASAR, ASET AND HERU: An Ancient Egyptian Legend (For Children)   Now for the first time, the most ancient myth of Ancient Egypt comes alive for children. Inspired by the books *The Asarian Resurrection: The Ancient Egyptian Bible* and *The Mystical Teachings of The Asarian Resurrection, The Story of Asar, Aset and Heru* is an easy to understand and thrilling tale which inspired

The Ancient Egyptian Path to Enlightenment

the children of Ancient Egypt to aspire to greatness and righteousness. If you and your child have enjoyed stories like *The Lion King* and *Star Wars you will love The Story of Asar, Aset and Heru*. Also, if you know the story of Jesus and Krishna you will discover than Ancient Egypt had a similar myth and that this myth carries important spiritual teachings for living a fruitful and fulfilling life. This book may be used along with *The Parents Guide To The Asarian Resurrection Myth: How to Teach Yourself and Your Child the Principles of Universal Mystical Religion*. The guide provides some background to the Asarian Resurrection myth and it also gives insight into the mystical teachings contained in it which you may introduce to your child. It is designed for parents who wish to grow spiritually with their children and it serves as an introduction for those who would like to study the Asarian Resurrection Myth in depth and to practice its teachings. 41 pages 8.5" X 11"   ISBN: 1-884564-31-3 $12.95

25. THE PARENTS GUIDE TO THE AUSARIAN RESURRECTION MYTH: How to Teach Yourself and Your Child the Principles of Universal Mystical Religion. This insightful manual brings for the timeless wisdom of the ancient through the Ancient Egyptian myth of Asar, Aset and Heru and the mystical teachings contained in it for parents who want to guide their children to understand and practice the teachings of mystical spirituality. This manual may be used with the children's storybook *The Story of Asar, Aset and Heru* by Dr. Muata Abhaya Ashby. 5.5"x 8.5"   ISBN: 1-884564-30-5 $14.95

26. HEALING THE CRIMINAL HEART BOOK 1 Introduction to Maat Philosophy, Yoga and Spiritual Redemption Through the Path of Virtue   Who is a criminal? Is there such a thing as a criminal heart? What is the source of evil and sinfulness and is there any way to rise above it? Is there redemption for those who have committed sins, even the worst crimes?   Ancient Egyptian mystical psychology holds important answers to these questions. Over ten thousand years ago mystical psychologists, the Sages of Ancient Egypt, studied and charted the human mind and spirit and laid out a path which will lead to spiritual redemption, prosperity and Enlightenment.   This introductory volume brings forth the teachings of the Asarian Resurrection, the most important myth of Ancient Egypt, with relation to the faults of human existence: anger, hatred, greed, lust, animosity, discontent, ignorance, egoism jealousy, bitterness, and a myriad of psycho-spiritual ailments which keep a human being in a state of negativity and adversity. 5.5"x 8.5"   ISBN: 1-884564-17-8 $15.95

27. THEATER & DRAMA OF THE ANCIENT EGYPTIAN MYSTERIES: Featuring the Ancient Egyptian stage play-"The Enlightenment of Hathor' Based on an Ancient Egyptian Drama, The original Theater - Mysticism of the Temple of Hetheru $14.95 By Dr. Muata Ashby

28.   GUIDE TO PRINT ON DEMAND: SELF-PUBLISH FOR PROFIT, SPIRITUAL FULFILLMENT AND SERVICE TO HUMANITY Everyone asks us how we produced so many books in such a short time. Here are the secrets to writing and producing books that uplift humanity and how to get them printed for a fraction of the regular cost. Anyone can become an author even if they have limited funds. All that is necessary is the willingness to learn how the printing and book business work and the desire to follow the special instructions given here for preparing your manuscript format. Then you take your work directly to the non-traditional companies who can produce your books for less than the traditional book printer can. ISBN: 1-884564-40-2 $16.95 U. S.

29.   Egyptian Mysteries: Vol. 1, Shetaut Neter ISBN: 1-884564-41-0 $19.99 What are the Mysteries? For thousands of years the spiritual tradition of Ancient Egypt, S*hetaut Neter,* "The Egyptian Mysteries," "The Secret Teachings," have fascinated, tantalized and amazed the world. At one time exalted and recognized as the highest culture of the world, by Africans, Europeans, Asiatics, Hindus, Buddhists and other cultures of the ancient world, in time it was shunned by the emerging orthodox world religions. Its temples desecrated, its philosophy maligned, its tradition spurned, its philosophy dormant in the mystical *Medu Neter*, the mysterious hieroglyphic texts which hold the secret symbolic meaning that has scarcely been discerned up to now. What are the secrets of *Nehast* {spiritual awakening and emancipation, resurrection}. More than just a literal translation, this volume is for awakening to the secret code *Shetitu* of the teaching which was not deciphered by Egyptologists, nor could be understood by ordinary spiritualists. This book is a reinstatement of the original science made available for our times, to the reincarnated followers of Ancient Egyptian culture and the prospect of spiritual freedom to break the bonds of *Khemn,* "ignorance," and slavery to evil forces: *Såaa* .

MEDITATION

30. EGYPTIAN MYSTERIES VOL 2: Dictionary of Gods and Goddesses ISBN: 1-884564-23-2 $21.95
This book is about the mystery of neteru, the gods and goddesses of Ancient Egypt (Kamit, Kemet). Neteru means "Gods and Goddesses." But the Neterian teaching of Neteru represents more than the usual limited modern day concept of "divinities" or "spirits." The Neteru of Kamit are also metaphors, cosmic principles and vehicles for the enlightening teachings of Shetaut Neter (Ancient Egyptian-African Religion). Actually they are the elements for one of the most advanced systems of spirituality ever conceived in human history. Understanding the concept of neteru provides a firm basis for spiritual evolution and the pathway for viable culture, peace on earth and a healthy human society.   Why is it important to have gods and goddesses in our lives? In order for spiritual evolution to be possible, once a human being has accepted that there is existence after death and there is a transcendental being who exists beyond time and space knowledge, human beings need a connection to that which transcends the ordinary experience of human life in time and space and a means to understand the transcendental reality beyond the mundane reality.

31. EGYPTIAN MYSTERIES VOL. 3 The Priests and Priestesses of Ancient Egypt ISBN: 1-884564-53-4 $22.95 This volume details the path of Neterian priesthood, the joys, challenges and rewards of advanced Neterian life, the teachings that allowed the priests and priestesses to manage the most long lived civilization in human history and how that path can be adopted today; for those who want to tread the path of the Clergy of Shetaut Neter.

32. THE KING OF EGYPT: The Struggle of Good and Evil for Control of the World and The Human Soul ISBN 1-8840564-44-5 $18.95   Have you seen movies like The Lion King, Hamlet, The Odyssey, or The Little Buddha? These have been some of the most popular movies in modern times. The Sema Institute of Yoga is dedicated to researching and presenting the wisdom and culture of ancient Africa. The Script is designed to be produced as a motion picture but may be addapted for the theater as well. 160 pages bound or unbound (specify with your order) $19.95   copyright 1998 By Dr. Muata Ashby

33. FROM EGYPT TO GREECE: The Kamitan Origins of Greek Culture and Religion ISBN: 1-884564-47-X $22.95 U.S. FROM EGYPT TO GREECE This insightful manual is a quick reference to Ancient Egyptian mythology and philosophy and its correlation to what later became known as Greek and Rome mythology and philosophy. It outlines the basic tenets of the mythologies and shoes the ancient origins of Greek culture in Ancient Egypt. This volume also acts as a resource for Colleges students who would like to set up fraternities and sororities based on the original Ancient Egyptian principles of Sheti and Maat philosophy. ISBN: 1-884564-47-X $22.95 U.S.

34. THE FORTY TWO PRECEPTS OF MAAT, THE PHILOSOPHY OF RIGHTEOUS ACTION AND THE ANCIENT EGYPTIAN WISDOM TEXTS <u>ADVANCED STUDIES</u> This manual is designed for use with the 1998 Maat Philosophy Class conducted by Dr. Muata Ashby. This is a detailed study of Maat Philosophy. It contains a compilation of the 42 laws or precepts of Maat and the corresponding principles which they represent along with the teachings of the ancient Egyptian Sages relating to each. Maat philosophy was the basis of Ancient Egyptian society and government as well as the heart of Ancient Egyptian myth and spirituality. Maat is at once a goddess, a cosmic force and a living social doctrine, which promotes social harmony and thereby paves the way for spiritual evolution in all levels of society. ISBN: 1-884564-48-8 $16.95 U.S.

Music Based on the Prt M Hru and other Kemetic Texts

Available on Compact Disc $14.99 and Audio Cassette $9.99

Adorations to the Goddess

Music for Worship of the Goddess

**NEW Egyptian Yoga Music CD
by Sehu Maa
Ancient Egyptian Music CD**
Instrumental Music played on reproductions of Ancient Egyptian Instruments– Ideal for meditation and reflection on the Divine and for the practice of spiritual programs and Yoga exercise sessions.

©1999 By Muata Ashby
CD $14.99 –

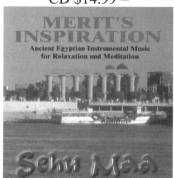

MERIT'S INSPIRATION
**NEW Egyptian Yoga Music CD
by Sehu Maa
Ancient Egyptian Music CD**
Instrumental Music played on reproductions of Ancient Egyptian Instruments– Ideal for meditation and reflection on the Divine and for the practice of spiritual programs and Yoga exercise sessions.
©1999 By
Muata Ashby
CD $14.99 –
UPC# 761527100429

ANORATIONS TO RA AND HETHERU
**NEW Egyptian Yoga Music CD
By Sehu Maa (Muata Ashby)
Based on the Words of Power of Ra and HetHeru**
played on reproductions of Ancient Egyptian Instruments **Ancient Egyptian Instruments used: Voice, Clapping, Nefer Lute, Tar Drum, Sistrums, Cymbals** – The Chants, Devotions, Rhythms and Festive Songs Of the Neteru – Ideal for meditation, and devotional singing and dancing.

©1999 By Muata Ashby
CD $14.99 –
UPC# 761527100221

MEDITATION

SONGS TO ASAR ASET AND HERU
NEW
Egyptian Yoga Music CD
By Sehu Maa

played on reproductions of Ancient Egyptian Instruments– The Chants, Devotions, Rhythms and Festive Songs Of the Neteru - Ideal for meditation, and devotional singing and dancing.
Based on the Words of Power of Asar (Asar), Aset (Aset) and Heru (Heru) Om Asar Aset Heru is the third in a series of musical explorations of the Kemetic (Ancient Egyptian) tradition of music. Its ideas are based on the Ancient Egyptian Religion of Asar, Aset and Heru and it is designed for listening, meditation and worship. ©1999 By Muata Ashby
CD $14.99 –
UPC# 761527100122

HAARI OM: ANCIENT EGYPT MEETS INDIA IN MUSIC
NEW Music CD
By Sehu Maa

The Chants, Devotions, Rhythms and Festive Songs Of the Ancient Egypt and India, harmonized and played on reproductions of ancient instruments along with modern instruments and beats. Ideal for meditation, and devotional singing and dancing.

Haari Om is the fourth in a series of musical explorations of the Kemetic (Ancient Egyptian) and Indian traditions of music, chanting and devotional spiritual practice. Its ideas are based on the Ancient Egyptian Yoga spirituality and Indian Yoga spirituality.
©1999 By Muata Ashby
CD $14.99 –
UPC# 761527100528

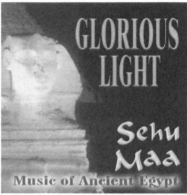

RA AKHU: THE GLORIOUS LIGHT
NEW
Egyptian Yoga Music CD
By Sehu Maa

The fifth collection of original music compositions based on the Teachings and Words of The Trinity, the God Asar and the Goddess Nebethet, the Divinity Aten, the God Heru, and the Special Meditation Hekau or Words of Power of Ra from the Ancient Egyptian Tomb of Seti I and more... played on reproductions of Ancient Egyptian Instruments and modern instruments - Ancient Egyptian Instruments used: Voice, Clapping, Nefer Lute, Tar Drum, Sistrums, Cymbals
— The Chants, Devotions, Rhythms and Festive Songs Of the Neteru – Ideal for meditation, and devotional singing and dancing.
©1999 By Muata Ashby
CD $14.99 –
UPC# 761527100825

GLORIES OF THE DIVINE MOTHER
Based on the hieroglyphic text of the worship of Goddess Net.
The Glories of The Great Mother
©2000 Muata Ashby
CD $14.99 UPC# 761527101129`

MEDITATION

Order Form

Telephone orders: Call Toll Free: 1(305) 378-6253. Have your AMEX, Optima, Visa or MasterCard ready.

Fax orders: 1-(305) 378-6253   E-MAIL ADDRESS: Semayoga@aol.com

Postal Orders: Sema Institute of Yoga, P.O. Box 570459, Miami, Fl. 33257. USA.

Please send the following books and / or tapes.

ITEM

_____Cost $_____
_____Cost $_____
_____Cost $_____
_____Cost $_____
_____Cost $_____

Total $_____

Name:_____
Physical Address:_____
City:_____ State:_____ Zip:_____

Sales tax: Please add 6.5% for books shipped to Florida addresses
_____ Shipping: $6.50 for first book and .50¢ for each additional
_____ Shipping: Outside US $5.00 for first book and $3.00 for each additional

_____Payment:_____
_____Check -Include Driver License #:
      _____

_____Credit card: _____ Visa, _____ MasterCard, _____ Optima, _____ AMEX.

Card number:_____
Name on card:_____ Exp. date:_____/_____

Copyright 1995-2005 Dr. R. Muata Abhaya Ashby
Sema Institute of Yoga
P.O.Box 570459, Miami, Florida, 33257
(305) 378-6253 Fax: (305) 378-6253

Made in United States
Troutdale, OR
10/22/2024